Discourse and Identity on Facebook

BLOOMSBURY DISCOURSE

Series Editor: Professor Ken Hyland, University of Hong Kong
Discourse is one of the most significant concepts of contemporary thinking in the humanities and social sciences as it concerns the ways language mediates and shapes our interactions with each other and with the social, political and cultural formations of our society. The *Bloomsbury Discourse* aims to capture the fast-developing interest in discourse to provide students, new and experienced teachers and researchers in applied linguistics, ELT and English language with an essential bookshelf. Each book deals with a core topic in discourse studies to give an in-depth, structured and readable introduction to an aspect of the way language is used in real life.

OTHER TITLES IN THE SERIES:

Discourse and Identity on Facebook

MARIZA GEORGALOU

BLOOMSBURY ACADEMIC
LONDON • NEW YORK • OXFORD • NEW DELHI • SYDNEY

BLOOMSBURY ACADEMIC
Bloomsbury Publishing Plc
50 Bedford Square, London, WC1B 3DP, UK
1385 Broadway, New York, NY 10018, USA

BLOOMSBURY, BLOOMSBURY ACADEMIC and the
Diana logo are trademarks of Bloomsbury Publishing Plc

First published 2017
Paperback edition first published 2018

A catalogue record for this book is available from the British Library.

Library of Congress Cataloging-in-Publication Data
Names: Georgalou, Mariza, author.
Title: Discourse and identity on Facebook: how we use language and
multimodal texts to present identity online / Mariza Georgalou.
Description: London; New York: Bloomsbury Academic, [2017] |
Series: Bloomsbury Discourse | Includes bibliographical references and index.
Identifiers: LCCN 2016058375 (print) | LCCN 2017024972 (ebook) |
ISBN 9781474289139 (epub) | ISBN 9781474289146 (epdf) | ISBN 9781474289122
(hb: alk. paper) Subjects: LCSH: Discourse analysis–Social aspects. | Discourse
analysis–Technology. | Facebook (Electronic resource)–Social aspects. |
Online social networks–Social aspects.
Classification: LCC P302.865 (ebook) | LCC P302.865 .G477 2017 (print) | DDC
302.23/10141–dc23
LC record available at https://lccn.loc.gov/2016058375

ISBN: HB: 978-1-4742-8912-2
PB: 978-1-3500-9470-3
ePDF: 978-1-4742-8914-6
ePub: 978-1-4742-8913-9

Series: Bloomsbury Discourse

Typeset by Deanta Global Publishing Services, Chennai, India

The companion website to this book can be found at
www.bloomsbury.com/Georgalou-Discourse-Identity-Facebook

To find out more about our authors and books visit
www.bloomsbury.com and sign up for our newsletters.

For Maria Georgalou, Antonis Georgalos and Konstantinos Georgalos

Table of contents

List of tables, figures and activities

Tables

Figures

Activities

Foreword

Greg Myers

As Susan Herring noted (2004), one problem for what was then called Computer-Mediated Communication is how quickly practices come to be taken for granted. Older researchers, coming to a new site for the first time, would see its possibilities as exciting and transformational or perhaps worrying. By the time they had written about it and integrated it into their teaching, younger researchers and students would see the same site as an unremarkable and uninteresting aspect of everyday life. One group needed to moderate its hopes and fears, while the other might need to see afresh media affordances that did, in fact, make a difference. Facebook, which began in the year that Herring was writing, is another case of this tension between seeing technology as new and taking it for granted. Mariza Georgalou's excellent study of Facebook manages to treat social networking sites as ordinary parts of life while still linking them to a broader sense of technological change and social change.

One way to tell people something new about what they do every day is to go broader, to gather huge amounts of data and look for patterns in them. This is a common approach in research on Twitter. Facebook has tended to get a different kind of study, partly because texts are not public; the way to tell us something new is to go deeper. For most studies of personal pages, there is no alternative to meeting the users who provide the data and gaining their interest in trust. With a smaller number of subjects, and more contact with them, one can look for richer connections to their practices and to what they think they are doing in their use of social media, what meanings it has for them. The emphasis on offline contact with users of the sites follows from the work of Jannis Androutsopoulos (2008) and others; the detailed exploration of how these practices fit within everyday life follows from work like that of Daniel Miller and his team (2011).

On rereading Georgalous's book, I am particularly struck by five aspects of what she has accomplished:

1) She takes care in presenting her informants, making them distinct and interesting characters, filling us in on those aspects of their lives that are important to them, but never intruding beyond their self-presentation on Facebook. After all, the last analysis chapter of this book is about ways that privacy is maintained, and her research respects that privacy.

2) She is as attentive to visual and audio modes as to language. Of course the language gets attention, in the choices of pronouns, deictics and the lively code-switching to Greeklish, Engreek, Spanish, English or Hungarian. But it is a truism that analysis of social networks must be multimodal. Not all researchers have the time and the space and the cultural knowledge to pursue the cues that a complex message can give, for instance, in the choice of a photo, a link to a video clip or the adaptation of a cartoon. She made me much more aware of the way musical allusions work; now I see how often they are used, and how subtly they are deployed, by my friends on Facebook (with a rather different playlist, though).

3) She is aware of the ways social media are part of daily life, work, leisure and relationships. She did not sit with the subjects as they typed their posts; it was not that kind of ethnography. But as she annotates these posts, she gives a rich sense of the particularities and rhythms of life. She considers the practices around the posts, for instance, copy-pasting, multiple posting and what boyd and Marwick (2011) called 'social steganography', in this case, hiding potential messages in song lyrics.

4) Her analysis connects these texts to all sorts of identities, from the more obvious (work, education, nation) to less obvious categories involving local places, shared memories and evaluations. The book includes a review of contemporary ideas of hybrid identities, but it can also be read as an interrogation of those categories.

5) And of course it is about the crisis. When she began her study, Georgalou could not have predicted the huge changes about to sweep through Greece, an economic crisis, but also a political crisis, a crisis of national identity and, for many people, a personal crisis. This is not an analysis of crisis discourse (see the special issue of *Discourse & Society* edited by Wodak and Angouri 2014). But many of the examples give us a sense of how ripples of the political and economic events reached into all aspects of everyday life, and what it might be like to have the landscape of one's life changed, with new holes, roadblocks and detours. The account is all the more effective for its being understated.

The particularity of the setting, in one European country, in a period of crisis, might put off some readers glancing at the book. They might think they are looking for a study of Facebook (or social media and identity, or multimodality on social media) in general, and they might think this book is just about Greece, or just about the crisis. The best answer to this was given by Daniel Miller and Don Slater in their ethnography of the internet in 2000, and again by Daniel Miller writing about Facebook in 2011, in explaining why they write about Trinidad: 'The internet was whatever any particular group of users had made it into. No one population was more "proper" and "authentic" than any others' (2011: xiii).

All ethnographic studies of media use have to deal with the situated culture and practices around the medium. There seems to be an academic convention that if one does a study of students at a large Midwestern US university, or if one has a large sample from around the world, the culture and practices can be taken for granted. And in many studies, the socioeconomic and political background hardly needs to be mentioned; it is assumed to be stable and known. Because Georgalou writes about people of a particular generation, in a particular country, when that country was undergoing a crisis, she has to give the kind of background that really should be in any study.

It takes time to write a book like this, and authors and readers may worry that the sites, terminology, affordances and practices of social media will have moved on. In one sense, this datedness is inevitable, as shown in Georgalou's notes on changes in Facebook in the course of the study. In another sense, good studies on the use of new media remain useful even when the media get old, and even after they are largely superseded, as shown, for instance, by the work of Herring, Miller and Slater, or boyd and Marwick.

Georgalou has a fascinating conclusion, in which she asks her subjects what they would do in a world that is currently unimaginable, a world without Facebook. She says, 'Facebook may be revamped, upgraded, transformed, merged, even replaced. It may acquire new roles, functions and practicalities wholly worthy to be assessed and researched.' All this will happen, but I am fairly sure that Georgalou's book will still prove to be a useful starting point for studies of whatever comes next.

References

Androutsopoulos, J. (2008). Potentials and Limitations of Discourse-Centred Online Ethnography. *Language@Internet, 5*, article 8. http://www. languageatinternet.org/articles/2008/1610 (accessed 23 September 2016).

boyd, d., and Marwick, A. (2011). Social steganography: Privacy in networked publics. *International Communication Association*. Boston, MA. http://www.danah.org/papers/2011/Steganography-ICAVersion.pdf (accessed 23 September 2016).

Herring, S. (2004). Slouching toward the ordinary: Current trends in computer-mediated communication. *New Media & Society*, 6(1), pp. 26–36.

Miller, D. (2011). *Tales from Facebook*. Cambridge: Polity.

Miller, D., and Slater, D. (2000). *The Internet: An ethnographic approach*. Oxford: Berg.

Wodak, R., and Angouri, J. eds. (2014). From Grexit to Grecovery: Euro/crisis discourses. *Discourse & Society*, 25(4), pp. 417–565.

Acknowledgements

This book, which started its life as a PhD thesis, was born in Athens (Greece), bred in Lancaster (UK) and matured in Jyväskylä (Finland). I owe my heartfelt gratitude and appreciation to a number of people from these three places for their support, direct or indirect, without whom this work would never have been possible.

I am deeply thankful to my supervisor Greg Myers and my host-supervisor Sirpa Leppänen, for sharing their wisdom, and for guiding and shaping me with active encouragement and substantial criticism.

I am especially grateful to my informants, Carla, Alkis, Romanos, Gabriel and Helen, for their enthusiasm in participating in my research, for patiently answering all the questions I had in different time spans and for offering constructive comments inside and outside Facebook.

Several colleagues at conferences, seminars and discussion groups expressed their interest in my work. I particularly benefited from insightful questions, comments and suggestions from Julia Gillen, Alexandra Georgakopoulou, Elina Westinen, Samu Kytölä and Saija Peuronen.

My gratitude also goes to the editorial and production staff at Bloomsbury, in particular Ken Hyland, Gurdeep Mattu and Andrew Wardell, who fully supported this project.

Parts of Chapters 4 and 7 have appeared as 'Small stories of the Greek crisis on Facebook', *Social Media & Society* (July–December 2015), parts of Chapter 5 as 'Beyond the Timeline: Constructing time and age identities on Facebook', *Discourse, Context & Media* 9: 24-33 (2015), and parts of Chapter 8 as '"I make the rules on my Wall": Privacy and identity management practices on Facebook', *Discourse & Communication* 10(1): 40-64 (2016). Relevant passages are reprinted here with permission kindly granted by Sage and Elsevier. I warmly thank: Jannis Androutsopoulos and Susan Herring, for permission to use Table 3.1; Woodrow Hartzog, for permission to use Table 8.1; Arkas, for permission to use Figure 7.5; and Jody Zucker and Warner Bros. Television, for permission to reproduce the epigraph from *Person of Interest* in Chapter 9.

I would also like to acknowledge the generous support of CIMO (Centre for International Mobility) in Helsinki, which made it possible for me to spend 7 productive months of research in Jyväskylä.

Finally, I am most grateful to my parents, Maria and Antonis, my brother, Konstantinos, and my partner, Konstantinos, for their endless caring, love, support and encouragement throughout and beyond my writing.

Σας ευχαριστώ. Thank you. Kiitos teille.

1

Introduction

A day in the (digital) life

12 September 2016. I wake up at 6.30. A quarter later, I turn my laptop on and decide to mark down the internet technologies I will use from that moment and during the whole day. I start with my emails. I have to send to a colleague some ideas on a research project that we are about to start. An incoming email notifies me that another colleague has uploaded new photographs on Flickr – my colleague is a loyal fan of the '365 project', a common photo project according to which users shoot and upload on Flickr one photograph a day for a year. I browse through his Flickr photo stream and **fave** a couple of pictures. In the meantime, I am responding to some other emails. In one of my mailing lists a link leads me to an article on language in the digital age. I read it and then post it on my Tumblr blog where I **curate** content about language, culture, society, **social media** and research.

At 8.10 I scroll down my Facebook **News Feed**. It is replete with posts related to the start of the new school year. The official **page** of the Beatles has shared on its **status** some information on the new film *Eight Days a Week: The Touring Years* and I click the **'Like' button** underneath it. I open a new browser tab and go to YouTube to watch the film's trailer. I keep on skimming through Facebook posts. I 'Like' one on places to visit while in Helsinki.

At 11.07 I accept a colleague's invitation to join a shared folder in Dropbox. We agreed to upload there our PowerPoint slides for an upcoming conference on **discourse** and European identity. Approximately one hour later I receive a contact update on LinkedIn: my cousin has now a new job in a brewing company. I write a **comment** below his update to congratulate him.

I have an incoming Twitter alert from a friend of mine on my smartphone. Following an offline discussion we had about the American TV series *The Sopranos* and *Mad Men* a couple of months ago, she now **tweets** me an article on both series' ambiguous final episodes. I tweet her back at 14.03. I return to my laptop screen. I have a short video call on Skype with my brother, who lives in Lancaster, UK. I use the same service for instant messaging with my partner for almost 20 minutes after 15.00.

At 17.15 I visit Facebook once again to wish 'happy birthday' on a friend's **Wall**. I also answer to another friend's private Facebook message to arrange a night out. At the same time I check on TripAdvisor the reviews of the bar theatre we are thinking of going to.

While sorting some bibliographies, it occurs to me that I am about to meet at a conference a bunch of academics who work on discourse analysis. I reach academia.edu to check if they maintain profiles there. I scan titles of their papers, download a couple of them and follow the academics' activity by clicking the relevant button.

By 19.00, I upload on Instagram a photo from yesterday's walk in Plaka, Athens. I scroll down my feed. I like a **selfie** posted by a newly-wed friend and a photo of my yoga teacher in a very difficult balancing pose. Further down, a food blogger I follow on Instagram has posted the picture of a babka cake she made. I search on Wikipedia for babka's name and origins.

At 22.24 I cast my eyes over the news, my emails and Facebook. I make a last Skype call and then turn the laptop off.

What is this book about?

As described in the **techno-autobiography** of a typical day of mine above, similar I guess to that of many other users', more than half of our awaken life is spent in front of a screen with unlimited access to the internet. New digital media technologies have been 'domesticated' in our everyday lives, allowing us to integrate our online with our offline discourse activities (Barton and Lee 2013) and, in the course of doing this, to express our identities.

It has been suggested that identity is a way of trying to make sense of the chaos in our lives, to organize our various feelings, ideas, beliefs, attitudes and values (Thurlow et al. 2004). This book examines how our identities are constructed, performed and experienced, namely typed, uploaded, shared, managed and protected, within such – chaotic too – online contexts (my digital media techno-autobiography above gives a fine taste of this 'chaos'). To this end, I have selected to focus on Facebook, one of the most popular and successful – at least at the time of writing – ***social network sites*** (henceforth SNS) worldwide.

Studying identity on Facebook is interesting for a number of reasons. First, Facebook is not a mere technology but a vibrant sociocultural arena which gives users unprecedented opportunities and ***affordances*** for self-presentation through the interplay of language and other semiotic means. Second, in view of the absence of face-to-face social cues, the expression of identity on Facebook is usually initiated more intentionally, selectively or consciously. Third, Facebook is largely structured around already existing offline relationships (some of them have existed long before Facebook), within friends, families and colleagues. So identities on Facebook are not necessarily constructed from scratch. What users do is constructing themselves in ways that they find meaningful to their familiar ones, based on their shared knowledge and experiences, as well as themselves.

Facebook, like all SNS, was initially designed as a self-report ***microblogging*** technology of the type 'been there, done that'. Hence, it comes as no surprise that untrammelled identity work is performed there, sometimes mundane, at other times overtly narcissistic and pretentious. My objective is to move beyond the brew of triviality, levity and light-heartedness that, according to traditional media comments, accompanies this new type of publicness. Instead, I am going to cast light on the ways in which users creatively deploy language to locate themselves, to assert facts, to argue, to evaluate and to define themselves – both explicitly and implicitly – in relation to their Facebook networks. In other words, I am interested in whether and how they repurpose the medium, questioning simultaneously its very use, to reconfigure their identities while working, studying, learning, bantering, travelling, consuming culture, being entertained and informed.

The key question underlying the book is how identity is discursively constructed within Facebook. In order to operationalize this question, I have broken it down into four smaller analytical questions:

1 How do Facebook users construct themselves?

2 How are they co-constructed by their Facebook friends?

3 What is the role of multimodality in these identity constructions?

4 What kind of textual practices do Facebook users adopt to construct their identities?

These questions were formulated as a response to four hypotheses I arrived at based on informal observation, preliminary research and previous literature:

1   **Facebook discourse, as any kind of public discourse, is inherently constitutive of identity**. Creating and updating a (semi)public profile on Facebook requires participants to reflect upon how they wish to represent themselves, enabling them to uniquely locate and combine their self-descriptions in the context of social connections (boyd 2008b).[1]

2   **Identity on Facebook is a product of online interaction.** A great deal of identity work is done by others, not just by oneself. Identity on Facebook is not solely a self-actualized task but an intrinsically interactive one, construed, maintained and challenged through processes of exchanging comments and 'Likes' (see Chapter 2) between the profile owner and their audience.

3   **Orchestrating meaning through a multimodal ensemble of modes is a crucial way of identity construction on Facebook**. Communication in social media is necessarily integrated into visually organized environments, and verbal exchanges appear to be more fragmented and reliant on multimodal context (Androutsopoulos 2011). Facebook makes 'a wide range of modes available, often in new inter-semiotic relationships with one another, and unsettle[s] and re-make[s] genres, in ways that reshape practices and interaction' (Jewitt 2013) and therefore identities.

4   **Facebook users adopt certain textual practices to present their identities online**. After conducting some preliminary interviews with Facebook participants, I figured out that they were very concerned about privacy and adopted specific textual practices to secure it. As a consequence, I became interested in what users do and achieve with Facebook texts more broadly and how this affects the final, textually visible, identity product.

The discussions in the chapters that follow cover a wide array of verbal and visual examples from five Greek Facebook users. The approach I take in discussing these examples synthesizes identity theories, discourse analysis, computer-mediated discourse analysis, multimodality studies and online ethnography. I will only very briefly outline each of these frameworks here, with more details provided in Chapters 2 and 3.

Starting with identity theories, this book is situated within a constructionist tradition, perceiving identity as dynamic, flexible and necessarily contextual – socially, politically, culturally and discursively. To fully address the purposes of the book, I employ a mix of discourse analytic approaches. The main thrust of my argument is that discourse constitutes a means of identity construction. As far as computer-mediated discourse analysis is concerned, I particularly espouse its premise that the technological features of new communication technologies can shape discourse (Herring 2004). Multimodality studies, on the other hand, offer me tools to explore the semiotic resources which users employ for the meaningful representation of their identities. Lastly, I draw on online ethnography and more specifically on **discourse-centred online ethnography** (Androutsopoulos 2008). I rely on users' insights as a backdrop to the choice and interpretation of the data, with a view to illuminating relations between digital texts and their production and reception practices.

By combining the above theoretical and methodological frameworks, this book gives a holistic and **emic** perspective on the construction of identity on Facebook, aiming to make an original contribution to discourse studies, digital literacies and the sociolinguistics of computer-mediated discourse.

Overview of the book

Following this introduction, Chapter 2 reviews the theoretical dimensions of the book. It outlines fundamental theories of identity explaining the relationship between identity and discourse. Thereafter, it centres upon identity online and argues that our identities online are in essence a series of identities in our everyday lives that we engender in order to handle different contexts. It defines SNS and touches on how they call for identity generation, reproduction and co-construction. It then goes back to Facebook's history and gives a brief description of its main features.

Chapter 3 lays out my methodological considerations and challenges. It positions this book within the discourse-centred online ethnographic paradigm and provides details on the research design: recruitment of participants, data collection, analysis procedures, ethical concerns and researcher's role and position. It also describes the blended discourse analytic approach that has been adopted in the discussion of the examples.

Chapters 4–8 comprise the empirical findings of this book. Focusing on a different facet of identity, each chapter starts with a short theoretical introduction specific to the given chapter before turning to the description, analysis and interpretation of the data.

Chapter 4 is devoted to the ways in which Facebook participants enact their identities by talking about and through places, seeing them not only as geographical, but also as social, political, cultural and emotional entities. In so doing, they communicate something about themselves: they confirm belonging, they disidentify with the stressful aspects of a place in crisis, they express respect to other cultures, they use different languages to affiliate with certain places and they raise awareness about local and national matters. I conclude that Facebook does not disconnect the users from their physical space but rather constitutes a versatile inventory of their routes as those are inscribed in maps, check-ins, updates, photographs and 'Likes'.

Chapter 5 explores how users construct themselves in time, namely how they time their social activities, think and talk about time and age, and enact time in Facebook discourse. Being involved in processes such as sharing songs, copying lyrics, liking, writing and receiving comments, participants are found to evoke certain periods of life, recollect memories, appeal to shared experiences, recall past tastes, generate past, present and future identities, argue about time's impact on appearance, and evaluate and express humorous attitudes to ageing.

Chapter 6 probes performances of professional and educational identity. The analysis reveals how people can utilize Facebook to announce and inform about undertaken tasks, complain about work, chat about work and study topics, promote their work, publicize achievements, organize and promote events, share expertise and bolster solidarity and collegiality with fellows. I maintain that Facebook provides a friendly and supportive environment that enables and invites participants' socialization in the process of constructing and advancing knowledge, a core aspect of professional and educational identity.

Chapter 7 looks at stance as a vital mechanism of identity construction. The Greek crisis (see Appendix), being ubiquitous in my participants' posts, becomes a handy criterion for selecting examples that enable me to illustrate a wide range of stance-taking modes. I argue that Facebook has stretched our conception of what stance-taking is as different Facebook affordances propel into different ways of developing stances within the medium. Most importantly, Facebook brings out the interpersonal nature of stance-taking, allowing the untangling of identity claims and relations to other people.

Chapter 8 amalgamates privacy theories with discourse analysis with a view to offering insights into how identity can be regulated online. It is shown that by adopting a series of privacy practices, my participants manage to assert control over their self-presentation, in other words, control of how they wish to craft and present themselves, to whom they want to do so, to what extent, in which contexts and under which circumstances.

Chapter 9 brings together the main findings dispersed in the five analytical chapters, addresses some overriding concerns on researching Facebook discourse and draws out some conditional conclusions about Facebook's role in our lives.

Each chapter starts with an overview of its contents. Chapters 2–8 end with methodological details, activities and useful resources for further engagement with the topics covered. At the end of the book I have included a glossary of key terms found in the text. There is also a companion website (www.bloomsbury.com/Georgalou-Discourse-Facebook) which provides supplementary data and screenshots.

The following format conventions are used throughout the book. *Italics* are used for interview excerpts and for mentioning words from the data. <u>Underlines</u> have been added to examples to indicate the feature I am discussing. ***Bold italics*** are added to key terms that have an entry in the glossary. All textual data (Facebook posts and comments, interviews) are rendered intact, including the use of different or transliterated scripts (e.g. ***Greeklish***), stress omissions (in Greek), typo and spelling mistakes, multiple punctuation, absence of or double spacing between words, incomplete meanings and unconventional usages. All Greek examples, as well as examples that draw on different languages (e.g. Spanish, French and Hungarian), are translated into English. The English translations are found within single inverted commas ('…'). When there is only English, without inverted commas, this means that the original example was in English. All interviews were conducted in Greek. In this book I have included their English translations only. The originals can be found in the companion website. The conventions +DIM (meaning that a diminutive suffix is attached to the word) and +AUG (meaning that an augmentative suffix is attached to the word) are followed in the translated data. Consider the following example:

άμα θες ΛΑΘ<u>ΑΡΑ</u> -όχι απλώς λαθ<u>άκι</u>- έχω μια ξεγυρισμένη
'if you want a MISTAKE<u>+AUG</u> -not just a mistake<u>+DIM</u>- I have a whacking one'

Facebook comments are enumerated for ease of reference. Metadata, such as time-stamps and 'Likes' in posts and comments, are also given. The acronym FBU is used for my informants' Facebook friends and stands for Facebook User. In longer threads of comments, different Facebook participants are enumerated (e.g. FBU1, FBU2, FBU3 …). Their gender is also inserted into the examples.

2

Identity, discourse and Facebook

Identity

Identity, simply put, is who and what you are. The root of the term is traced back to the Latin *identitas*, meaning 'sameness, oneness', which in turn derives from *idem* (the same) and abstracted from *identidem*, a coalescence of the phrase *idem et idem* (over and over). The question of identity has become central to the research agenda of many disciplines and intellectual paradigms within humanities, including psychology (social, discursive, developmental and psychoanalysis), sociology, anthropology, political science, history, philosophy, communication and cultural studies, literature and linguistics. Within these fields we come across a plethora of often near-synonymous terms for identity, yet with no unanimity on how they apply, like self, self-hood, position, positioning, identification, role, personality, category, person, person formulation, person description, subjectivity, subject, subject position, agent, agency, persona, being, ethos, soul and psyche (Ivanič 1998; Thurlow et al. 2004; Benwell and Stokoe 2006; Lemke 2008).

Identity theories are roughly classified in either essentialist or constructionist terms. According to essentialists (e.g. classical, Renaissance and Enlightenment humanists), identity resides inside persons 'as a product of minds, cognition, the psyche or socialisation practices' (Benwell and Stokoe 2006: 9) and is constructed only through binary oppositions: nature versus culture, insiders versus outsiders. It follows from this that identity is a taken-for-granted, absolute, knowable and invariant feature of self-hood (ibid.). Such perceptions are presupposed by expressions like 'I must find myself'; 'I need to understand what I want from my life'; 'Above all, be yourself' (Archakis and Tsakona 2012).

Conversely, for social constructionists (e.g. social psychologists as well as conversation analysts, anthropological linguists and ethnomethodologists) identity is not the product of individuals' minds but is consistently in flux and alters on the basis of particular beliefs, values and possibilities available to them in their social, historical and cultural context. This should be taken to mean that identity is not socially determined but socially constructed (Ivanič 1998). Within this alternate framework, identity is seen as a key tool in explaining how the economic, cultural, technological and psychological changes and processes have affected our lives showing the way towards postmodernity (Widdicombe 1998). These perceptions are presupposed by expressions such as 'How you've changed, I don't recognize you'; 'My friendship has softened him'; 'In just a few months her behavior deteriorated/improved considerably' (Archakis and Tsakona 2012).

Social constructionist theory has been richly furnished by social interactionist theory. Its most pivotal figure, Erving Goffman, in his seminal work of 1956, introduced that the self performs multiple different roles in daily life and therefore cannot be understood as a wholly unified entity. He further distinguished between the 'expressions we give' and the 'expressions we give off'. The former refers to the consciously stated messages indicating how we wish to be perceived, while the latter concerns subtler – and often even unintentional – messages conveyed through action and nuance (Donath 1998).

Social constructionism converges with post-structuralism in that both consider that identity is shaped by discourse. Nonetheless, the latter conceives discourse as a vehicle of ideologies and power asymmetries (see Althusser 1976 and Foucault 1980). People consent to particular formations of power because the dominant cultural group producing the discourse convinces them of their 'truth', 'desirability' and 'naturalness' reproducing in this way social inequalities (Benwell and Stokoe 2006). Yet, Althusser's and Foucault's identity frameworks have been roundly criticized as being one-sided.

Confluence of social and personal identity

In its very term, identity encloses a paradox, as it implies both absolute sameness and distinctiveness (Buckingham 2007). Not only is it something unique to us, but it also suggests a bond with a broader group. In trying to answer the seemingly plain question 'Who am I?', I must take into consideration what I know and think about who I am; what I know and think about others; what stories I tell others about myself; what others know and think about who I am, what stories they tell about me and so on, opening up in essence an ongoing dialogue between me and them (Thurlow et al. 2004; Schiffrin 2006; Jenkins 2008).

Identity appears to have two analytically distinct aspects: social identity and personal/individual identity (personality). Social identity is defined as 'the active negotiation of an individual's relationship with larger social constructs' (Mendoza-Denton 2001: 475) and encompasses two kinds of identities: master and interactional (Tracy 2002). Master identities refer to the social circumstances into which we are born and inherit, and initially have no choice about: age, generation, sex and sexuality, race, family, capacity (abilities and disabilities of various kinds), social class, language, geographical region, nation and religion. Interactional identities pertain to our early socialization, which naturally is expanded as we grow up, including education, occupation, institutional setting and interactional activities. Hence, social identity is infused with the individual identification with a group: a process which presupposes reflexive knowledge of group membership, identification with, involvement in and emotional attachment to this belonging (Benwell and Stokoe 2006), in addition to the readiness to lock the 'others' out of this collective, which entails that we are also defined by who we are not (Hall 2000).

On the other hand, personal identity is about our personality, character and attitude, 'what goes on inside our skins' (Fortes 1983: 393). We become personalities when we are able to formulate our reputation and ultimate goals as well as to balance and prioritize our socialization in proportion to these (Fairclough 2003). Personal identity, rather than being a given and stable inner entity in space and time, becomes an open-ended and lifelong project of the self-constructed by subjective and unique choices and wishes from a vast reservoir of discourses and practices (Chouliaraki 2003).

Nevertheless, these two formations of the self, the social and the personal, should not be seen as independent from one another, contrastive or contradicting to one another, but in a dialectal, interdependent relationship: the personal (individual/private) is social (group/cultural/sociohistorical) and vice versa (Bamberg et al. 2011). When people socialize, specific aspects of their personal identity are projected onto their social identity enabling them to perform in a variety of social situations (boyd 2002). As such, individual self-hood constitutes a social phenomenon in the sense that it is shaped by interactions and negotiations with other people (Grad and Rojo 2008). As Fairclough (2003: 223) pithily remarks: 'The full social development of

(question of agency)

one's identity, one's capacity to truly act as a <u>social agent</u> intervening in and potentially changing social life, depends upon "social roles" being personally invested and inflected, a fusion between social identity and personality.'

One's identity, thus, should be understood as a synthesis of interacting aspects of different group and personal identities (Meyerhoff and Niedzielski 1994).

Identity and discourse

Identity, be it individual or group, cannot be exclusively condensed into a way of being or assigning a label; it also presupposes the inbuilt need to represent ourselves, to record our lives. Identity is a concept filled with ideas, beliefs, attitudes and values, passions, experiences, memories, influences, repulsions, attractions, interests, hobbies, idols, fetishes, problems, addictions and aspirations (Thorne 2008). All these abstract entities need to be framed in some social, cultural, economic or political context, and given some form: presented, communicated, compared, shared, adjusted, disputed, defended, resisted, managed and negotiated – in a word, 'mediated' (Gauntlett 2008).

Our identity is mediated, constituted and reconstituted, via the varied discursive practices in which we participate. As Rose (2001) has properly maintained, we sense ourselves through the operation of discourse. By discourse here I mean language as a social practice, the way in which it is used in interactions between people (Fairclough 1989). Every time we use language, we instantly disclose – either intentionally or unintentionally – something about ourselves and who we take ourselves to be. In using language, we portray ourselves in terms of both linguistic content (what we say/write) and linguistic form (how we say/write it) (Kristiansen 2003).

The relationship between discourse and identity is a mutual one. The identities we fetch to our interactions influence the way we communicate. Simultaneously, the specific discursive practices we choose shape how we perceive ourselves as well as our interlocutors (Tracy 2002). So identity is not an externalized and static notion merely reflected in discourse but is actively, incessantly and dynamically produced and reproduced by means of and in language (Benwell and Stokoe 2006).

A common denominator in discourse-analytical approaches to identity is the rejection of the essentialist position, according to which identities are fixed possessions, as a shibboleth. Instead, identity is seen as a multifaceted, fluid, dynamic, contingent, shifting and malleable attribute. Thus, from a discursive point of view, it can be realized in two ways: as a discursive performance or construction of identity in interaction, or 'as a historical set of structures with regulatory power upon identity', which in turn can challenge, transform and destabilize the discursive order (Benwell and Stokoe 2006: 29, 34). This book espouses the former discursive view.

In concurrence with Blommaert (2005), the following points should be taken on board when studying identities in discourse:

- Performing identity is not a matter of articulating a single identity, but of mobilizing a whole repertoire of momentarily positioned identity features.

- Identities are constructed in practices that produce, enact or perform identity; identity thus is identification, a product of socially conditioned semiotic work (e.g. symbols, narratives and textual genres).

- Identities can exist long before an interaction starts and thus can condition the course of this interaction.

- Identities are established when ratified by other people.

- Identities can be attributed and ascribed in hindsight.

As noted above, it is of paramount importance to think of identity as 'a process – identification' and 'not a thing' because identity 'is not something that one can have, or not; it is something that one does' (Jenkins 2008: 5) principally, we could argue, via discourse. The ways in which we identify ourselves as well as the ways in which we are identified by others can differ radically across contexts: self- and other-identification are fundamentally situational and contextual (Brubaker and Cooper 2000).

Seeing that this book investigates manifestations of identity in computer-mediated discourse, at this juncture I proceed to placing identity within the online landscape.

Online identity, identity online

Back in the end of 1990s, Horn (1998: 81) expressly stated that in the internet we are 'stripped of everything but our words'. Since then the online realm has undergone radical transformations owing to the upsurge of social media, yet the kernel of our online practices remains almost intact. All our interactions take place by means of discourse: we type on a keyboard (or touch screen) and read from a screen. Hence, our identities are created and recreated as we actively type (or touch) and post ourselves into being (Sundén 2003).

Online identity, also called virtual identity, digital identity, cyber identity or e-identity, is 'the representation of one's persona in a digital context' (Russell and Stutzman 2007). Benwell and Stokoe (2006: 278) have defined it as 'identity work performed and enacted online', 'a unique product of the linguistic qualities and technological properties of CMC'. For Markham (2005:

249), 'The first step toward [online] existence is the production of discourse, whether in the form of words, graphic images, or sounds.' Correspondingly, Androutsopoulos (2007: 282–3) views identities on the Web as 'processes in which individual relationships to larger social constructs are constructed and negotiated through text and talk' and other symbolic resources such as image, animation and sound.

The clash between online and offline identities has long constituted a conundrum among researchers. Online identities, in the frequent absence of any corporeal traits, have been seen as ambiguous, especially due to cases of trolling, category deception (e.g. gender), impersonation and identity concealment (see Donath 1998; Hardaker 2013). In lieu of thinking that we are transformed into different people in either of the offline/online environments, it would be more sensible to see our online selves as just one more series of selves in our daily lives that we generate in order to cope with various contexts (Yus 2011: 39–40). Depending on the situation we find ourselves in, the people we interact with, the stage of life we are at, our mood and motivations, we opt for expressing or make salient different aspects of our multiple and dynamic identity (Thurlow et al. 2004). As Wertheim (1999) has vividly illustrated, our 'multiple self-ing' online does not entirely differ from the 'chameleon-like behavior' we display offline. Interestingly, Barton and Lee (2013) do not differentiate between online and offline identities, but between offline and online situational contexts in which communication takes place. They are certainly right when they say that many of our contemporary social practices entwine online and offline activities (see my techno-autobiography in Chapter 1), and therefore cannot be separated.

On that account, Thurlow et al. (2004) have already suggested that it is preferable to talk about identity online rather than online identity (hence the title of this section) as the latter connotes that we have an identity somewhat distinct from an offline identity. In this line of reasoning, the kinds of identities which we bring online and those we have offline are part of one and the same ongoing process, that of identification (ibid.). A necessary desideratum then is to learn and develop the significant skill of coordinating, rather than disentangling, our communicative behaviours in these two spheres (Zhao et al. 2008).

Regarding the online/offline chasm and its implications for researchers, instead of questioning whether people on internet are actually who they say they are, the empirical focus should shift on how, where and when identities become available on the internet (Hine 2000). In other words, questions of who a given individual is offline (man or woman, young or old) or whether his or her identity appears idealized, pretentious, anti-normative or socially desirable ine become of less importance. Our exploration should focus on who, how with what kinds of resources) and why this identity is made relevant or ascribed to self or others within the various modes of sociality available in computer-mediated communication (CMC) spaces (Georgakopoulou 2006; Zhao et al. 2008). As Gee (2011: 106–7) has put it: 'As discourse analysts, we do not care whether there is a really core self or exactly what it is. We care about how people express their sense of who they are and their multiple other identities through language.'

SNS: New arenas for the construction of identities

The term Web 2.0 refers to a combination of economic, social and technological trends that laid the foundation for the next generation of the internet in late 2004 – a more mature, distinctive medium marked by collaboration and participation, openness and network effects (Musser et al. 2007). Social media are a Web 2.0 innovation and describe digital applications and services which promote social interaction between participants through the exchange and sharing of user-produced content. Examples of social media sites include SNS (e.g. Facebook), microblogging sites (e.g. Twitter), photography-sharing sites (e.g. Flickr and Instagram), music and video sharing sites (e.g. YouTube), meme-generating websites (e.g. 9GAG), location-based services (e.g. Foursquare), virtual worlds (e.g. Second Life, World of Warcraft) and livecasting services (e.g. Skype). Yet, the term 'social media' can be used more broadly (see Leppänen et al. 2014) to refer to any digital environment that promotes interaction between participants irrespective of whether it was launched before or after Web 2.0. In that sense, blogs, discussion forums, chatrooms and consumer review sites (e.g. TripAdvisor) can also be considered as types of social media.

SNS are accessible anytime from virtually anywhere (home, office, on the road) via any possible device (PC, notebook, netbook, mobile phone or tablet). What emerges from such a 24/7 sociability is a hybridized, networked self which constantly seeks opportunities for expression and connection (Papacharissi and Yuan 2011). SNS are defined by Ellison and boyd (2013: 158) as networked communication platforms in which participants

1 have uniquely identifiable public or semi-public profiles that consist of user-supplied content, content provided by other users and/or system-provided data;

2 can publicly articulate connections that can be viewed and traversed by others; and

3 can consume, produce and/or interact with streams of user-generated content provided by their connections on the site.

These profiles contain a bricolage of personal biographical information, in both textual and visual forms, presented via a template structure. In the majority of SNS, users are invited to launch profiles with brief résumés adding contacts with similar tastes. The SNS of Facebook, more precisely, deals in the main with physical friendships and acquaintances that are initiated offline and then transferred to the virtual scenario. Unlike other SNS, Facebook is not meant to address and meet strangers (although this is perfectly possible) but to sustain, deepen and extend offline relationships (Ellison et al. 2010) with known actors who share common (offline) experiences, knowledge and backgrounds.

Profiles in all SNS function as 'digital bodies' (boyd 2007), as public displays of self where users have a unique opportunity to disclose and deeply enmesh aspects of their social and personal identity, ranging from their date of birth, gender, hometown, relationship status, religious and political beliefs to current moods, feelings, thoughts, activities, interests, likes and dislikes combining language(s), imagery and other multimedia. Such identity information in the profile assists users in engaging in 'people sense-making' (Ellison et al. 2010: 138), the process of understanding 'who someone is and to determine how and why that user should interact with someone' (DiMicco and Millen 2008: 1 in Ellison et al. 2010: 139). Creating a text like an SNS profile is essentially a self-reflexive act since it involves the selection and gluing of self-related episodes and attributes (Brake 2008). Yet, it is a collaborative act as well, whereby the user's identity is shaped and validated by those with whom they share a 'friendship' (see below for the meaning of friendship on Facebook). Baym (2010) underscores that to the pool of information we have put about ourselves in SNS, by filling in slots and writing status updates, other users can also contribute by posting further details about us, **tagging** us in photographs, linking to us and discussing us (for privacy implications related to these matters, see Chapter 8). Against this backdrop, Web 2.0 self-presentations are variable among users, driven by the technological affordances available and the immediacy of social context.

Facebook

History and features

Facebook, co-founded by the then roommates and fellow Harvard University students Mark Zuckerberg (computer programmer), Eduardo Saverin (business manager), Dustin Moskovitz (computer programmer), Andrew McCollum (graphic artist) and Chris Hughes (spokesperson), made its debut on 4 February 2004 in the United States. It originally started as a network, at that time called *Thefacebook*,[1] aiming to facilitate communication within the niche communities of Harvard, initially, and then Stanford, Columbia and Yale college students. Sean Parker, co-founder of the file-sharing computer service Napster, played a pivotal role 'in helping Facebook transform from a college project into a real company' (Zuckerberg in Bertoni 2011) by finding benevolent investors and suggesting the site's renowned clean interface. In September 2006, Facebook expanded registration so that anyone could join. In no time, it spread all over the world at astounding rates becoming a 'global online giant' (Papacharissi and Yuan 2011). Its mission nowadays is 'to give people the power to share and make the world more open and connected', 'to stay connected with friends and family, to discover what's going on in the world, and to share and express what matters to them' (Facebook 2016). On average, 1.18 billion Facebook users across the world were active daily in September 2016 (Facebook 2016).[2]

Facebook participants can post on a text box (publisher box) status updates, that is to say, short messages in which they report what they are doing, thinking or feeling, share photos, photo albums and links, create **groups** of connected individuals, as well as write comments on the material they or other users, the so-called 'friends', post.[3] Note here that the traditional meaning of friends is stretched to include anyone with whom a user is connected on Facebook, be that offline actual friends or casual acquaintances, parents, colleagues, lovers, friends of friends, people they only know or have met online and so on (for the collapse of various social relationships in a single Facebook profile, see Chapters 6 and 8). Friend relationship is reciprocal (Page 2012): once a friend is confirmed by a Facebook member, both can see and post to each other's Wall or **Timeline**,[4] unless privacy settings are customized differently by the profile owner. Moreover, Facebook participants can like status updates, comments and other postings by clicking the 'Like' button at the bottom of the content.[5]

Expanding Parks's (2010) taxonomy on MySpace (SNS launched in 2003) social affordances, I have grouped Facebook features in terms of four types of affordances: participation, space, personal expression and connection. Affordances of participation pertain to creating a profile, with a profile picture, a **cover photo** and other (optional) information about one's self according to a series of preset fields, and setting it to private or public. Affordances of space refer to the environment that users face each time they log in to Facebook, namely their News Feed and Timeline. Affordances of personal expression involve profile customization by means of posting status updates, photos, videos and links. Affordances of connection deal with friending and ways of contacting and linking with others through comments, the 'Like' button, tagging, private messages, instant messaging, groups, pages and **events**.

This categorization gives us an overall picture of Facebook's infrastructure. Of course, it should not be taken as exhaustive as some of the features in this categorization unavoidably overlap (e.g. a user can connect with a friend via posting a video on their Timeline). What matters is that Facebook users deploy and/or play with these affordances, and their constraints, to 'make meaning' and 'shape their identities' (Adami and Kress 2010), based on their perceptions and knowledge of how these affordances are experienced and appropriated as well as on their wider sociocultural assumptions and values. This book abounds with examples on how people can utilize affordances to that end, with Chapter 8, in particular, looking at this issue in greater detail offering some critical reflections as well.

Facebook has been given numerous facelifts over the years; however, its core experience has remained mostly unchanged since its launch: posting self-relevant information on a customizable profile page as well as connecting and interacting with other members, with the major spaces for writing being still available (Barton and Lee 2013). Whether or not findings from Facebook studies are considered obsolete, each time Facebook refurbishes its interface is touched upon in the concluding chapter.

A convergent and emergent discourse phenomenon

As can be deduced from the previous section, Facebook's nature is fluid, flexible and dynamic: members can edit or update their profile information, communicate with others publicly and privately, synchronously and asynchronously, whereas their News Feed is continually changing, friend lists fluctuate as contacts are added or removed, and as developers update the site's layout and infrastructure (Page 2012). It is not then overstatement to argue that Facebook represents the epitome of 'convergence culture' (Jenkins 2006). Within the social media ecosystem, convergence is understood as the multiple co-occurring of various formerly separate Web spaces and modes of communication – verbal and visual – in one single platform (Lee 2011). For twenty-first-century media, as Meikle (2010) contends, convergence defines content, computing and communications: new platforms mushroom, audiences are reconfigured and digital contexts become bustling with shareable and remixable multimodal products, all in real time and universally. These convergences, he elaborates, beget the convergence of different kinds of media texts (e.g. a comic that becomes videogame and then film), the convergence of professional and non-professional (e.g. citizen journalism) and the convergence of personal communication with public media.

Although the concepts of convergence and participation do not directly refer to language, they have significant implications for online discourse phenomena (Androutsopoulos 2010). Inspired by Crowston and Williams (2000), Herring (2013) has classified these phenomena into three categories:

'familiar', 'reconfigured' and 'new' or 'emergent'. 'Familiar' phenomena are those known from older computer-mediated discourse modes (e.g. email, chat and forums) that appear in the rhetoric of Web 2.0 as well with minor differences (e.g. non-standard typography and orthography, code-switching, gender differences, flaming, trolling and scams). 'Reconfigured' phenomena seem new at first blush (e.g. status updates, quoting and retweeting), but in fact they already have online antecedents (in Internet Relay Chat, massively multiplayer online games and discussion forums). Lastly, the label 'new', or 'emergent', is reserved for phenomena that did not exist – or if they did, the public was not aware of them – before the Web 2.0 era.

Herring highlights that we should be very careful in claiming that any phenomenon is entirely new. Concerning Facebook, as she rightly observes, it started as a fusion of the format of 'face books' from Harvard University dormitories with Web-based features such as commenting; therefore, it was adapted. However, over time it has assembled and combined manifold features (from graphics to a mixture of CMC modes) that it can presently be regarded as emergent. According to Herring, it is not the plethora of features that make Facebook a new discourse phenomenon, but the fact that as a whole differs qualitatively from the sum of its parts, on the one hand, and that it does not have any other precedents, on the other. Plausibly, these new forms of discourse entail and enable new forms of discourse analysis (Jones et al. 2015), as we will see in the following chapters.

Identity in this book

According to Brubaker and Cooper (2000: 1), identity 'tends to mean too much (when understood in a strong sense), too little (when understood in a weak sense), or nothing at all (because of its sheer ambiguity)'. In view of all that has been discussed so far in this chapter, this book takes on a constructionist approach to identity and is built upon the following premises:

- identity is the fusion of social identity and personality;
- identity is a form of socially meaningful practice;
- identity is constructed in discourse;
- the relationship between discourse and identity is reciprocal;
- identity involves a semiotic process of representation;
- identity is multifaceted and is not a single entity;
- identity is contextual;

- identity is an interactive task;

- analysis is interested in the discursive manifestation(s) of a given identity and not in its authenticity;

- identity online is not separate from identity offline;

- identity formation is enabled and restrained by available Facebook technologies.

The subsequent chapters further deepen, extend and enrich the concept of identity, as constructed in the SNS of Facebook, in relation to place (Chapter 4), time and age (Chapter 5), profession and education (Chapter 6), stance (Chapter 7) and privacy (Chapter 8). The reasons why identity was chosen to be investigated through the prism of these particular facets are addressed in Chapter 3, which delineates my methodological considerations.

ACTIVITY 2.1: AFFORDANCES

Consider the examples given below and discuss how the users perceive the affordance of the 'Like' button.

Example 1

A male user (undergraduate student preparing for a presentation) is tagged in a photo depicting him in an uncomfortable position trying to fix a paper jam in a photocopy machine. The photo receives a number of likes. This is what the user commented underneath the photo:

> what do the above likes mean?? I had 5 strokes up to that moment and then I foamed from the mouth (the exorcist came a bit later!)

Example 2

Status update by a female user:
it's been 19 years since my first trip to London and my first obsession with the Smiths. mom, I'm growing old. [Smith's song *Last Night I Dreamt That Somebody Loved Me* is embedded in her status.]
8 people like this

Comments underneath the status:

1   Male friend: The 'Like' is for London and the Smiths:-)

2   Status updater: do you mean you don't like the way I'm getting old? hahahahaha!:p

3   Male friend: I have learnt not to comment on ladies' age issues;-)

Useful resources

Print

One of the most comprehensive books on the relationship between discourse and identity is written by Benwell and Stokoe (2006). The volume on discourse and identity edited by De Fina, Schiffrin and Bamberg (2006) is also very wide-ranging and illuminating.

Concerning Facebook, since its advent, it has constituted a novel and challenging context for research in various fields. Wittkower's (2010) philosophical work as well as Miller's (2011) and Miller and Sinanan's (2017) anthropological work on Facebook are ideal starting points. Wilson et al. (2012) have carried out a comprehensive review of Facebook research in the social sciences that tackles descriptive analysis of users, motivations for using Facebook, identity presentation (with authenticity and idealization of identity being the main foci), the role of Facebook in social interactions, and privacy and information disclosure.

As far as the sociolinguistics and discourse analysis of Facebook are concerned, recent work has focused on issues of

- translation and language policy (Barton and Lee 2013; Lenihan 2011 and 2014);
- literacy (Eisenlauer 2013; Lee 2011);
- multilingualism (Androutsopoulos 2013b and 2014; Barton and Lee 2013);
- minority languages (Honeycutt and Cunliffe 2010);
- facework (West and Trester 2013; Bedijs et al. 2014);
- compliments (Maíz-Arévalo 2013; Maíz-Arévalo and García-Gómez 2013; Placencia and Lower 2013);
- humour and language creativity (Lewin-Jones 2015);
- gender (García-Gómez 2011);
- narration (Page 2012; Georgakopoulou 2013a,c);
- addressivity and audience design (Tagg and Seargeant 2014 and 2016);
- linguistic reflexivity, enregisterment and normativity (Stæhr 2015a,b).

I have not yet found any books exclusively on Facebook discourse and identity. The particular topic mainly constitutes a slice of larger-scale linguistic research on social media and not a full-fledged study per se. Some useful linguistic case studies on Facebook and identity can be found in Bolander and Locher (2010; 2015), Locher and Bolander (2014; 2015), Page (2012, Chapter 4), Barton and Lee (2013, Chapter 6), Seargeant and Tagg (2014, Chapters 1, 2, 4 and 5), Tyrkkö and Leppänen (2014), and more particularly the article by Jousmäki (2014), and Koteyko and Hunt (2016).

On language-focused research on digital communication more generally, see Georgakopoulou and Spilioti (2016).

Web

Facebook features
www.bloomsbury.com/Georgalou-Discourse-Facebook

Bibliography of research on SNS
http://www.danah.org/researchBibs/sns.php

Bibliography of research on Facebook in the social sciences
http://psych.wustl.edu/robertwilson

Facebook in discourse studies
http://www.discourses.org/resources/bibliographies/Facebook.doc

Language and Superdiversity: (Dis)identification in Social Media
https://www.jyu.fi/hum/laitokset/kielet/tutkimus/hankkeet/lgsd

British Association for Applied Linguistics Special Interest Group in Language and New Media
http://www.baal.org.uk/sig_lnm

The impact of new media on forms and practices of self-presentation
http://www.ego-media.org

Why we post: Social media through the eyes of the world
https://www.ucl.ac.uk/why-we-post

Video

Cinematic portrayal of how Facebook was founded:

The Social Network (2010), [Film] Dir. David Fincher, USA: Columbia Pictures.

Television portrayals of SNS and their founders:

Killer App (2011), [Episode from the television series *Lie to me**], Fox, 31 January, 21.00.

One Percent (2013), [Episode from the television series *Person of Interest*], CBS, 7 February, 22.00.

3

An online ethnography of Facebook discourse

Chapter overview

From ethnography to online ethnography

Principles of ethnography

Seeing that Facebook envelops technology, language, culture and self-hood, I approached my project as an online ethnographic study. This modus operandi enabled me to explore thoroughly the rich situated meanings of Facebook communication making sense of participants' practices and experiences in the context of day-to-day usage of the service. Facebook consists of faces, that is, people, and I wished for my data to have a human face, to have an identity since this is a book about identity. The unique asset of ethnography lies in that it can give a vivid output 'with human resonance impossible to recreate by the application of other methodologies' (Hobbs 2006: 102).

Ethnography, deriving from the Greek words ἔϑνος (ethnos, meaning 'folk, people, nation') and γράφω (grapho, meaning 'I write'), is a qualitative research approach, which embarks on close, in-depth examination of social groups and social activities in their real-life settings. The ethnographer participates in people's everyday lives for a prolonged period of time, watching what happens, listening to what is said and asking questions so as to gain illuminating insights into the issues upon which the research focuses (Hammersley and Atkinson 2007). Ethnography has been located in the heart of sociologists' and anthropologists' practice – its founding figure was Bronisław Malinowski (1884–1942), an anthropologist who carried out field research near Papua New Guinea – but is also widely employed across the social science disciplines. With respect to linguistics, it was Dell Hymes (1927–2009) who championed the merits of ethnography in the study of language in society establishing the framework for the ethnography of communication (Hymes 1964).

The principles, as summarized by Papen (2005), upon which ethnography is founded are as follows:

- Ethnography is holistic (not isolating individual factors).

- It includes engagement in the lives (or in selected aspects of the lives) of those being studied, usually for long periods of time.

- It studies real subjects in real-life contexts.

- It draws out the insiders' (emic) perspective.

- It is based on an interpretive process that involves both the researcher's and the research subjects' perspective on the issues in question.

The main research techniques, or research methods, that ethnography employs are *participant observation*, interviews (unstructured, *semi-structured* and, occasionally, structured in the form of questionnaires and surveys), document analysis and visual methods (e.g. photography, videos, film) (Papen 2005).

Online ethnography

Online ethnography, also termed digital ethnography, internet ethnography, virtual ethnography (Hine 2000), netnography (Kozinets 2002), cyberethnography (Domínguez et al. 2007) and webnography (Puri 2007), 'transfers the ethnographic tradition of the researcher as an embodied research instrument to the social spaces of the Internet' (Hine 2008: 257). Robinson and Schulz (2009) have distinguished three waves in the evolution of the ethnographic practice in response to the internet and digitally mediated environments: (1) pioneering, (2) legitimizing and (3) multimodal. In the beginning of 1990s, pioneering cyberethnographers (e.g. Rheingold 1993; Turkle 1995) focused on uncovering the centrality of identity play and deception that separated online and offline realms conducting fieldwork on technophile user populations, whose main online activities revolved around role-playing games. Then, in late 1990s, legitimizing ethnographers (e.g. Markham 1998; Baym 2000; Hine 2000; Miller and Slater 2000; Kendall 2002) were concerned with transforming offline methodological approaches to online spaces. Viewing the digital *field site* as part of a flow between online and offline realities, they formed the bedrock of much of what is nowadays known as 'online ethnographic practice'. Current online ethnographers (e.g. boyd 2014; Lange 2014) tackle the burgeoning multimodal-mediated communication occurring in Web 2.0 venues turning their analytical gaze to visual, aural and other non-text modalities, immersing themselves in pop culture, and moving between multiple field sites, including offline ones.

Discourse-centred online ethnography

The data of this book draw on what Androutsopoulos (2008) has conceived and proposed as discourse-centred online ethnography strongly influenced by previous research into CMC, Hine's virtual ethnography and Hymes's linguistic ethnography. Androutsopoulos's (2008) springboard is that 'research based exclusively on log data is not ideally positioned to examine participants' discourse practices and perspectives or to relate these practices and perspectives to observable patterns of language use'.

TABLE 3.1 Guidelines for doing discourse-centred online ethnography

Practice-derived guidelines for systematic observation
• Examine relationships and processes rather than isolated artefacts.
• Move from core to periphery of a field.
• Repeat observation.
• Maintain openness.
• Use all available technology.
• Use observation insights as guidance for further sampling.
Practice-derived guidelines for contact with internet actors
• Contacts should be limited, non-random, and include various participation formats.
• Pay attention to the initial contact.
• Formulate and customise interview guidelines.
• Confront participants with (their own) material.
• Seek repeated and prolonged contacts.
• Make use of alternative techniques whenever possible.

Source: Androutsopoulos (2008)

He, therefore, advocates that online ethnography has necessarily two dimensions: a screen-based and a participant-based one. The former centres on systematic and longitudinal observation of online discourse (Facebook discourse in this book), while the latter draws upon direct (face-to-face and/or mediated) engagement with online actors, that is, the producers of this online discourse (specific Facebook profile owners in this book). Discourse-centred online ethnography coalesces both these dimensions and is complementary to the textual analysis of *log data*.

In the remainder of this chapter, I provide an account of how I designed and carried out my research as a discourse-centred online ethnography, inspired by the guidelines shown in Table 3.1. Note, however, that there are certain things that I did not take from this approach. I will come back to that at the end of the chapter, where I also assess the benefits accruing from doing discourse-centred online ethnography.

Facebook participants

My very first step was to write a solicitation through email, in which I explained the purposes of my study. In this message I also included a brief online questionnaire to be filled in by the potential participants. The survey covered questions pertaining to the reasons for creating online profiles, the types of shared and shareable content as well as a mini-assessment of the users' presence in social media venues. In order to find participants for my study, I adopted a convenient sampling strategy; that is, I chose the nearest individuals to serve as informants and continued that process until I obtained the required sample size from those who were available and accessible at that particular time. To that end, I asked my own friends and family who had a Facebook account to forward my message to Facebook contacts of theirs. The simple reason I did not recruit friends and acquaintances of mine was to avoid subjectivity and bias in my analysis. Instead, my friends and relatives functioned as 'insider assistants' (King and Horrocks 2010) who helped me in two ways: one, by establishing further credibility for my study, and, two, by nurturing honesty and commitment on the part of the interviewees. In the end, five participants[1] agreed to be interviewed and have their Facebook profiles and Timelines painstakingly observed. Their demographics and background information are found below (valid as of the completion of my ethnography in April 2013) under pseudonyms.

Romanos

Romanos was born in 1989 and lives in Athens, Greece. He has studied videogame programming in a private institute of vocational training and has worked for the Greek branch of an IT company with an international reputation, offering technical support. He speaks Greek (native) and English. In September 2012, he started serving his mandatory military service, with 14 months of regular duty in the army. Romanos accepted to participate in my research in April 2010. He joined Facebook on 24 November 2007. He visits his profile every day and posts once in ten days. His posting activity was significantly reduced when he joined the army (see also Chapter 5). His main incentives for creating a Facebook profile (Cha 2010) were of interpersonal utility (to keep in touch with friends and acquaintances, communicate with people he knows and cannot meet face-to-face, bantering with close friends even if he sees them every day), boredom relief (to kill time, browse photos) and learning (to spot events). His friends' list has remained rather steady, with 143 friends upon his recruitment, on 13 May 2010, and 146 friends on 23 September 2012.

Gabriel

Gabriel was born in 1990 and originally comes from Athens, Greece. He holds a BA in International and European Studies (University of Piraeus, Greece). In 2012 he moved to the United States to pursue an MA in European and International Economics. He speaks Greek (native), English, French and

Spanish. He was recruited in July 2010. He has maintained a Facebook account since 27 November 2008, primarily to stay in contact with people he already knows offline. He had 404 Facebook friends on 17 July 2010 and 708 friends on 23 September 2012. He visits his profile almost everyday and posts 5 times per month maximum.

Carla

Carla was born in 1975 and lives in Athens, Greece. She has a BA in Translation and Interpreting from the Ionian University in Corfu, Greece. She has been working as a translator, principally of Latin American literature. She speaks Greek (native), English, Spanish, Portuguese and French. She was recruited in October 2010. She has been monitoring two Facebook profiles: a personal one (since 5 November 2007) and a professional (since 20 January 2009). Her main motives for setting them up were interpersonal, that is, to keep in touch with friends, acquaintances and colleagues as well as entertainment and learning, that is, to express and share interests, views and ideas (see also Cha 2010). She visits her personal profile almost everyday posting once or twice per week. Her professional profile is updated less often, 3–4 times per month. On the day of her recruitment (26 October 2010), Carla had 109 friends in her personal profile and 92 friends in her professional one. Two years later (23 September 2012), she counted 142 and 128 friends, respectively.

Alkis

Alkis was born in 1981 and lives in Athens, Greece. He has gained a BA in Translation and Interpreting from the Ionian University in Corfu, Greece, as well as an MSc in Services Management from Athens University of Economics and Business. He has worked as a freelance translator, a project manager and a real estate agent. In 2009–11 Alkis was a postgraduate student working simultaneously full-time as a project manager. From December 2011 (he was preparing his MSc dissertation then) until June 2012, he was unemployed. He speaks Greek (native), English, French and Italian. He was recruited in December 2010. He created his Facebook profile in November 2007 in order to maintain contact with friends and acquaintances as well as to express himself. He visits his profile almost every day and uploads posts 2–6 times per week. His friend list is hidden from all his contacts for privacy reasons (see Chapter 8). However, in our first interview (December 2010), he claimed he had 430 Facebook friends.

Helen

Helen was born in 1979 and lives in Athens, Greece, while she visits the UK for one month every year working as an English for Academic Purposes (EAP) tutor in various British universities. She has a BA in English (American College of Greece, Athens), an MA in English Language and Literary Studies (Lancaster University, UK) and a PhD in Linguistics (Lancaster University, UK). She works as a lecturer in Academic English in Athens. She speaks Greek (native), English and Spanish. She was recruited in October 2011. She has been a Facebook member since 9 September 2007. She too visits her profile almost every day posting once a week. The chief reason she opened her account was to sustain bonds with networks that are geographically dispersed. Her Facebook friend list included 175 people in 30 November 2011 and 216 in 23 September 2012. Given that many of Helen's friends are international, she writes her updates and comments mainly in the English language.

Except for Romanos, the other four informants were not owners of smartphones or tablets during the data collection period. This means that their posts were made from a desktop computer and/or a laptop.

Interviews

As my purpose was to study phenomena that occur online, I opted for mediated engagement with my participants; that is, I made use of online settings to conduct my interviews. I employed different procedures and methods for interviews as my participants were given the initiative to select their preferred interview technology (e.g. email for Carla, Gabriel and Alkis; instant messaging for Helen and Romanos) at their convenience and in accordance with their schedules and various commitments. After plunging into participant observation and starting my analysis, new questions grew organically. I sent to the participants multiple messages, either via email or Facebook private messages, with various follow-up questions for further clarifications at different stages of the analysis and different time spans. These interviews enabled me to learn about and comprehend my informants' elicited narratives and representations of their social worlds, namely beliefs, ideologies, justifications, motivations and aspirations. They also offered me the opportunity to learn about their histories, internal power struggles and unofficial customs (see also Boellstorff et al. 2012: 92–3), especially with regard to privacy matters.

For their time and invaluable contribution to the study, the participants received a small compensation prize, that is, €10 vouchers from an Athenian bookstore (Carla, Alkis, Helen) and $15 vouchers from Amazon (Gabriel,

Romanos). The prize was provided as a 'thank you' token rather than as an inducement to take part in the research.

Researcher's position

Undertaking online ethnography presupposes that the researcher has to introduce themselves in the epistemological space of the practice under investigation (Rybas and Gajjala 2007). My research motivations originated in my personal participation and interest in Facebook. My position then as a Facebook researcher was largely facilitated by my role as an active Facebook user. In Schaap's (2001) terms, I developed a 'divided self', acting both as a participant in and as an observer of Facebook activities. This insider status of mine played a vital role in my participants being 'at ease' with me as their researcher and as their Facebook friend too (see also Robards 2013).

As part of the Facebook setting, I had a prior intimate view of users' practices building and maintaining my own network. I came to the decision not to set up a separate profile on Facebook for research purposes. Instead, I added my informants as friends to the profile I already owned to allow a degree of mutuality with them. As I was given access to their profiles, I thought it would be fair they were also given access to mine. Taking into account the challenging aspect of this choice, I adjusted some of my privacy settings pertaining to visibility of content and list of friends. I speculate my respondents may have done similar customizations.

I clicked 'Like' on their status updates or other posts I found interesting, wished them on name days and birthdays, and vice versa on their part. Alkis once sent me a Christmas card by post while Carla sent me a book she had co-translated. Beyond research purposes, I exchanged emails with Carla when she asked me for some travel information. I also had a Facebook messaging communication with Romanos talking about our jobs and his decision to join the army. At some point, I sought Helen's advice on professional issues. Whenever I heard about a translation or editing job vacancy, I immediately notified Carla and Alkis to spread the word to their networks. I even became very fond of The National, an American indie rock band previously unknown to me, thanks to Carla's frequent postings of their songs.

On 8 March 2013, we arranged with Helen to meet face-to-face for a coffee in Athens city centre to get introduced to each other. As we sat opposite each other, I felt I had known Helen long before I met her. I knew her favourite singers and authors, the place of her last holidays, the bantering with her partner, her worries about the Greek crisis. To my surprise, she told me exactly the same thing: she felt she had known me from before. In essence, we had built commonality on Facebook through words and bits and pieces of other semiotic material, and that was truly fascinating.

A second, rather different, meeting with Helen followed. On 9 May 2014, I gave a conference presentation in Athens. My topic was about the Greek crisis as narrated and discursively represented on Facebook. The data I had chosen to discuss came from Helen's profile exclusively as the crisis has been a very frequent theme in her Facebook posts (see Chapters 4 and 7). Three days prior to the conference I had asked her whether she would be able to attend my talk. And indeed, on 9 May, there she was sitting in the fourth row of the conference theatre. While I was talking, I could see Helen taking notes. Some members of the audience were taking photographs of my slides depicting Helen's posts. Others appeared really interested in her case and asked several questions (e.g. about her choice of language, her sarcasm towards Greek politicians). It felt surprisingly strange for me answering for her in front of her. Right after the talk I had a very brief follow-up with Helen on her notes. She too confessed it felt surprisingly strange for her listening to the audience and me talking about her.

After the completion of my ethnography, an informal, face-to-face **post hoc interview** with Carla took place in an Athenian café on 8 October 2014. Carla (and the other four informants as well) had received my analysis via email prior to our meeting. Apart from reflecting on my analysis, Carla offered detailed and emotionally laden accounts on her decision to learn Spanish and follow a career in literary translation as well as on the relationship she maintains with her teacher of Spanish. She bantered on the pseudonym *Carla* (see below) while she admitted that occasionally, while composing a status update, she was momentarily thinking that I was about to see the update and perhaps analyse it. Such a thought, however, did not prevent her from her original posting. The moment she was about to press the button to publicize her update, she had already forgotten my existence as a researcher, as she told me. Initially, I was surprised that Carla revealed so many things to me that had not come up in our online, text-based interviews. Yet, I realized that she is so open now because, after having the whole picture of what this research has been about, she can trust me more.

As I write these lines (July 2016), my informants and myself are still friends on Facebook, occasionally exchanging messages on various topics other than research, likes and wishes.

Data

From the time my informants and I became 'friends' on Facebook, I conducted bi-weekly observation of their profiles. The hours spent browsing their

Facebook Walls varied according to their frequency of posting and the wealth of interactions unfolded. As they were recruited at different periods, I reached the decision to have May 2010 as a starting point of my observation for all five of them. My observation lasted almost three years, ending in April 2013. My data comprised Facebook profile information, status updates, comments, video and article links, photos my informants have taken themselves or have found elsewhere in the internet, interview excerpts, survey and field notes as well my informants' comments on my drafts. This latter extra data set, on the one hand, brought my participants closer to the core of my research and proved helpful for me in gauging reconstructions of my analysis through their standpoint. On the other hand, such a practice 'empowered' (Cameron et al. 1992) them in the research, as they participated in the analysis itself. I have been benefited greatly from the fact that Carla, Helen and Alkis, thanks to their studies and jobs, showed metalinguistic awareness and critically reflected upon their posts.

Once in a while, Carla shared Facebook updates relevant to the reports I was sending her. Figures 3.1 and 3.2 illustrate two posts she made after

FIGURE 3.1 *Carla comments on drafts of the analysis.*

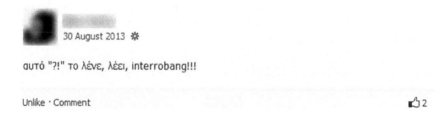

FIGURE 3.2 *Carla shares her discovery after reading a draft of the analysis (her status reads: 'This "?!", they say, is called interrobang!!!').*

reading an earlier version of Chapter 5. In Figure 3.1 Carla teasingly refers to my evaluation of her age in relation to the other participants. In the status, she speaks in the first person while in her follow-up comment she writes ήρθα στα ίσια μου (now I'm back on my feet) and then quotes my words ('she is just 37'). Elsewhere, within the same chapter, I had mentioned the use of the interrobang, a non-standard punctuation mark which combines the functions of the question mark and the exclamation mark (?!). Carla got enthusiastic in reading that the particular punctuation mark has a proper name and posted her new discovery as shown in Figure 3.2. Notice that in both posts Carla is very careful: she does not specify the context in which she is the oldest participant nor does she reveal where she learnt about the interrobang settling for the impersonal λέει (they say).

Status updates, interactions and interviews were manually imported in Word documents. Field notes were inserted as comments in the documents or as in-text information in different colouring. For screen captures of statuses, comments and photos, as well as their resizing, I used the free screenshot app PicPick Image Editor (www.picpick.org), whereas for image editing (cropping, blurring, adding brightness filters), Pixlr editor (http://pixlr.com/editor) and Pixlr o-matic (http://pixlr.com/o-matic), two free cloud-based sets of image tools and utilities. It should be noted that I have chosen English (UK) as my primary language in Facebook and as a result the hypertext links of Facebook interface (e.g. Home, News Feed, Like, Comment, Share) appear in English in my screenshots irrespective of whether my participants have chosen Greek or any other language. Furthermore, all timings in the data are plus two hours Greenwich Mean Time, that is, Greek time.

Table 3.2 gives a rough idea of my data corpus in numbers. Differences in numbers, as shown in the tables, are contingent on my informants' activity on Facebook. For example, in marked contrast to Helen, Gabriel usually delves into lengthy interactions with his Facebook friends. Alkis, on the other hand, as the most active user of all, posts almost every day and exchanges many comments with friends. Carla's two profiles, personal and professional, were examined in parallel, so I opted for having one document with textual information from both profiles. Interviews and feedback on my analysis are merged into one document for each participant as in a number of circumstances follow-up questions emerged from participants' commentary. Lastly, my archive comprises brief handwritten pages with notes (not mentioned in the table) I kept during my meetings with Helen and Carla, and two printed pages, with my analysis on an interaction taking place in Helen's profile, upon which Helen herself jotted down some notes (see Chapter 4).

TABLE 3.2 Data in numbers

Documents	Romanos	Gabriel	Carla	Alkis	Helen
Screenshots	59	67	31 (professional) 113 (personal)	106	89
Textual information from profiles	2,271 words	10,226 words	6,915 words	17,847 words	3,804 words
Interviews and feedback on analysis	1,056 words	797 words	1,224 words	1,809 words	2,591 words
Fieldnotes	17,040 words				

Ethical concerns

A significant first leap was already taken by my informants themselves who had set their profiles private so their content was neither searchable nor retrievable (more details on how they dealt with privacy in Chapter 8). On my part, they were asked to sign a consent form in which they were assured that their material (information they added about themselves, status updates, their comments, their friends' comments, images, other multimedia) would remain confidential and would be used for academic purposes solely.[2] It was highlighted that they could withdraw from the study at any time they wished.

Throughout my data I have preserved pseudonymity for my informants and anonymity for other Facebook users. My informants were welcome to choose their own fictive names. Carla confessed to me there was a personal story behind her choice of the particular pseudonym. She and a good male friend of hers had at some point constructed an imaginative scenario parodying Latin American soap operas (a popular TV genre in Greece). He would be the rich and powerful boss of a big company and she would be his 'naughty' secretary. Both agreed that *Carla* would be a suitable name for the secretary. Since then *Carla*, both as a fictional character and as a proper name, started recurring as an inside joke between the two friends.

Romanos asked me to think of a name for him while I rejected Gabriel's initial pseudonym. He wanted to be called *paralias* (the beach guy), which I thought it detracted from the seriousness of his profile as well as from the development of my argument.

Moreover, I have blurred images depicting faces and other revealing personal information. In the same vein, I have deleted comments or parts of comments referring to individuals by name or other information (e.g. place names). Handling third-party data, that is, data on my informants' profiles from users that had not given their consent, constituted a thorny matter. Just asking for their permission to use their comments was not always enough. Sending them samples of textual analysis of their Facebook interactions gave them a clearer picture of my research and secured their approval. I also asked my subjects to inform their Facebook friends on the issue. Yet, not all Facebook users were willing to give their consent so their comments were not included in my analysis.

Processing data

My analysis draws on the principles of **grounded theory** (Glaser and Strauss 1967). This means that my theoretical understanding of the observations was fully grounded in and developed on the basis of my observations in the data. I started with an orienting theory on identity, online identity and social network sites, already unfurled in Chapter 2, which functioned as a compass in my research design. My data (Facebook material and interviews) were gathered on an ongoing, recursive basis, and I kept on adding to my set until there was sufficient data that would allow me to create a theoretical explanation of what was happening and its key features.[3] My analysis started once I had any data (May 2010), continued and got revamped throughout and beyond the period of data garnering (April 2013).

I came up with the categories of place, time, profession and education, stance and privacy after multiple and close readings of my data. In this fashion, I identified themes, sub-themes and concepts and then consulted the relevant literature. Put it differently, the existing literature on the specific thematic contents became part of the analysis – it did not determine a priori the nature of the research. Adopting a thematic approach proved to be very useful for dealing with a variety of data (archival Facebook posts, visuals, interviews and notes) and theorizing across a number of cases. What I did was identifying common thematic elements across the five research participants and the events and practices they reported.

I was cycling back and forth between theory and data to identify patterns and systematize my data. I compared, contrasted, linked and sorted new and already existing data. I coded, defined and refined categories and subcategories in terms of broader themes (e.g. profession, privacy) as well as linguistic features (e.g. time references, mental verbs). Besides revisiting data and theory, I was visiting my informants' Facebook profiles over and over again to observe anew my data in their original context and check if I had missed anything.

Sometimes the analysis zooms in on a specific informant (e.g. Carla's two profiles), at other times on a concrete theme (e.g. advancing knowledge). Some of the discussion and analytical points connect more with some informants and not others. This is mainly due to the fact that they were quite uneven in when, how often and what kinds of things they posted. We will see, for example, in Chapter 4 that place is a key component in Helen's identity but not in Romanos's. Valuating youth and recycling memories (Chapter 5) is central in Gabriel's, Carla's and Alkis's posts but not in Helen's. Yet, in Chapter 8, all five informants appear equally concerned with ways of shielding their personal information.

It should also be stressed that my participants' voices, beyond their direct quotes, are mainly mediated by me. Their words (as appeared in questionnaires, interviews, comments on my drafts, Facebook posts) are selected by me and contextualized in the text by my words (see also Barton and Hamilton 1998: 72).

A vast volume of my data was in Greek, which meant that I had to translate them into English. In my translation, I pursued both loyalty and functionality. Loyalty refers to the closest possible match in form and content between source and target version while in functionality, the impact of the target-text on target-readership is aimed to be equivalent to that of the source-text on original recipients (Sidiropoulou 1999). Additionally, I relied on my intuition as a native speaker of Greek as well as a user familiarized with the style of writing on Facebook having used writing of that ilk myself. Throughout the book, I frequently provide further explanations or contextual information in endnotes regarding culturally specific words and phrases as well as in-text clarifications within square brackets. By and large, my main concern was to maintain the communicative force of the Greek message through culturally preferred patterns of linguistic behaviour in English.

I was fortunate enough in having the chance to triangulate my translations with my participants. Particularly, Carla and Alkis, who are professional translators themselves, upon receiving drafts of my reports, were commenting not only on the content of the analysis but also on the quality of my translation of their posts. Carla provided constructive suggestions for amelioration, whereas Alkis appeared very satisfied with how his puns and other humorous phrases had been rendered.

Discourse analysis

Discourse analysis is interested in how people use language 'to do things in the world: exchange information, express feelings, make things happen, create beauty, entertain themselves and others, and so on' (Johnstone 2008: 3). According to Baxter (2010), the core features of discourse analysis are the following:

- **Principle of variability:** Language is used for various functions and its use has variable consequences. The same phenomenon can be described differently according to audience, purpose and context, with significant variation in accounts. Accordingly, these accounts are received and interpreted in a gamut of diverse but context-appropriate ways.

- **Constructed and constructive nature of language:** The kinds of linguistic events (e.g. descriptions, narratives, accounts, comments and jokes) that occur in the data are constructions that rest on the context in which they are produced and the objectives their producers wish them to serve.

- **Interpretative or linguistic repertoire:** Research accounts often provide evidence of distinctive vocabulary, particular stylistic and grammatical features, as well as the occurrence of specific features of speech, idiomatic expressions, metaphors and other figures of speech (Wooffitt 2005).

- **A combination of micro- and macro-analytical approaches:** Identifying linguistic repertoires in the data can provide evidence for wider patterns of language use as well as for speculating about the role of the broader psychological and sociopolitical context that may inform the speech or writing of research participants.

This book combines different approaches within discourse analysis as a result of the varied theories and concepts deriving from my data. In this manner, I have developed a data-driven, bottom-up approach of discourse analysis. Starting with Chapter 4, on place and identity, my discourse-analytical methodological toolkit includes frameworks from van Dijk's (2009) classification of places into (1) personal and interpersonal, (2) social and (3) geographical as well as insights from Scollon and Scollon's (2003) and Jaworski and Thurlow's (2009a) semiotic approaches in relation to physical world and tourism.

Chapter 5, on time and identity, is informed by Coupland and colleagues' (1991) taxonomy of age identity-marking, Myers's (2010b) categorization of functions of time references in blogs as well as Georgakopoulou's (2007) small stories framework for the narration of past, present and future events.

The orientation taken in Chapter 6, on professional and educational identity, was influenced by Achugar's (2009) research on the construction of professional identity, Fasulo and Zucchermaglio's (2002) typology of identity markers in work meetings, Jacoby and Gonzales's (1991) study on the construction of expertise as well as van Leeuwen's (1996) framework of the representation of social actors.

Du Bois's (2007) stance triangle, Martin and White's (2005) appraisal theory, Myers's (2010a) investigation into stance-taking in blogs, and Myers and Lampropoulou's (2012) study on stances in social research interviews have given direction to my discussion in Chapter 7, on stance-taking.

The most central notion in Chapter 8, on privacy, is that of practice as discussed in Barton and Hamilton (1998) and Barton and Lee (2013). The focus is on discourse practices that my five informants followed to secure privacy and, concomitantly, identity. Part of the discussion has been benefited from van Leeuwen and Wodak's (1999) processes of *recontextualization*.

In managing my data, I always kept in mind that they constituted computer-mediated discourse, the analysis of which differs from other forms of discourse analysis in that it essentially allows for the technological affordances of Facebook (see Chapter 2).

With the relevant tools, concepts and frameworks sketched out above (more details in the respective chapters), in my analysis I look at choice of lexis, language mix, *code-switching*, *tropes*, pronoun use, *presuppositions*, attitudinal vocabulary and *modality*. In the generation, reproduction and co-construction of identity, I also consider the effects of:

- **intertextuality:** the traces one text bears of preceding texts, for example, by means of alluding, quoting, echoing, paraphrasing or linking;

- **interdiscursivity:** the reciprocal relationships of discourses and the connection, intersecting or overlapping of different discourses within a single linguistic product;

- **multimodality:** the co-existence of resources from more than one semiotic mode in digital content itself (e.g. written language, audio, images and videos).

Advantages of discourse-centred online ethnography

This chapter featured my research methods for data harvest, processing and interpretation. My starting point has been that language does not just exist in the abstract but is inculcated with social meanings. Applying online ethnography to discourse-based research proves especially useful in understanding the social functions of Facebook's computer-mediated discourse (see also Barton and

Lee 2013). A significant caveat is that in no way does the present study purport to represent a full, in-depth ethnography of a specific community in Facebook. Central premises within discourse-centred online ethnography, such as the investigation of participant roles and relations as well as the comparison between core and periphery were not followed, as a much bigger sample would have been needed, or were followed to a much lesser extent.[4] Other ethnographic methods such as diary keeping of social media engagements were also left out. I fully acknowledge the importance of having integrated these processes into my project as they would have yielded a potentially more fruitful and ethnographically holistic enterprise. Yet, constraints of time, space and ethical considerations (as fully informed consent should have been sought for tens of Facebook participants) as well as opting for a tighter focus, which would favour a more discourse-oriented approach, dictated that these methodological lines were excluded from the present research design. What I applied to my topic was the two key tenets of discourse-centred online ethnography, that is, 1) prolonged and systematic observation of discourse activities and semiotic production, and 2) qualitative interviews with specific social actors, which supported the analysis of the online text. So, although this is not an 'ethnography', it could be argued that it is an 'ethnographic approach' in the sense that the users' perspectives are brought to the fore and the analysis is situated within a broader sociocultural context seeking to be naturalistic with minimal intervention (see also Barton 2015). Designing and conducting my research in this way proved valuable to me in manifold ways:

- I developed a firm grip on the content my participants posted along with their frequency of posting as well as the discourse styles they adopted and the discourse activities they engaged in. For example, Romanos favoured bantering while Gabriel revealed his rhetorical strengths. Carla and Alkis often shared songs accompanied with personal comments, while Helen conveyed her messages by means of images.

- I acquired an emic understanding of my participants' semiotic practices. It was my interview with Helen that enlightened me about, and allowed me to frame, her persistent sharing of photos from demonstrations against austerity policies held in Athens. In the same vein, only after interviewing Alkis did I manage to grasp his habit of choosing to upload impersonal profile pics.

- I gained some of the 'tacit knowledge' (Kytölä and Androutsopoulos 2012) underlying my informants' 'invisible' discourse practices regarding the subtle issue of privacy (e.g. self- and other-censorship).

- I situated my informants' discourse styles and activities in multiple, frequently imbricated, contexts: the context of Facebook itself (e.g. Alkis wrote in a comment: *Ρε σεις παιδιά, μόνο εγώ ακούω όπερα;; Ούτε ένα λάικ;; – Hey guys, is it only me that I listen to opera? Not even one like??*), the broader interactional context as other Facebook friends entered, contributed to and/or diverted discussions, as well as the overall sociocultural and historical context, mainly Greek (e.g. one of Helen's status updates read: *have stayed too long in this country…*).

- I worked with various discourse analysis strands, as they emerged from the data at hand, validating in this way the dynamic, flexible character of discourse analysis as a research approach.

- I made participants realize the value of their communication on Facebook. Upon sending Carla one of my reports, she wrote me back: *δεν φανταζόμουν ποτέ ότι οι βλακείες που ανεβάζουμε στο FB θα γίνονταν αντικείμενο τέτοιας ανάλυσης!* (I could never imagine that the nonsense we upload on Facebook could become the object of such an analysis!).

- I learnt how to exploit Facebook to design research projects after witnessing how Alkis wrote his MSc dissertation utilizing Facebook as a research tool (see Chapter 6).

- I reconsidered my own participation in and usage of Facebook in terms of content posted and audiences addressed.

This chapter set out the book's research design and methods. The next chapter moves on to the analysis of properly engaging with how place and identity can be articulated in Facebook posts.

ACTIVITY 3.1: FRIENDING PARTICIPANTS

As was described in this chapter, a significant step in approaching Facebook ethnographically is to friend one's participants in order to study them. Discuss:

(a) What advantages might the researcher and the participant gain from this friending?

(b) What challenges/disadvantages might they experience?

(c) How can such a friending be affected when the participants are vulnerable (e.g. children, teenagers) or when sensitive types of information (e.g. religious affiliation, sexual preferences, health issues), concerning both the researcher and the participant, have to be dealt with?

Useful resources

Print

For a brief yet concise history of the development of ethnographic methods, see Boellstorff et al. (2012; Chapter 2). For those especially interested in the history of linguistic ethnography, Creese (2008) provides a thorough account.

Christine Hine's *Virtual Ethnography* (2000) could be considered as the keystone in the field of online ethnography. More recent studies with detailed guidance on designing ethnographic research online are Markham and Baym (2009) and Varis (forthcoming). Of the various handbooks on how to conduct online interviews, Salmons (2015) is very accessible and lucidly written. Interesting insights on the subject can also be found in Kendal (2008).

For the use of Facebook as a source of data and as a research tool within humanities and social sciences, see Baltar and Brunet (2012), Brickman Bhutta (2012), Giglietto et al. (2012), Baker (2013), Stirling (2014) and Taylor et al. (2014).

On linguistics, Androutsopoulos (2013c) provides a balanced, well-organized discussion on the conceptual, methodological and analytic conditions that may affect online data (both the collection of data from existing online sources and the creation of new data, via interactions with language users). For a fuller introduction to social media ethics in sociolinguistic research, see D'Arcy and Young (2012). Page et al.'s (2014) guidebook offers detailed practical advice on researching language and social media, including qualitative and quantitative approaches. An excellent resource on doing discourse analysis in the digital age is by Jones et al. (2015).

Web

Christine Hine on virtual ethnography's E3 internet
http://ethnographymatters.net/blog/2013/11/29/christine-hine-on-virtual-ethnographys-e3-internet/

Annette Markham's work on research methods for studying networked culture
http://www.markham.internetinquiry.org/research/

Microanalysis of online data (MOOD)
http://moodnetwork.ruhosting.nl/

Practical tips for conducting online interviews
http://vision2lead.com/design/

Data collection tools for social media
http://socialmediadata.wikidot.com/

Ethical guidelines in internet research compiled by the Association of Internet Researchers (AoIR)
http://aoirethics.ijire.net/2012aoirgraphic.pdf

Social media research: A guide to ethics
http://www.dotrural.ac.uk/socialmediaresearchethics.pdf

Council for Big Data, Ethics, & Society
http://bdes.datasociety.net/

4

Place and identity
on Facebook

Chapter overview

Place

Who we are is entwined with where we are, where we have been or where we are going (Barnes 2000). Facebook's prompt in content sharing is straightforward: 'Share where you are. Let people know where you've been, where you're heading and where you are now.'[1] How do Facebook users refer to places? Where are these references tied up to places? What do they imply or infer about place identities in these references? These matters will be addressed in this chapter.

Place is not just a position in space; it is the location plus everything that occupies that location, that is, tasks, practices, routines, everyday life, seen as an integrated and meaningful phenomenon (Relph 1976; Myers 2006). van Dijk (2009) classifies places into three basic types: personal and interpersonal, social and geographical. Personal and interpersonal places deal with where we are now (in the sense of where our bodies are now) as well as our interlocutors; in other words a space that organizes our interaction, perspective and discourse. Social places, on the other hand, locate our activities in everyday life: at home, at work and during leisure time; hence they are usually defined in terms of what people do in these places – many of which are institutional. Examples in this category comprise outdoor places, residential places, commercial places, commercial service places, community service places, government agencies, educational places, leisure places and workplaces. Ultimately, the third kind of place, although called geographical, in essence embraces social, political and cultural dimensions. These places can be represented by their scope, range, size or level, and are progressively inclusive, for example, home, street, neighbourhood, city, state, province, country, region, continent and world.

Place, identity and language

French philosopher Gabriel Marcel (1889–1973) (cited by Relph 1976) propounded the idea that individuals are not distinct from their place – they are that place. All of us have a strong bond with the places where we were born and grew up, where we live or where we experience particular stirring moments. Humanist geographer Relph (1976) sees this bond as a starting point from which we can orient ourselves to the world. By the same token, environmental psychologists duly acknowledge that 'who we are' is intimately related to 'where we are', arguing that identity is not only shaped by place, but we ourselves may also serve as contextual markers for shaping place identities (Dixon and Durrheim 2000). In their seminal article, Proshansky et al. (1983) view place identity as consisting of cognitions about the physical world in which we are located. These cognitions, they maintain, represent an assortment of memories, conceptions, interpretations, ideas, attitudes, values, beliefs, social meanings, preferences and feelings about specific physical settings. Put it plainly, place identity refers to the ways in which we understand ourselves by attributing meanings to places. As such, it should not be understood as a separate part of identity related to place, since all aspects of identity often contain significant references to place or incorporate locations or trajectories as crucial constituents (Twigger-Ross and Uzzell 1996; Blommaert 2005).

For sociolinguists and discourse analysts, a place acquires its meanings by the ways it is represented, that is, written, talked about and photographed, as well as by the situated interactions that 'take place' within it (Myers 2006; Thurlow and Jaworski 2011). Language can form and transform our everyday experiences of 'self-in-place' (Tuan 1991; Johnstone 2011) so that places are constructed in ways that carry profound implications for who we are, who we can claim to be (Dixon and Durrheim 2000) or where we belong (Taylor 2003). Through this spectrum, language should not be seen as a mere means to represent or describe external environments. It is also a symbolic resource through which constructions of place can do rhetorical work, such as making contrasts, justifying statements, giving a perspective on the topic, narrating stories and – what is of interest here – claiming an identity (see also Myers 2010b).

Facebook and multiple-placed identities

The practice of writing and uploading other multimedia content on Facebook is a self-reflexive process which is not situated in a particular location; it can exist anywhere, allowing the en route construction of a hybrid place identity as mobile, shifting. Consider the case of my informant, Helen, who experiences a triple spatial reality: She lives and works in Athens; she has stayed for seven years in the UK (2002–9) while she has been serving as a visiting EAP tutor in British universities for one month per year since 2010; her partner is Hungarian and lives in Budapest. While observing her profile, I noticed that in several instances it was difficult for me to decipher in which of the three places (UK, Greece, Hungary) she was located at the time of posting on Facebook. Interestingly, friends of hers have encountered the same difficulty. Here is a comment-question written by a friend to a Helen's status on the Eurovision song contest in 2012: *se poia xwra eisai twra?* (in which country are you now?). During 2011, the bulk of Helen's posts were related to the Greek crisis.

Hence, one of my very first questions in my instant messaging interview with her dealt with her location while posting. (We were both located in Athens at the time of the interview.) She stated that

1   *I was here most of the time*

2   *but some posts were made when I was in Hungary*

3   *and if I wrote some posts in September then I was in England*

4   *but mainly I was here*

5   *and I participated in what was happening*

6   *hm.. even if I'm not in Greece I write posts on issues related to the situation here*

7   *moreover, on the other hand, when I'm in Greece I write posts that concern the UK*

8   *for example, when the fees increased in UK universities*

9   *I was in Greece*

10 *and I was very worried about this issue, as far as I can remember from my profile*

11 *or other issues related to UK universities*

12 *but when the big demonstrations were held and I wrote some [status] updates I was here*

13 *I also posted some photos*

14 *I shot them the day after the demonstrations*

15 *sometimes I write posts that concern Hungary*

16 *even if I'm not there*

17 *oh, this identity is too complicated..*

18 *a mess!*

Helen acknowledges the complication of her place identity by jokingly characterizing it *a mess*. Having Greece as the location of her immediate proximity (*here* in turns 1, 4, 6, 12), her place posts revolve around the three countries: Greece (turns 6, 12, 13), UK (turns 7, 10, 11) and Hungary (turn 15). Helen feels entitled to comment on her Facebook on issues about the Greek crisis wherever she is, because she still has a legitimate interest in Greece when she is in the UK. In these posts, she often draws on English language

shared a link.
19 October 2011 at 12:34 · 👥

Strike shuts down Greece before austerity vote
www.reuters.com

ATHENS (Reuters) - Greek unions began a 48-hour general
strike on Wednesday, the biggest protest in years, as
parliament prepares to vote on sweeping new austerity

FIGURE 4.1 *Using English language resources for the Greek crisis.*

resources as illustrated in Figure 4.1. But she also has a special entitlement to
speak from experience on these matters: when she is in Greece, she takes
part in demonstrations and then uploads relevant material on Facebook, as we
will see later on.

With posts like this in Figure 4.1, Helen navigates multiple places
simultaneously: the one she is physically located in, the one she is thinking of
as well as Facebook space itself. Facebook is brought into the places Helen
occupies, and, likewise, those places are brought into Facebook. In line with
Gordon and de Souza e Silva (2011: 86), the ability to navigate multiple places
at the same time is in effect 'the ability to consolidate and locate the spaces
and information that we associate with our "digital selves" into something of a
hybrid space'. In these hybrid spaces, and in light of social media affordances,
the boundaries between remote and contiguous contexts, be that Greek,
English or Hungarian, can no longer be clearly defined. Thus bringing these
contexts together in Facebook is not *messy* – there are just many 'theres'
there, to rephrase Fernbank (1999).

Place marking in profile information

'About' section

The most explicit and direct references to place on Facebook are found in
the demographic information on top of the users' profiles and concern social
places such as school, university and workplace, as well as geographical ones
like neighbourhood, city and country. By way of illustration, on her professional
profile, Carla has added the university where she spent her undergraduate
years: Ιόνιο Πανεπιστήμιο (Ionian University). Although not straightforwardly

stated, readers with previous exposure to Greek education know that the Ionian University is located in the island of Corfu. Similarly, Gabriel has filled in his university, Unipi (University of Piraeus, nearby Athens), and his hometown, Athens. Romanos writes that he lives in Athens, having specified that he comes from the municipality of Nea Smirni, a southern suburb of Athens. Helen provides information on location of the university she studied (Lancaster, UK) as well as her hometown (Athens).

Notwithstanding, the completion of these profile fields is optional. For instance, Alkis, as I discuss elsewhere in Chapter 8, gives no indication of where he lives or comes from. The same goes for Carla in her personal profile. Along the lines of Gordon and de Souza e Silva's (2011) net locality, our perception of place is dictated both by Facebook affordances and by our own desire to be or not to be located.

Pages

The pages that Facebook users 'Like' and follow can also give us a glimpse of place in relation to what they care about: their studies, jobs, dwellings, civic engagement and travelling. For example, on both her profiles, Carla has clicked 'Like' on *atenistas* (an open community of Athens citizens) and *PlusCorfu.gr* while in her professional profile she has included *Ionian University Library and Information Center* and *ΜΕΓΑΡΟ ΚΑΠΟΔΙΣΤΡΙΑ* (Kapodistrian Mansion – a historical building of the Ionian University). Gabriel likes *European Parliament Simulation (Euro.Pa.S) at University of Pireaus* and *ΘΕΛΩ ΝΑ ΤΑΞΙΔΕΨΩ ΣΕ ΟΛΟ ΤΟΝ ΚΟΣΜΟ*!!. (I want to travel all over the world!!). Romanos follows *ΠΛΑΤΕΙΑ ΝΕΑΣ ΣΜΥΡΝΗΣ*, a central square in his neighbourhood, Nea Smirni, whereas Helen likes *Lancaster University*, *Secret Budapest*, *atenistas* and *PIGS: Portugal, Italy, Greece & Spain*.

As a word of caution, what I am arguing here is not that liking specific pages as such is tantamount to asserting a specific place identity. Instead, I view these 'Likes' as snippets that can complement, enhance and consolidate respondents' already existing – and articulated elsewhere in both their Facebook posts and their interviews with me – place identities.

Facebook places

Facebook allows users to add a location to their posts as shown in Figure 4.2. Each time they add a location to their post, it is added to their map. Figures 4.3–4.6 provide samples of Facebook maps. These locations in the main pertain to social places (restaurants, bars, coffee shops, landmarks, beaches

FIGURE 4.2 *Carla has added a London tag to the photo.*

FIGURE 4.3 *From Gabriel's maps.*

FIGURE 4.4 *From Romanos's maps.*

FIGURE 4.5 *From Carla's maps (personal profile).*

FIGURE 4.6 *From Helen's maps.*

and so on) and constitute an indication of what users are doing there: eating, drinking, doing sports and touring, among others.

In addition to communicating users' presence in a given location, these software tools 'communicate the location's presence with the user' via pictures, comments and anything else that can be tied to a specific location (Gordon and de Souza e Silva 2011). Hence, I see Facebook mapping not as sheer pointing to a universal geographical space but as selecting specific moments and boundaries that have actual meaning for the identities that users construct. In Figure 4.4, Romanos maps a significant period in his life, that of being a soldier, adding the places where he served his military service: Tripoli, Rhodes and Orestiko. Carla, in Figure 4.5, does not just mark a trip to France but her visit to her sister and her newborn nephew, permanent residents in France. What Helen plots in Figure 4.6 is the Christmas holidays she spent at her partner's home in Budapest. Such mapping of the self 'goes further than retelling the story and producing narrative accounts of identity. Maps represent another way of attempting to pin down identity, to structure what matters by picking out the key places, the main links and attempting to secure them. Maps chart what matters, where we have been and where we are going' (Woodward 2002: 68).

I will now turn to examples in which my informants, other than exploiting Facebook affordances, further localize their posts by making both direct and indirect references to particular places.

Place marking in posts

Verbal locating of self

Users specify where they are, where they are heading towards or where they are departing from, namely where their bodies are, at the moment of writing the status update. With this type of contextual relevance of place, users organize their perspective and orient readers (van Dijk 2009: 47). Example 4.1 offers a brief insight:

4.1
Helen
27 December 2011 at 19:40

At a cafe in <u>Budapest</u> marking students' final exams and in a good mood! Everyone should get an A!
5 people like this

Here there is a reference to a social place, and particularly a commercial service place, a café and a geographical place, the city of Budapest. Helen, however, is located at the café not only for the typical activity of drinking coffee but also for working. That the formulation of this place is littered with feelings of euphoria and optimism (*in a good mood!*) is not due to marking but to the fact that she is in her partner's home city with him (according to my ethnographic observation). In this status we observe two things. First, Helen, beyond just defining where she is, she discloses how she feels while being in the specific place too. Second, Budapest triggers certain emotions in her ongoing activities, marking exams in this case.

Saying where you are going can be done in more inventive ways as shown in Figure 4.7. Helen adopts an **entextualization** process (Blommaert 2005; Leppänen et al. 2014), namely she extracts an instance of culture (the song 'First We Take Manhattan', which includes the lyric 'First we take Manhattan, then we take Berlin') and relocates it in her discourse as first we take Budapest (where she will meet her partner) *and then we take Berlin* (where she will participate in a conference) to adjust it to her own situation and give us a flavour of her itinerary.

Users can less openly define where they are by means of tropes to refer to places. In Example 4.2, *Greek summer* is a **metonymy** standing for islands, the sea, beaches and the sun, and it is likened to a drug or habit that Helen

 shared a link.
5 August 2012

first we take Budapest..and then we take Berlin

joe cocker - FIRST WE TAKE MANHATTAN - Ultimate Collection
www.youtube.com

Download this track for free from http://YOUTUBEMUZIK4FREE.INFO
joe cocker - FIRST WE TAKE MANHATTAN - Ultimate Collection

Like · Comment · Share   👍 2 💬 4

FIGURE 4.7 *Entextualizing a song to locate the self.*

perhaps cannot imagine herself without. She is not saying *I am in Greece right now* – we can effortlessly deduce it.

4.2
Helen
25 June 2011 at 12:48

addicted to the <u>Greek summer</u>
8 people like this

4.3
Helen
2 October 2011 at 16:23

bye bye <u>Lancaster</u>
1 person likes this

Helen, in Example 4.3, marks her corporeal departure from the place yet at the same time, through its **personification**, she expresses a kind of affection similar to that of bidding farewells to people: that she will miss it. Of course the same expression could be used of a place one was glad to leave. Helen's attitude to Lancaster is known to me through observations and interviews.

Visual locating of self

Though text is sufficient to give a location, it is not the only mode that is used on Facebook. Uploading profile pictures with landscapes and cityscapes in the background has specific resonance for identity claims as well. It serves as a performative exercise of identity and belonging, which documents and validates the subjects' experience of being at particular places (see also Mendelson and Papacharissi 2010) experiencing particular moments. Following Goffman (1956), Scollon and Scollon (2003) suggest that our own bodies give and give off their meanings because of where they are and what they do 'in place'. In the same line of reasoning, Jaworski and Thurlow (2009a) argue that this type of photographic posing constitutes a kind of placement action which indicates and locates the self. The following examples will illustrate this point.

Carla in her professional profile is pictured surrounded by the sea of Havana, Cuba (Figure 4.8), while Gabriel is photographed at Granada, Spain (Figure 4.9). Helen, in Figure 4.10, enjoys the Hungarian countryside as a biker. Interestingly, more than half of Helen's profile photos depict her relaxed and smiling in various places in Athens, Greek islands, Budapest and the UK, shot within both urban and rural settings, at restaurants and cafés, beaches, island towns, with monuments as a backdrop, while travelling, at the university or in her kitchen. Alkis, on the other hand, in lieu of posing, he just gives a picture of the beach Sarakiniko in Parga, Greece (Figure 4.11), personifying it in his comment: *Την έχω ερωτευτεί αυτήν την παραλία…* (I'm in love with this beach…).

These photographs (Figures 4.8–4.11) were taken during holidays. Tourism provides a strong impetus for identity construal as the processes of travelling and narrating – textually and visually – holiday stories enable people to think of and present themselves as specific types of person (Desforges 2000; McCabe and Stokoe 2004). The practice of posting tourist profile pictures, albeit commonplace at first blush,[2] forms a process of selective representation of lived bodily experience in place similar to that of mapping. Amid an array of

FIGURE 4.8 *Carla's profile picture (11 January 2011).*

photos, the users choose to identify themselves with one depicting a place that matters – it is not just sightseeing. Carla is tied to Cuba professionally, as she has translated Cuban literature, whereas Helen is tied to Hungary emotionally because of her partner.

Let's shift our focus now from profile pictures to place-themed photographic albums. Carla has created albums with photographs of the places she has visited both in Greece and abroad, with Athens, Havana and Paris taking centre stage. One of the most challenging aspects in this social networking activity is Carla's journalistic kind of writing in choosing witty intertextual titles to name her photo albums. In Table 4.1, I have gathered some of her albums together with the sources to which their titles pay dues. As can be seen, Carla presents the places neither in purely visual terms (i.e. through

FIGURE 4.9 *Gabriel's profile picture (23 June 2012).*

FIGURE 4.10 *Helen's profile picture (23 August 2011).*

FIGURE 4.11 *Alkis's profile picture (31 August 2011).*

TABLE 4.1 Carla's photo albums and intertextual references

Album thumbnail	Places depicted	Title of album	Intertextual link
city sickness 58 photos	Athens (Greece)	city sickness	Song title by Tinderstics
city sickness II 57 photos	Athens (Greece)	city sickness II	Song title by Tinderstics
looking for a girl in a washing 26 photos	-Havana (Cuba) -Barcelona (Spain) -Corfu (Greece)	looking for a girl in a washing machine?	Song title by The Big Sleep
à paris (banlieue) tombe la n 12 photos	Paris (France)	à paris (banlieue) tombe la neige_ janvier 2013	'Tombe la neige à Paris' is a song performed by Adamo

Album thumbnail	Places depicted	Title of album	Intertextual link
la france, j'aime :-) 46 photos	French countryside	la france, j'aime :)	—
Lisbon stories 60 photos	Lisbon (Portugal)	Lisbon stories	*Lisbon Story* is the title of a film directed by W. Wenders
panic in the streets of 77 photos	London (UK)	panic in the streets of	'Panic on the streets of London' is a song title by The Smiths
Habana Blues 67 photos	Havana (Cuba)	Habana Blues	Title of a Spanish-Cuban film directed by B. Zambrano
ο ουρανός είναι εφτά φορές γ... 33 photos	Monemvasia (Greece)	ο ουρανός είναι εφτά φορές γαλάζιος (transl.: the sky is seven times light blue)	Verse by Greek poet Yannis Ritsos
We'll always have Paris 106 photos	Paris (France)	We'll always have Paris	Line from the film *Casablanca*
fotoVivaCuba 29 photos	various places in Cuba	fotoVivaCuba	*Viva Cuba* is a Cuban film, directed by J. C. Cremata and I. M. Cabrera

photos) nor in purely verbal terms (i.e. through titles and captions) but takes up a multisemiotic combination. Her multilingual (English, French, Greek and Spanish) and multilayered blending of song lyrics, poetry verses, film titles and lines with place images in one multisemiotically complex product points to a cornucopia of ideas, feelings, memories and trains of thought attached to the particular locations. This use of indexicality, on the one hand, puts on display Carla's linguistic and **cultural capital** (Bourdieu 1984), while, on the other, it offers her audience the potential of playful engagement. For example, one has to click on the album *panic in the streets of* to decipher that the photos are taken in London. By leaving the lyric 'panic in the streets of' unfinished, it is as if Carla invites viewers to reconstruct the place themselves.

The identity work done by Carla in taking these photos and then creating, editing and sharing albums including them is twofold. On the one hand, in consonance with Jaworski and Thurlow (2009a: 261), she locates herself implicitly:

> The camera function[s] as extension of the body (McLuhan, 1974) enabling a kind of double location of Self: first, as a prosthetic pointing gesture (which others will often follow) and, second, as a representation (or record) of the space and one's place in it. This representational locating of Self can be explicit (i.e. when posed in front of the camera) or implied (i.e. when taking the image).

On the other hand, she constructs herself not simply as a traveller but also as a photographer. If one browses photographs in her albums, they will instantly notice that from a technical perspective Carla is highly competent in taking photographs with a deep aesthetic appreciation of what is characteristic of a place.

Places are not only interwoven with pleasure and leisure but also with work and duty. Gabriel, as a student of international and European relations, has participated as delegate in several academic simulations of the United Nations (MUN – Model United Nations) around the world. He has shared on Facebook two albums with visual material from these trips, entitled *all around* and *still all around*. He never writes place names in captions, yet some can be easily recognized by particular signals such as the Spanish, the American and the UK flag, the London Eye, the Big Ben clock tower and the Atomium in Brussels. Most of them portray both modern and historical buildings, mainly in European countries, as well as indoor places where MUN conferences have been held. In these latter pictures, Gabriel appears with formal clothing either preparing or giving a presentation or posing after the conferences with other students from different cultural backgrounds. Gabriel uses the cultural capital of travel as a form of distinction that helps him enhance his status (see also Desforges 2000) by adding a set of international experiences to his professional biography, as he expounds below:

> The uploading [of these photographs] was within the framework of attempting to build a profile of a more international experience, which I

think is necessary for international relations students. Of course, this attempt mainly addressed fellow students and mainly people who are involved [in international relations] and they especially appreciate this kind of activities.

In deliberately crafting such a cosmopolitan profile, Gabriel points at the same time to his intended audience: fellow students and the cognoscenti (more details on Facebook audiences in Chapter 8).

Culinary experiences and placemaking

Social media, and principally Facebook, Flickr and Instagram, have played an instrumental role in the explosion of interest in food, and food photography more specifically. Apart from a biological need, food is robustly interlaced with place within the geographic imagination and has become central to our lived worlds and thereby our sense of identity (Bell and Valentine 1997; Lakoff 2006). As Cook and Crang (1996: 140) have aptly put it, 'Foods do not simply come from places, organically growing out of them, but also make places as symbolic constructs, being deployed in the discursive construction of various imaginative geographies.' Building upon this argument, Lockie (2001: 241) views place as both signifier and signified, namely as 'a site at which food consumption may take place' as well as 'a contingent and potentially contested set of meanings that may themselves be consumed through those practices associated with food'. To explicate these points, I will provide four examples: the first relates to local cuisine, as an inextricable part of people's collective national consciousness; the second weaves local cuisine with memory and autobiography; the third pertains to culinary tourism, as an opportunity to 'taste' the Other (Molz 2007); and the fourth is concerned with food as a displaced symbol of home.

Figure 4.12 is a photo that Helen shot and then posted on her Timeline. It pictures a traditional Greek dish she made herself, called *gemista* (stuffed vegetables).

The comments, in Example 4.4, produced by some of her international friends (I have indicated their nationality for ease of reference) underneath the picture set in motion a series of place identities, confirming van Dijk's (2009: 128) argument that places can be interactionally construed by dint of past experiences and sociocultural knowledge.

4.4

1. Helen: food just out of the oven:-)
29 April 2012 at 14:40 · Like · 2

FIGURE 4.12 *Helen's* gemista *(stuffed vegetables).*

2. Greek friend [male]: Mmmmmmmmmmmmmmmmmm
29 April 2012 at 14:54

3. Iranian friend [female]:
yummmmmmmmmmmmmmmmmmmmmmmmmy!
29 April 2012 at 15:15

4. Iranian friend: Very nice! We have exactly the same dish in Iran and call it 'Dolme'. What do you call it?
29 April 2012 at 15:16

5. Greek friend [male]: Gemista ('stuffeds':-). We also have 'dolmades', but it's only for vine leaves, and the preparation is different.
29 April 2012 at 15:21

6. Iranian friend: Thanks. We have it too. Just we differenciate them by the name of the covering vegetables as: Peper Dolme, Tomato Dolme, Aubergine Dolme, or Vine leave Dolme!!!!
29 April 2012 at 15:30 · Like · 1

7. Helen: Dolme was good:-)In the UK we can't make proper dolme though, because vegetables are tasteless (at least the ones you can get from Sainsburys)
29 April 2012 at 15:40 · Like · 2

8. Iranian friend 2 [male]: yammmmmiiiiii :)
29 April 2012 at 15:54 · Like · 1

9. Helen: wondering if the Iranian version is exactly the same..what spices do you use? if you find an English version of the recipe send it to me:-)
29 April 2012 at 16:01

10. Austrian friend [male]: get your veggies a) in season and b) from a nice, organic supplier (e.g. at a market, or somewhere like single step) and they won't be bland!
29 April 2012 at 16:03 · Like · 1

11. Helen: will do that next time I'm in Lancaster, thanks! problem is that in the UK, you need to make an effort to find something organic, whereas this should be the default and what is labelled as organic in different countries is yet another issue.
29 April 2012 at 16:06

12. Austrian friend: Yes, totally agree! My point was mainly that there's no point in complaining about bland veggies if you buy out-of-season ones grown thousands of miles away.... It is possible to find delicious veg in the UK, despite the obvious disadvantages of the northerly climate
29 April 2012 at 16:09

13. Greek friend 2 [male]: why don't you try Booths,[3] much better
29 April 2012 at 16:14

14. Helen: I used to buy stuff from Booths ages ago, when I lived in Hala[4]... quality is better than Sainsbury's, but they are more pricey, I think. Next time I'll try the market/single step[5] and see how that goes...For now, I'm OK with fresh Greek vegetables:-)
29 April 2012 at 16:19 · Like · 1

15. Austrian friend: Sigh... yes – it is amazing what a difference it makes to be able to buy nice veggies from just about any shop!
29 April 2012 at 16:21

What is worth discussing here is the evocation of the inclusive *we* via which the Iranian friend (comments 4 and 6) and the Greek friend (comment 5) speak for the culinary traditions of their countries seeing food standing in a metonymic relationship for their whole nations, the Iranian and the Greek, respectively. Helen, on the other hand, deploys a different kind of *we* in comment 7. Taking into account that all of the participants in this thread have been or are still UK residents, this *we* comprises all those who come from different cultural and culinary backgrounds than the UK and find it difficult to prepare their local dishes there because the ingredients differ in taste (comment 7) or good ones are scarce to find (comments 11 and 12), constructing thus the UK as a rather hostile place for gastronomy. In this thread, Helen claims intimate knowledge of the UK and identifies with it by finding it appropriate to criticize it.

As was corroborated by Helen herself in our first face-to-face meeting (see Chapter 3), during which we discussed the foregoing example, the mere uploading of a local food photo and the accompanying comments provide a sense of continuity to her past, present and future place selves and actions through specific references to social places (Booths, market/single step), **toponyms** (Hala, Lancaster), **toponymic anthroponyms** (Greek) and time expressions (past: *I used to buy, when I lived*; present: *For now, I'm*; future: *will do that next time, Next time I'll try*).

Similar issues are treated in the next example as well only with the difference that what gives the handle is not a photograph but a language play. In her post, Carla makes a pun based on **homophones**: the song title 'Sofrito' and a special dish from Corfu (the place where she studied and feels tied to it) under the same name, which consists of veal steak cooked in a white wine, garlic and herb sauce, and is usually served with rice.

4.5
Carla
14 November 2010 at 14:11

να 'χαμε κι ένα <u>κερκυραϊκό</u> σοφρίτο μαζί με αυτό του mongo santamaria.... χαχαχα!
(πώς το έλεγαν <u>το μαγέρικο πίσω από τη σχολή</u>... τα παλιά τα χρόνια; κόλλησα...)
'if only we had a <u>Corfu</u> sofrito along with that of mongo santamaria.... hahaha!
(how was <u>the tavern behind the school</u> called... back in the old years? I can't remember...)'
[she embeds video song *Sofrito* by Mongo Santamaria]
4 people like this
[2 comments follow]

1. FBU1 [female]: stou <u>Papirh</u>?....
'at <u>Papiris</u>?....'
14 November 2010 at 22:53 · Like · 1

2. Carla: NAIIIIIIIIIIIIIIIIIIIIIIIIIIIIIIIII ΠΑΠΙΡΗΣ!!!!!!!!!!!!!!!!!!!!!!!!!!!!!!!!!!
πωπωπω! πολλά χρόνια πίσω όμως, ε;;;
'YEEEEEEEEEEEEEEEEEEEEEEEES PAPIRIS!!!!!!!!!!!!!!!!!!!!!!!!
wooow! many years ago though, ah???'
15 November 2010 at 01:07 · Like · 1

3. FBU2 [male]: Παπίρης λέμε, ντροπή σου που το ξέχασες.
'Papiris we say, you should be ashamed you have forgotten it.'
15 November 2010 at 11:30

4. Carla: δεν ξέρεις πως ντρέπομαι, αλήθεια!
τι να κάνω όμως που γερνάω κι εγώ;
αλλά μπουρδέτο, σοφρίτο και παστιτσάδα ΔΕΝ ΞΕΧΝΩ!!!

'you don't know how ashamed I feel, truly!
but what can I do when I'm getting old?
I NEVER FORGET bourdeto, sofrito and pastitsada though!!!'
15 November 2010 at 18:00
[another 6 comments]

Continuity of identity can be maintained through references to places that belong to individuals' past and have emotional load for them (see also Twigger-Ross and Uzzell 1996). 'Papiris', the tavern where Carla used to eat Corfu dishes like *sofrito*, *bourdeto* (fish cooked in tomato sauce with onion, garlic and red spicy pepper) and *pastitsada* (chicken or rooster in tomato sauce with onion, red pepper, cinnamon, garlic and lots of pasta), becomes a **synecdoche** of a whole period in her life as a student in Corfu. That Papiris's food is surrounded by such nostalgic implications plays an active role in the construal of her identity, representing continuity and change over time (*back in the old years, I can't remember, many years ago, I'm getting old, I never forget*). So places for food consumption can become autobiographical as well. One more point merits mentioning here. The invocation of places 'can achieve immediate interactional currency through related memories' (Boden and Bielby 1986: 77). FBU1 and FBU2 have also been students in Corfu. It is due to their comments that the place is co-constructed filling the gap in Carla's memory.

Having touched upon tourism in the previous section, I will now move on to discuss culinary experiences as a form of tourist practice. Culinary tourism has been described as the intersection between food and travel, and refers to the practice of exploratory eating as a way to encounter, know and consume other places and cultures, experiencing thus new ways of being (Long 2004; Molz 2007). In this light, food functions as a transportable symbol of place, a moveable sign of Otherness (Molz 2007). In Figure 4.13, included in an album with photos from Katowice and Krakow in Poland, Helen is holding – as if she is serving the viewer – a *Zapiekanka*, a popular type of Polish street food. Having a photo album under the name of the place and including food pictures of this place, Helen re-circulates an imagined geography that differentiates places on the basis of their cuisines (Molz 2007). In the caption of the photo, she writes: *Zapiekanka..miam!!!* (Zapiekanka yummy!!!). But she is not only eating Zapiekanka – she is also eating 'the differences mobilities make' (Molz 2007: 91). What Helen exhibits here is openness and desire to consume difference as well as competence in the other culture. By posting this photo on Facebook, she almost literally puts on display these qualities of hers.

According to Cook and Crang (1996), foods should not solely be viewed as placed cultural artefacts, but as displaced materials and practices as well, which can inhabit many places. Consider Figure 4.14. While being in the UK (one perhaps can see the British buildings in the background, emphasizing

FIGURE 4.13 *Polish Zapiekanka.*

the out-of-placeness), Helen noticed and shot a tin of Greek olives used as plant pot (the tin reads: *εκλεκτές ελιές εξαιρετικής ποιότητος* – 'selected olives superior quality'). For Helen, the Greekness of the olives, as represented in their packaging, is no longer ordinary and mundane because it is embedded into another, fresh context and therefore stands out, deserving to be captured and shared as a symbol of home. In this example, Helen manifests a dual kind of geographical knowledge (Cook and Crang 1996): first, knowledge of the origins of the olives; and second, knowledge of the meanings of place, and regional identity, evoked among her Facebook audience who will look at this photo (and perhaps smile), especially the Greek members.

Sociopolitical aspects of places

Physical environments are necessarily social environments (Ittelson et al. 1974). Economic, political and social upheavals such as unemployment, governmental instability, intergroup conflicts and other sources of frustration can have a corrosive effect upon one's place identity (Proshansky et al.

FIGURE 4.14 *Greek olives tin in the UK.*

1983: 65). The following examples tackle this matter with regard to the Greek crisis (it is advisable to consult the crisis timeline in the Appendix).

Protesting and documenting

Harking back to Helen's interview in the beginning of this chapter, she says about the demonstrations in Athens that *I was here and I participated in what was happening*. Indeed, she was an active and conscious citizen both physically and digitally. For instance, in heading to Athens Syntagma Square to protest against austerity together with the Greek Indignados (Aganaktismenoi) in June 2011, she wrote on Facebook: *off to syntagma*. Such a status update should not be viewed as a mere check-in but as a discursive practice embedded in a broader sociopolitical and historical context.

The same goes for the uploading of photographs she had taken herself of the places where events related to the protests took place. In Figure 4.15, we see Athens Syntagma Square, outside the Greek parliament, while Figure 4.16 is shot outside Marfin Bank in Stadiou Street, Athens, where three employees died during the nationwide strike on 5 May 2010. Figure 4.17 is an instance of

FIGURE 4.15 *Syntagma Square (posted by Helen on 30 May 2011).*

FIGURE 4.16 *Stadiou Street (posted by Helen on 6 May 2010).*

what Scollon and Scollon (2003) call ***transgressive semiotics***, namely when a sign violates either intentionally or accidentally the conventional semiotics at that place. The photo shows an empty Athenian store, probably one of the thousands that have closed down on account of the crisis, with two labels on its window, *ΠΩΛΕΙΤΑΙ* (for sale) and *ENOIKIAZETAI* (to rent), and underneath

FIGURE 4.17 *Empty store in Athens (posted by Helen on 23 October 2011).*

FIGURE 4.18 *Flyer in Syntagma Square (posted by Helen on 18 October 2012).*

them a poster that promotes tourism in Greece. At any moment in time, before the Greek crisis (i.e. before 2009), these three signs could function independently from one another. Nonetheless, because of the sociopolitical situation in Greece, this triptych functions on a symbolic level: Greece (the land, its people) is available for sale to or to be rented by its creditors. In Figure 4.18, which reads *MENOYME ΣYNTAΓMA* (We stay at Syntagma), the place, Syntagma Square, is represented as a symbol of resistance placed within the same contextual conditions as in *off to syntagma* above.

All these examples lead us back to Jaworski and Thurlow's (2009a) path. By recording the place in crisis, Helen simultaneously represents her place in it. Since she is the one taking the image, and not posing in front of the camera, her representational locating of self is implied. Her identity claim is 'I'm there, at the heart of the events, protesting and documenting'.

Responding to 'unattractive' places

It goes without saying that under the crisis circumstances, places become 'unattractive' causing stress to people, who in turn feel displaced. As a consequence, their discourses about these places can become deterritorialized characterized by an irritated style (Blommaert 2005: 223; van Dijk 2009: 59). Here is a simple example:

4.6

Helen

24 February 2012 at 14:19

Dear politicians, I'm fed up with your dilemmas! The only dilemma I have in 18 degrees sunshine is: coffee break from work in Exarcheia or Monastiraki? 6 people like this

By polarizing the unstable political situation in Greece, which distresses Greek people, with the sunshine that typically lifts their spirits, Helen polarizes two aspects of her place identity. On the one hand, it is the sociopolitical place to which she does not feel attached because of its governors. On the other hand, by referring to the two toponyms, the two Athenian neighbourhoods Exarcheia and Monastiraki, she mobilizes a kind of intimacy associated with the activities of strolling in pedestrian streets and sitting at outdoor cafés, meaningful only to Athenians.

In the next two examples, without mentioning any place names at all, Helen renounces her identification with Greece.

4.7

Helen

25 May 2012 at 20:22

have stayed too long in this country ...
2 people like this

4.8

Helen

16 June 2012 at 12:43

surrealand

The frustration-littered update in Example 4.7 is unpacked if we take into account that it was posted just after the May 2012 elections in Greece and the failure of political parties to form a new government as none of them had won an absolute majority of parliamentary seats. While in the interview excerpt in the beginning of the chapter Helen deployed the spatial adverb *here* to designate Greece, in this status update she displaces and distances herself by selecting the **demonstrative** *this country* which in this context has a pejorative nuance seen as attitudinal dissociation and depersonalization from the place. Her estrangement from Greece is even more accentuated by choosing English as the language of her status.

One day before the new elections, on 16 June 2012, Helen's status (Example 4.8) included just one **coined word**: *surrealand*. Her Greek contacts as well as those who keep in touch with the proceedings in Greece can easily deduce that the *surrealand* is Greece. The coined term bears the connotations of absence of rationality, coordination and planning in the country which Helen implicitly condemns.

Helen's irritated style continued after the elections and the announcement of the final result. Centre-right New Democracy was the largest party and Antonis Samaras became the new prime minister. Helen wrote on this:

4.9
Helen
18 June 2012 at 10:25

Elections part II: Ο τρελαντώνης, ο μάγκας και τα μυστικά του <u>βάλτου της Ελλάδας</u> ....
'Elections part II: Crazy Anthony, mangas and the secrets of <u>Greece's swamp</u> ...'
2 people like this

In this status update, and relying upon her cultural capital, Helen wittingly draws intertextual parallels between the result of the elections and Penelope Delta's books. Delta (1874–1941) was one of the most prominent Greek authors of children's books, who drew inspiration from historical events in Greece. She was also Samaras's great grandmother. *Ο τρελαντώνης* (Crazy Anthony), *Ο Μάγκας*[6] and *Τα μυστικά του βάλτου* (The secrets of the swamp) are three of her most well-known and influential books. Helen's mapping goes like this: Antonis Samaras is crazy Anthony who, like Mangas, has come to the difficult position of governing and has to prove if he has the guts to confront crisis while Helen likens Greece to a swamp insinuating (and again disapproving of) predominant mentalities of the Greek society including bureaucracy, nepotism, lack of meritocracy, political instability, corruption, apathy and prioritization of the personal over the collective interest (Chalari 2014). By employing this derogatory metaphor, Helen directs attention to negative features of Greece as a sociopolitical place dismantling in this way aspects of her national identity.

Facebook as a tool for raising local awareness

Helen's photos in the centre of Athens in the previous section constitute tokens of **citizen journalism**. As Allan (2013) explains, in citizen journalism newsmaking contributions come from ordinary individuals, who are present on scenes of crisis, accident, tragedy or disaster, and can vary including first-person eyewitness accounts, audio and video recordings, mobile phone and digital camera photographs, shared online. Among its various alternative names, citizen journalism is also interestingly called 'hyperlocal journalism'. Apart from radically inverting the traditional model of news production and distribution, citizen journalism empowers people to produce news about their neighbourhoods, thereby contributing to a deeper awareness of their places (Gordon and de Souza e Silva 2011: 117). Allan (2013) underscores that the true value of citizen journalism lies in being there, on the ground, documenting and disseminating what you have seen, felt or heard at the scene, as Helen exactly has done. But when you feel affixed to a place, you do not always have to be on the ground to show that you care and know about your place. You can use Facebook while being on the sidelines.

In my last example, I look at the ways in which Facebook, a global technology, can be used for a local purpose. Before that, it is necessary to provide some contextual grounding. Until 2012 all students from the Department of Foreign Languages, Translation and Interpretation of the Ionian University in Corfu, Greece, were expected to spend a compulsory semester abroad with a view to broadening their horizon and getting a head start in the competitive translation job market. Notwithstanding, the Greek Ministry of Education, in line with the austerity policy, decided that the semester in question should become optional and stopped providing any funding. On 17 January 2013, fifty students from the department, together with their representatives, visited the dean's office to discuss this unexpected development. The dean, though, got locked into her office and refused to meet the students who, in turn, remained there determined not to leave until she would talk to them. Although there were no violent deeds, the police arrived and arrested twenty-seven students who were released later that night.

Table 4.2 contains all posts from Carla's professional profile that concerned this serious incident. As can be seen, Carla was alert and posted across different time spans (4 posts on 18 January, 2 on 21 January and 1 on 22 January; both at noon and at night). To build up a complete and spherical picture of the episode, she aggregated information from a range of media sources (local and mainstream media sites, blog, official university webpage, educational portal) sharing her Facebook friends' links as well (exploiting the **Share** facility). Moreover, she provided evaluations of the situation in her comments: *disgrace,*

TABLE 4.2 Carla's activity on the 17 January 2013 incident in the Ionian University

Date & time of post	Opening comment	Article title	Link	Via	Comments underneath post
18 January 2013 at 12:41	Αίσχος και ντροπή για την κατάχρηση εξουσίας από την πλευρά της Πρυτάνεως και την αδικαιολόγητη παρέμβαση των ΜΑΤ!!! 'Disgrace and shame on the Dean's abuse of authority and the riot police's unjustified operation!!!'	Επέμβαση ΜΑΤ στο Ιόνιο Πανεπιστήμιο! 'Riot police operation at the Ionian University!'	www.enimerosi.com/component/content/article/119-2010-02-12-06-59-39/14783-2013-01-17-17-55-17.html [from a Corfu news website]	—	**Carla:** πολλές αναδημοσιεύσεις στο διαδίκτυο τα έγγραφα της διαύγειας για οικονομικές ατασθαλίες και αδικαιολόγητες δαπάνες … <u>επίσημες απαντήσεις θα έρθουν άραγε;</u> (ενδεικτικά http://papaioannou-giannis.net/…) 'many repostings on the internet the documents of transparency for financial misconducts and unjustified expenses … <u>will we ever have official responses?</u> (e.g. http://papaioannou-giannis.net/…)' **FBU1 [female]:** Μα τι λέτε;;; Για όνομα του Θεού!!! Τα ΜΑΤ στο Ιόνιο Πανεπιστήμιο; 'What is going on??? For God's shake!!! Riot Police operation at the Ionian University?' **Carla:** <u>δυστυχώς! χωρίς κανένα λόγο</u>, οι φοιτητές περίμεναν <u>απλώς</u> μια απάντηση από την Πρύτανη '<u>unfortunately!</u> with no reason, the students were <u>just</u> waiting for a reply from the Dean'

(Continued)

TABLE 4.2 Continued

Date & time of post	Opening comment	Article title	Link	Via	Comments underneath post
18 January 2013 at 12:56	–	Ανακοίνωση ΜΑΣ για την εισβολή των ΜΑΤ στην Ιόνιο Ακαδημία 'Announcement for the Riot Police operation at the Ionian University'	www.pluscorfu.gr/index.php/news/kerkyra/33278-mat-ionios-akadimia.html [from a Corfu portal]	PlusCorfu.gr	–
18 January 2013 at 13:23	–	Κέρκυρα: Προσαγωγές 27 φοιτητών στην Ιόνιο Ακαδημία 'Corfu: 27 students arrested in the Ionian University'	tvxs.gr/news/ellada/kerkyra-prosagoges-27-foititon-stin-ionio-akadimia [from an Athenian news website]	friend	–
18 January 2013 at 18:06	–	ΟΤΑΝ ΣΠΕΡΝΕΙΣ ΑΝΕΜΟΥΣ, ΘΕΡΙΖΕΙΣ ΘΥΕΛΛΕΣ .... 'SOW THE WIND, REAP THE WHIRLWIND'	fasma-txgmd.blogspot.gr/2013/01/blog-post_18.html [from a blog maintained by independent students at the Department of Foreign Languages, Translation and Interpretation]	friend	–

| 21 January 2013 at 14:57 | — | Οι πανεπιστημιακοί καταγγέλλουν την παραβίαση του Πανεπιστημιακού Ασύλου στο Ιόνιο Πανεπιστήμιο 'Academics denounce the violation of university asylum in the Ionian University' | esos.gr/article/eidisis-tritovathmia-ekpaidefsi/panepistimiakoi_kataggelloyn_parabiasi_panepistimiakoy_asyloy_ionio_panepistimio [from an educational portal] | friend | — |
| 21 January 2013 at 23:42 | για να κλείσει το καρέ … 'to finish off …' | Ανακοίνωση της Πρυτανείας σχετικά με την 17η/01/2013 'Dean's announcement in relation to 17/01/2013' | www.ionio.gr/central/gr/news/read/3534#.UP1aen-Oeg8.facebook [from the official website of the Ionian University] | friend | — |

(Continued)

TABLE 4.2 Continued

Date & time of post	Opening comment	Article title	Link	Via	Comments underneath post
22 January 2013 at 00:58	δημοσιευμάτων συνέχεια 'postings continue'	Ερώτηση στη Βουλή & μπαράζ, ανακοινώσεων για τα γεγονότα στο Ιόνιο Πανεπιστήμιο! 'Question at the Parliament & barrage of announcements for the event at the Ionian University!'	www.corfupress.com/ news/1page/26734- mparaz-anakoinoseon- gia-ta-gegonota-sto- ionio-panepistimio [from a Corfu news website]	–	–

shame, unjustified, misconducts, unjustified expenses, will we ever have official responses?, unfortunately, with no reason, just waiting. All these elements set up an interesting multivocal blending of news, fact, opinion, subjectivity and objectivity, emotion and meaning (see also Papacharissi and de Fatime Oliveira 2012). The persistent posting on the event shows, on the one hand, that Carla strives to keep her audience (a great deal of its members are Ionian University alumni as well as current translation students) abreast undertaking somehow the role of a reporter. On the other hand, and taking into consideration that a significant period in Carla's life was located in Corfu (as an educational, residential, leisure and outdoor place), it confirms that place identity can exist beyond the confines of distance transcending time.

Writing status updates here

Hall (1990) has eloquently articulated that we are the product of the routes we have traversed. In this networked era, Facebook could very well be seen as a versatile inventory of our routes as those are inscribed in maps, check-ins, updates, photographs and likes. What this chapter brought to the fore is that place identity can have several components and overlapping layers, be that geographical, social, political, cultural and emotional. My informants could bring together on Facebook these components and layers from virtually anywhere. The findings provide valuable insights into the nature of place identity as unfurled in Facebook.

To commence with, place identity is different for different users. This was evidenced in my participants' posts. The largest volume of the data presented here was abstracted from Helen's profile, including a number of posts by Carla too. For Helen especially, in comparison to the other informants, place seems to be at the core of her identity. The following extract is from our interview after my initial observation of her Facebook activity:

Mariza: what has struck me most is your place identity
Helen: well, indeed
now you're saying it ...
I knew it to a certain degree, but it impresses me that it comes across so strongly to someone else

Not only does *it come across so strongly*, to borrow Helen's words, but also we witnessed how references to places in her posts endowed her with a sense of continuity to her identity.

The users identify with different scales or types of places, from micro (e.g. a café) to macro (e.g. Budapest) and from specific (e.g. Hala) to general (e.g. Hungarian countryside). Moreover, place identity differs with respect to our role in given places. It is one thing to be a traveller in Cuba (Carla) or a delegate in a conference in Brussels (Gabriel) and another to be a protester in Syntagma (Helen) or a soldier in Rhodes (Romanos). Place identity is also associated with different representations of personal meanings (e.g. eating at Papiris) as well as sociopolitical meanings (e.g. Greece as a swamp). Furthermore, it is associated with different types of discursive means (e.g. place naming, inclusive *we*, distancing deixis, metonymy, synecdoche, insinuation, intertextual links, artistic photography, protest photography, food photography).

Place identity on Facebook is found to have two intrinsic values. First, it is fluid, often divorced from where the body is physically located. Strictly speaking, the body is situated together with a portable device and posts on Facebook. As shown, however, Helen is in England but thinks and posts about the demonstrations in Athens. Likewise, Carla is located in Athens but cares and shares information about her former university in Corfu.

Second, place identity is an essentially interactive, collaborative task, constructed through processes of negotiation between the profile owner and their Facebook audience. Participants work together on place identities, picking up certain aspects and playing with them, as revealed in the stuffed vegetables photo and the Papiris sequence. It is through their comments to posts that different facets of the hybridity of place identity are brought out, functioning as complementary parts of the profile owner's asserted identity.

As emerged from the data at hand, the users do not just communicate about place, but most importantly they communicate through place, that is to say, by means of the place they communicate 'something about themselves that goes beyond the descriptive characteristics of a place' (Humphreys and Liao 2011: 415). For instance, they assert or eschew belonging, they communicate openness and respect to other cultures, they convey cosmopolitanism, they organize their memories, they use different languages as a mark of affiliation with (or disaffiliation from) certain places, they make political statements, they disidentify with the stressful aspects of a place, and they raise awareness about local and national issues.

Besides place, time is also a significant orientation device for the self (Georgakopoulou 2003). How this happens on Facebook is the topic of the next chapter.

Place identity: Why and how

Carla's constant references to Corfu and her practice of uploading photo albums depicting places as well as Helen's attachment to the UK and

Hungary directed me to the topic of place identity. I categorized my examples based on:

- page 'Likes' that show place;
- toponyms (e.g. Athens, Corfu, Lancaster);
- toponymic anthroponyms (e.g. *Greek*);
- demonstratives and **deictics** (e.g. *this* country);
- adverbs of place (e.g. *here*);
- personal/possessive pronouns that refer to nationality (e.g. *we* as Greeks);
- language alternation (e.g. code-switching, code-mixing);
- references to events occurring in a place (e.g. marking essays, protesting);
- references to people related to a place (e.g. politicians);
- visual symbols/metonymies of a place (e.g. food);
- reasons places are photographed (e.g. tourism, business, citizen journalism).

Here I should note that there is a distinction between place references and place references as identity; not all place references are identity. Place identity is a much more complex entity than mere references to a place. The aspect of place identity I was particularly interested in was references to different places that are used as identity. In my analysis, I did not include every single reference to a place – just the ones my interpretation of them was offered as identity marker (e.g. places that were meaningful to my participants for personal, professional and national/ethnic reasons).

ACTIVITY 4.1: FACEBOOK AS PLACE

Digital communication can be approached either as text (i.e. written language) or as place (i.e. a discursively created space of human interaction) (Androutsopoulos 2013c). Seeing Facebook as place, consider how people use it to report on or coordinate social action regarding a particular event. How can their usage shape the course and meaning of that event (see also Androutsopoulos 2013c: 240)? How can this be significant to users' identity?

ACTIVITY 4.2: FOOD PHOTOGRAPHY AND PLACE IDENTITY

Gather a small corpus of photos depicting food, together with their accompanying captions and/or comments, from Facebook, Flickr, Instagram, Pinterest and/or food blogs. How and to what extent can such kind of posting be related to place identities?

Useful resources

Print

There is a vast amount of literature on place and space. Here I have followed studies that mainly focus on place and/or place identity from a discourse-analytical and multimodal perspective. I have also tried to include studies with a specific focus on place and digital media. More references are also found in the next chapter as place and time are often studied in unison. A good starting point on place identity in discourse is Benwell and Stokoe (2005; Chapter 6). The volumes edited by Jaworski and Thurlow (2010) and Bamford et al. (2014) are concerned with the textual/discursive construction of place and place identity as well as the use of space as a semiotic resource in our present, globalized, and technologically saturated era. Myers (2010b, Chapter 4) zooms in on how bloggers signal place in their posts and to what effect: identity claim, comparison and contrast, justification and explanation of one's views, storytelling or celebration of one's routine. Aguirre and Davies (2015) provide an interesting study of place and belonging as communicated via Facebook through the spectrum of migration. Goodings et al. (2007) treat the dialectic between (mediated) community and place identity examining interactions occurring on MySpace. Kytölä (2016) gives a comprehensive account of 'translocality', namely the connectedness between physical and cultural places, in digital communication. Gómez Cruz and Lehmuskallio's volume (2016; Part II) includes empirical case studies on digital photography and transformed localities. If you are particularly interested in the discursive construction of place as a political arena in times of crisis and the role of SNS as places for communication and meeting, the articles in Mártin Rojo (2015) provide interesting insights drawing on the examples of the Arab Spring, Indignados and Occupy movements. For general theorizations of place in the context of digital media, see Gordon and de Souza e Silva (2011) and Evans (2015).

Web

Space, place and digitalization reading list
https://danielderkunzelmann.piratenpad.de/airl-space-place-lit?

Selfies and visual placemaking
http://paulmullins.wordpress.com/2014/06/30/imagining-heritage-selfies-and-visual-placemaking-at-historic-sites

Visualising Facebook within local contexts (Miller and Sinanan 2017)
http://discovery.ucl.ac.uk/1543315/1/Visualising-Facebook.pdf

5

Time, age and identity
on Facebook

Chapter overview

Time

Όλα είναι συμβατικά, τι προχθές, τι χθες τι σήμερα!
(τι σήμερα, τι αύριο τι τώωωωωρααααα!).

Everything is conventional, the day before yesterday, yesterday, today,
what difference does it make!
(today, tomorrow, nooooooooow, what difference does it make!).

This is a comment written by Alkis. The comment is a reaction on a belated birthday wish on his Facebook Wall. In lieu of expressing irritation because of the delay, Alkis suggests that time is a conventional concept, what Jenkins (2002: 269) has appositely called an 'abstraction of human construction'. Alkis's suggestion is intertextually livened up by means of alluding to a Greek rebetiko[1] song in the parenthesis, entitled *Τι Σήμερα, Τι Αύριο, Τι Τώρα* ('Today, Tomorrow, Now, What Difference Does It Make').[2] Alkis's comment illustrates two main topics of this chapter, namely, the relative and relational construction of time in discourse and the key role of music (by embedding and/or referring to songs, lyrics, clips, artists) in how Facebook users engage with the theme of time.

Facebook, like any type of social media, is essentially time-bound. At the bottom of every Facebook post there is always a date and a time. Thus, users' content (status updates, photos, videos, links) is categorized according to the period of time in which it was posted in the form of a Timeline. Nevertheless, time is not only indicated by the time-stamp. Time is also made relevant in the content of the posts by Facebook participants, who employ intricate ways to talk about how they integrate and accumulate identity, experience and meaning across different timescales. That is, across who they are in this event and that, at this moment or the other, with this person or another, in one role and situation or another (Lemke 2000). In this chapter, I will attempt to give answers to the following questions: How do Facebook users discursively construct themselves as 'chronological beings' (Jenkins 2002)? How do they position themselves vis-à-vis time? How do they make aspects of time relevant in their Facebook interactions? What is the role of music in all of this? My discussion will be informed by elements from Myers's (2010b: 68–75) categorization of functions of time references in blogs and the Coupland et al. (1991) taxonomy of age identity-marking.

Time is an abstract notion with manifold and complex meanings. In this section I describe different approaches to the notion of time drawing on semantics, philosophy and anthropology. Starting with semantics, time is a polysemous lexical category between units, periods and events, which, according to Evans (2005: 49–70), bears eight distinct senses: duration, moment, instance, event, matrix, agentive, measurement system and commodity. Table 5.1 summarizes these senses providing representative examples from Evans's work (2005). At the end of the chapter, I will revisit some of these meanings to discuss how they fare in terms of experienced and lived time in light of my data.

From a philosophical perspective, time is conceived in a 'tensed' way, that is to say, in terms of past, present and future, as well as in a 'tenseless' way, namely as clock times and relations of succession and simultaneity (Baker 2009). For Chafe (1994: 205), tense linguistically marks the relationship between 'the time of an extroverted consciousness and the time of a representing (not represented) consciousness'. To substantiate this point,

TABLE 5.1 Senses of time

Senses	Time as ...	Examples
Duration	Assessment of magnitude of duration.	*It was a long time ago that they met.*
Moment	A discrete or punctual point or moment without reference to its duration.	*The time for a decision has arrived.*
Instance	A particular instance (i.e. occurrence) of an event or activity, rather than an interval or a moment.	*The horse managed to clear the jump 5 times in a row.*
Event	A boundary event.	*The barman called time.*
Matrix	An unbounded elapse conceived as the event subsuming all others.	*Time has no end.*
Agentive	A causal force responsible for change regarding humans and animals.	*Time has aged me.*
Measurement-system	A means of measuring change, duration and other behaviours, events etc.	*Eastern Standard Time is five hours behind Greenwich Mean Time.*
Commodity	An entity which is valuable, and hence can be exchanged, traded, acquired etc.	*They bought more advertising time.*

Source: Adapted from Evans (2005).

Chafe (1994: 205–6) says that in the example 'I was there for about six years', the time of the extroverted consciousness preceded the time of the representing consciousness. Conversely, in the example 'then I'll go my own way', the time of the extroverted consciousness is expected to follow the time of the representing consciousness.

In anthropological parlance, an influential definition of time comes from Jenkins (2002: 277), who places weight upon human activity:[3]

> Time is something that humans do, naturally, and human life without time is unthinkable. What we call 'time' is, in fact, perhaps best understood as an inevitable consequence of our need to have a working sense of the here-and-now if we are to go about the business of everyday life, in a universe of perpetual, and in a very real sense timeless, transformation.

Time, thus, is not just a chronometric or categorical measure, conventionally segmented by the members of a culture into seconds, minutes, hours, days, weeks, months, years, centuries and millennia. It is also a social, interactional and irreducibly subjective construct related to one's personal history, experience, self and episodic memories (van Dijk 2009: 129). Put it another way, it is related to one's personal identity.

Identity is a temporal process (Mead 1932). Every human action, social practice or activity takes place on some timescale – the characteristic time or rate of a process (Lemke 2000). Humans, therefore, are essentially 'chronological beings' (Jenkins 2002: 268) – they cannot live without time: they need to have a past so as to situate who they are in a biography and history (memory); they need a future to envision what they are in the process of becoming (anticipation); and they need to build a sense of the present, of where they are now (perception) (Flaherty and Fine 2001: 151; Jenkins 2002: 268). Memory, perception and anticipation can come together in narrative action and emplotment (i.e. the process of weaving events together, viewing them as a coherent whole; Ricoeur 1984). As Ricoeur (1984: 52) explains, 'Time becomes human to the extent that it is articulated through a narrative mode, and narrative attains its full meaning when it becomes a condition of temporal existence.' The following sections will discuss how these views of time and identity relate to Facebook.

Facebook and temporality

The resources for temporality on Facebook are of two kinds: 1) date- and time-stamps which articulate the 'here and now' of telling and 2) the content produced by Facebook members, which constructs the time relative to the reported events in their lived experience. Starting with the time of telling, this is indicated by means of time-stamps appended automatically by the system to both posts and follow-up comments. If we hover the mouse over the date of a specific post (or comment), we can get the precise time of posting, with day of the week and exact time. A poster's content is organized in the form of a Timeline (Figure 5.1), which replaced Facebook profile as a new and more interactive virtual space where participants can collect their stories and experiences, add landmarks along with their dates, go back to stories from their past by clicking on particular years and months, as well as see highlights from each month (I will return to the Timeline and its implications for the researcher towards the end of the chapter). On 24 March 2015, Facebook launched the feature 'On This Day', which shows users content from that particular day in their Facebook history (e.g. statuses and photos from one year ago, two years ago and so on), enabling them to share it anew if they wish.

Frobenius and Harper (2015) have suggested that the time-stamps of updates and comments constitute resources for and obstacles to the production of meaning and sense on Facebook on account of the medium's **asynchronous** nature of interaction. More precisely, they contend that the relationship between time and commenting turns (a relationship presumed to bear similar characteristics to the temporal patterning of face-to-face turn-taking) has a different nuance on Facebook since not all users are participating all the time or at the same time. A comment may appear after a status or another comment hours or even days later. Frobenius and Harper conclude that users need to accommodate different affordances (e.g. employ name mentioning/tagging to address a particular individual) to make their comments conditionally relevant.

FIGURE 5.1 *Time-stamps and the menu of dates on the right side of Gabriel's Timeline (as of 2014).*

Statuses are archived in reverse chronological order, so that the most recently added content appears always at the top of a user's profile. Conversely, a sequence of comments has a different spatial configuration with older text appearing uppermost and newer text underneath. This kind of chronological and spatial sequencing in Facebook posting bears consequences for how status update stories evolve and are interpreted. As different Facebook participants weigh in to an ongoing story at different times and points of ongoingness, their modes of engagement can be instrumental in shaping the tale and telling (Georgakopoulou 2013c).

Turning to the relative construction of time through content, since its conception, Facebook has been present-oriented: its initial prompt was 'What are you doing right now?' and users had to start their post with the verb 'is' appearing automatically (e.g. Carla *is* listening to Sarah Vaughan and almost forgets she's still at the office. Almost ...). Despite major changes in the social network's infrastructure since 2010, the 'pre-eminence of the present moment' (Page 2010: 429) remains at the heart of all Facebook use. Narrativity in Facebook status updates is characterized by the present tense of announcing and sharing breaking news, namely the reporting of very recent events (e.g. 'this morning', 'just now') or events as unfolding near-simultaneously with the act of narration (Georgakopoulou 2013a).

Adding an interesting addendum to Georgakopoulou (2007), Page (2010) has approached Facebook status updates as belonging to the genre of small stories. Small stories are non-canonical stories (i.e. they do not necessarily fulfil prototypical definitional criteria of the narrative enquiry such as beginning–middle–end, a complicating event, and a clear evaluation of the events), normally small in length, typified by fluidity, plasticity and open-endedness, occurring in the small moments of discourse, and within everyday life situations, rather than constituting distinct, full-fledged units (Georgakopoulou 2007). Notably, in the case of Facebook, small stories are influenced by the given online discourse situation (Page 2010): they are afforded and constrained by certain temporal and spatial specificities, with the recency of events and the ongoingness of telling being predominant, and are circulated among a multidimensional network of Facebook friends.

Taking these features together, it could be plausibly argued that time on Facebook is multifaceted and multilayered. On the one hand, Facebook's automatic time-stamps along with the Timeline metaphor imply a representation of life created out of uniform divisions (years, months, days, hours, minutes). On the other hand, as we will see in the analysis, the sense of identity linked to time and age is actively constructed, and is done in interaction with other Facebook friends. The main issues addressed in my examples are nowness; cyclical time; future and hypothetical projection; and age and lifespan. The first three categories derive support from Myers (2010b), while the latter comes from Coupland et al. (1991). More details on both frameworks will be given in the course of the discussion.

Nowness

As Jenkins (2002: 275) has conceded, 'Identity and "the present" are mutually implicated in each other.' For him, 'The stability of identity … depends in part on having a working interactional space of the here-and-now – "the present" – in which to be stable.' Extending his argument to contemporary social media, we could claim that Facebook can easily undertake the role of this interactional space (see previous section on the present-orientedness of Facebook). Below I present four examples in which Carla and Romanos stress the importance of the present moment by means of naming the day, telling a story and counting down.

Carla in Example 5.1 specifies the day of writing her post (*Sunday*, *today*), with a view to emphasizing, and promoting, the vitality of the current event (Myers 2010b: 68–9), namely her culinary inspiration and creativity, which would be appreciated by the friend-cook addressed in the postscript. Of course Carla could have omitted saying *today* as this can be easily deduced.

5.1

Carla [personal profile]
7 November 2011 at 02:50

η πιο ευωδιαστή <u>κυριακή</u> έβερ! εκεί που το σαφράν συναντάει το κόλιαντρο, την κανέλλα και την πάπρικα και το κάρυ το γάλα καρύδας … απόλαυση!!!
πι.ες. [όνομα φίλης], θα ήσουν πολύ περήφανη για μένα αν μ' έβλεπες <u>σήμερα</u> στην κουζίνα!:-)

'the most fragrant <u>sunday</u> ever! where saffron meets coriander, cinnamon and paprika and curry [meets] coconut milk … delight!!!
p.s. [name of friend], you would be very proud of me if you saw me <u>today</u> in the kitchen!:-)'
3 people like this

Nowness can be invested with meaning by way of narratives, that is to say, telling stories about the self, recounting and commenting on recent or ongoing happenings and events (future and past events are discussed later on), and putting together explanations and plans (Georgakopoulou 2002; Jenkins 2002). Narrating events and actions is integral to self-discovery and the process of storying ourselves, namely, integrating ourselves in time (McAdams 1997). Let's see an example suggestive of the small story genre.

5.2

Carla [personal profile]
6 November 2011 at 10:59

ξυπνάς πρωί πρωί. αφήνεις τον ταξιδιώτη στο ελ βενιζέλος. και πάνω που πας να φύγεις τον βλέπεις. περπατά σκυφτός, με το αδιόρατο χαρακτηριστικό τρέμουλο. κουβαλάει στο καροτσάκι τη λύρα του. και μόλις διασταυρώνεστε σηκώνει το κεφάλι και σε καρφώνει με αυτά τα μάτια τα απίστευτα και δεν μπορείς να μην του πεις 'Καλημέρα Μάστορα!'. απαντά ένα μακρόσυρτο χαμογελαστό 'Γειαααα!'. 9.30 π.μ. συνάντηση με τον Ψαραντώνη.:-)

'you wake up early in the morning. you leave the traveler at Eleftherios Venizelos [Athens airport]. and as you're ready to go you see him. he is stooping with his indiscernible typical tremor. he is carrying his lyra on a trolley. and as soon as you cross each other he raises his head and stares at you with these unbelievable eyes and you can't help not telling him 'Good morning, Master'. he answers with a persistent smiling 'Hiiii!'. 9.30 a.m. meeting with Psarantonis.:-)'

9 people like this

Carla describes in detail her meeting with one of her favourite Greek artists, Psarantonis (born 1942), a Cretan composer, singer and performer of lyra, a traditional bowed string instrument. Carla's account pertains to a recent key event rooted in an old admiration of hers for Psarantonis's music. She deploys present tenses (*you wake up, you leave, you're ready to go, you see, he is stooping, he is carrying, you cross each other, he raises, stares, you can't help, he answers*), with *you* being synonymous with *I*, creating vividness and immediacy to her description. What Carla is doing here is taking a moment, that is, a greeting, which would otherwise be unimportant (for instance, she could have just written 'Glimpsed Psarantonis at the airport'), and builds it into an event that has value for her and her readers. As a nice stylistic choice, Psarantonis's name comes last, revealing the meaning of the whole story.

Carla specifies she met Psarantonis at 9.30 am. The time of narration indicated by Facebook's time-stamp is 10.59 am. I assume that had she been an owner of a smartphone at that time, she might have posted this story even earlier, just a few minutes after her meeting with Psarantonis. Thanks to Facebook, Carla does not need to wait until she gets together with her friends to recount to them all the details as she has the opportunity to share her story and reach her audience in the closest possible proximity to the event.

Stepping away from the minutiae of everyday life often encountered in status updates, both examples below report present events crucial for the informants: summer vacations for Romanos (Example 5.3) and Morrissey's[4] concert in Athens for Carla (Figure 5.2).

FIGURE 5.2 *Carla's countdown for Morrissey's concert in Athens.*

5.3

a. Romanos

23 August 2010 at 12:00

Countdown set... 2 kai simera!
'Countdown set... 2 [days] and today!'

b. Romanos

24 August 2010 at 12:53

Misi kai simera!
'Half [day] and today!'
1 person likes this

c. Romanos

25 August 2010 at 13:25

Today! Bye-Bye...
4 people like this

d. Romanos

1 September 2010 at 01:23
Back...

Although countdowns are generally inherently future-oriented, they embody a working sense of present continuity. In Romanos's case, the countdown is purely textual, complementing the temporal deictic *today*, while in Carla's it is backed up by Morrissey's lyrics ('last night I dreamt', 'A double bed / And a stalwart lover for sure / These are the riches of the poor', 'Yeah, I've made up your mind') and audiovisual material (Morrissey's video clips). Such kind of daily persistence, not only does it accentuate the importance of the event but it also keeps their audiences in suspense. Even after the completion of the event, both of them provide their readers with further feedback (*back* by Romanos and *last night* by Carla from a Morrissey's lyrics).

Cyclical time

Daily, weekly and annual cycles of recurring events at the sociocultural or organizational level are of paramount importance to identity as they provide a basis of stability and self-continuity (Lewis and Weigart 1981). This section examines how the informants position themselves cyclically within everyday events, seasons and festivities.

Everyday cycles

Example 5.4 and Figure 5.3 impart a flavour of how tastes and habits embedded in everyday life cycles are multimodally treated in Facebook posts. Alkis in 5.4 shares an extract from the Greek comedy *Η Παριζιάνα* (*La Parisienne*),[5] filmed in 1969, employing time adverbials of frequency (*HOW many times, always*) to highlight the all-time amusing impact of the particular video scene on him.

5.4

Alkis
30 May 2011 at 21:05

ΟΣΕΣ <u>φορές</u> και να το δω πάντα γελάω ...!!:-)
'No matter <u>HOW MANY times</u> I watch it I <u>always</u> laugh...!!:-)'
[He embeds from YouTube the video *Vlaxopoulou: Souzi trws!*.]
23 people like this

Romanos, in Figure 5.3, accompanies a ***meme*** based on *Futurama*, an American animated science fiction sitcom, with the opening comment *Story of my life...*. The particular phrase, according to the Urban Dictionary (2016), is said when something negative happens very often. Notably, Romanos does not explicitly say that the negative phenomenon is his forgetfulness; this is humorously conveyed by dint of the meme.

FIGURE 5.3 *Romanos's post about forgetting.*

Seasons

Seasons are a key cycle which can bind Facebook posts into larger idiosyncratic narratives. Examples 5.5 and 5.6 treat the season of summer as triggered by particular pieces of music.

5.5

Romanos
19 April 2011 at 10:48
Song reminds me of <u>summer</u> ...
[He embeds from YouTube the song *Lights* (Bassnectar Remix) by the English sythpop singer Ellie Goulding.]
1 person likes this

5.6

[Carla embeds from YouTube in her personal profile the song *Kissing A Fool* by the English dance-pop singer and songwriter George Michael.]
9 August 2011 at 02:07

FBU1 [male]: <u>καθε τετοια περιοδο</u> σε πιανει η αρρωστια των <u>80s περσι</u> ειχαμε την σοφια βοσσου και το εγω και ο πουφ
'<u>every year such period</u> you suffer from the <u>80s</u> sickness <u>last year</u> we had Sofia Vossou [a Greek 80s singer] and *Me and Pouf* [title of a Greek 80s pop song]'
9 August 2011 at 11:21

[Carla writes a comment about FBU1 and another mutual friend]

Carla: <u>φέτος</u>, ε, μου ρθε μια νοσταλγία βρε αδερφέ (αλλά η αλήθεια είναι ότι δεν την παλεύω, αν δεν καταργηθεί ο <u>αύγουστος</u> δε με σώζει τίποτα)
'<u>this year</u>, ah, I have felt some nostalgia bro (but the truth is that I can't stand it, if <u>August</u> is not abolished nothing will save me)'
9 August 2011 at 17:14 · Like · 1

The present tense (*reminds me*) in 5.5 suggests that whenever Romanos listens to the particular track, he imagines sunshine and beaches, he relaxes or he even anticipates summer to come (as his post was written in April). In 5.6, it is FBU1 who detects (*every year such period*) that every August Carla's posts are entirely different from what her audience is accustomed to reminding her exactly what she had posted last year. While Carla acknowledges that she feels nostalgia for 80s music, in effect she cannot put up with the fact that she is working during summer. Hence, this kind of unusual posting can be viewed as an iterative ritual to exorcize her summer stay in the city.

Festivities

On New Year's Eve, as well as on the New Year's Day, Facebook News Feed is normally teemed with pictures of gatherings at friends' houses or social outings at bars and clubs. In Example 5.7, Romanos reports how he was about to spend New Year's Eve away from family and friends while he was in the army.

5.7

Romanos
31 December 2012 at 19:44

Σχέδια για αλλαγή χρόνου: Σκοπιά
Φαγητό: Βραστά αυγά με τηγανητές πατάτες
Τοποθεσία: Φυλάκιο
Εξοπλισμός: Ουίσκι, ρακί, κρασί, ξηροκάρπια, όπλο, κράνος, εξάρτηση
'Plans for New Year's Eve: Night watch
Food: Boiled eggs with French fries
Place: Guardroom
Equipment: Whiskey, raki,[6] wine, nuts, gun, helmet, harness'
10 people like this

From time to time, depending on various personal and sociocultural reasons (e.g. joining the army in the case at hand), the sense of 'here we go again' (Myers 2010b: 74) in one's life is breached and, consequently, routines, customs and habits are not followed with the same reverence. Romanos here uses Facebook to record what is different and irregular and, of course, to seek support while the rest of his Facebook contacts enjoy the typical celebration.

To sum up, references to the present are crucial for the solidity of identity as the users instantly recognize the significance of particular moments and attach meanings to them. Cyclical repetitions, on the other hand, have a different kind of meaning to their identity, either reassuring (e.g. liking the same things over time) or upsetting (e.g. forgetting, working in the summer, keeping a night watch on New Year's Eve).

Future projections

Mead (1938) has differentiated future into immediate and hypothetical. The immediate future is pertinent to what actually happens. The hypothetical future, conversely, refers to those moments during which individuals contemplate alternative responses and possibilities to a specific situation. Put it another way, immediate and hypothetical futures 'correspond to alternating phases of the self in action and reflection' (Flaherty and Fine 2001: 156), respectively.

Talking about the immediate future constitutes part of a description or evaluation of the present (Myers 2010b: 73) as appears from Example 5.8. Alkis had sent his fellow student, FBU1, via email some materials relevant to a presentation on advertising and marketing they were going to deliver as part of their MSc. Adhering to the guidelines of their professor, the presenters were not supposed to accompany their talk with PowerPoint slides. Both Alkis and FBU1 appear to worry about the success of their 'slideless' presentation, which is arranged a few days before Christmas with everyone being in a mood for celebration and not concentrated on studying and working.

5.8

Alkis
15 December 2010 at 21:42

'Πάρτο αλλιώς διαφορετικά χάσαμε', 'sorry κιόλας', με και για την αγορά – με και για την κοινωνία (ουπς ... από αλλού αυτό!)
'"Take it differently otherwise we'll lose," "ahem sorry," with and for the market – with and for the society (oops ... this is from elsewhere!)'[7]

1. FBU1 [female]: tuxaio???de nomizw .....
'Accidental??? I don't think so .....'[8]
15 December 2010 at 22:34

2. Alkis: ΤΙΠΟΤΑ δεν είναι τυχαίο!!
'NOTHING is accidental!! :)'
15 December 2010 at 22:51

3. Alkis: Meanwhile δες τα emails σου και πες μου αν έκανα καλά που έστειλα ό,τι έστειλα!
'Meanwhile check your emails and tell me if I did well for sending what I sent!'
15 December 2010 at 22:52

4. FBU1: ta eida idi kai ekanes polu kala!!vevaia to <u>pws tha ta parousiasoume</u> proforika kai tha einai kai kali i parousiasi pragmatika den xerw!!!!!sigoura tha eprepe na uparxei ena pp na exeis kai mia eikona alla ....
'I've checked them already and you did very well!! however I really don't know <u>how we will present them</u> orally and how the presentation will be good!!!!! definitely there should be a powerpoint to give a picture but ....'
15 December 2010 at 22:54

5. Alkis: OXI AΛΛΑ PP!!!!!!!!!!!! Έχεις δίκιο βέβαια αλλά εκείνη το είχε πει ....

'NO MORE POWERPOINTS!!!!!!!!!!!! You're right of course but she [the professor] had asked it ....'
15 December 2010 at 22:56

6. FBU1: to xerw!!genika pisteuw oti tha ginoume rompa alla allou pappa euaggelio auto!!!

'I know!! generally I believe that we'll become a laughing stock but that's a different story!!!'
15 December 2010 at 22:58

7. Alkis: Mas kovw na to kouventiazoume me kafe kai koulourakia sti megali aithousa pou exoun aplws... Ki etsi na ginei plaka tha exei!! 8 to vradu tis Deyteras kai proproproxristougenniatika mallon tetoia atmosfaira prepei na epidiwxoume!

'I guesstimate we'll just discuss it with coffee and cookies in the big hall they have... Even if it happens this way it'll be fun!! 8 at night on Monday and on the day before Christmas Eve perhaps we should pursue such an atmosphere!'
15 December 2010 at 23:00

Chiming with Georgakopoulou's (2002) observations on the collaborative construction of hypothetical narratives, Alkis here functions as the elicitor of the projected event of their upcoming presentation inviting suggestions in comment 3 (*tell me if I did well*). FBU1 enacts the role of the assessor or evaluator of the event invoking a future group identity (comment 4: *I really don't know how we will present them orally*; comment 6: *I believe that we'll become a laughing stock*). Alkis aids the narrative by offering a potential scenario in comment 7 (*I guesstimate we'll just discuss it with coffee and cookies in the big hall*) and elaborating on the story's evaluation deploying a conditional (*Even if it happens this way it'll be fun!!*).

Future in this example is constructed as a fact, namely shaped by present choices and actions (Adam 2009), in which identities are galvanized by planning a joint course of action. Hovering the mouse over the time-stamps of the thread, one will notice that Alkis asks for feedback on the material he forwarded to his fellow student on a Sunday night. The thread takes place on 15 December while we can easily deduce that the presentation is scheduled for 23 December (*on the day before Christmas Eve*). Instead of sending a private message to FBU1, Alkis opts for writing a public comment under his post. In this fashion, his audience, consisting of other fellow students too, is indirectly informed that Alkis is working on Sunday and is getting prepared several days prior to the presentation. The same goes for his fellow student, who answers him *I've checked them already*. Both of them therefore, beyond the humorous performance, craft themselves as being responsible and committed to their upcoming project.

Moving now to hypothetical future, I focus on wishing which, by and large, involves desired future states (King and Broyles 1997). Alkis, every year on 31 December, enjoys the annual textual ritual of issuing wishes to all of his Facebook friends as illustrated in Examples 5.9, 5.10 and 5.11.

5.9

Alkis

31 December 2010 at 13:11

ΠΟΛΥ καλή χρονιά σε όλες κι όλους και με μία ευχή: το 2011 σε ΠΕΙΣΜΑ όλων των απαισιόδοξων <u>εμείς να είμαστε</u> – έστω και ανεξήγητα – τιγκαρισμένοι στην αισιοδοξία!!
'VERY Happy New Year to everyone with one wish: in 2011 IN THE FACE OF all pessimists <u>we should be</u> -even inexplicably- full up with optimism!!'
17 people like this

5.10

Alkis

31 December 2011 at 15:46

Μακάρι κάτι μαγικό να γίνει και <u>να μας εκρφάζει όλους</u> αυτό το υπέροχο κομμάτι, τη νέα χρονιά που έρχεται. ΠΟΤΕ δεν ξέρεις …!
ΠΟΛΥ πολύ καλή χρονιά σε όλους!:-D
'May something magical happen so this wonderful song <u>will express all of us</u>, in this new year that is coming. You NEVER know …!
VERY very happy New Year to everyone!:-D'
[He embeds from YouTube the song *Feeling Good* by the Canadian pop/jazz singer Michael Bublé.]
14 people like this

5.11

Alkis

31 December 2012 at 18:06

Πολλές πολλές ευχές σε όοοολες κι όλους για μια νέα χρονιά (και όλες τις επόμενες!!) με όμορφες προθέσεις που να γίνονται πράξεις, (θετικές) σκέψεις και ιδέες που να γίνονται και αυτές πράξεις, την ευχή <u>να ξέρουμε/μάθουμε όλοι</u> τι θέλουμε και πώς να το διεκδικούμε σωστά, το μυαλό μέσα <u>στο κεφάλι μας</u> και <u>την καρδιά μας</u> ανοιχτή κι όχι μπλοκαρισμένη!
Ξέχασα κάτι; Α, βέβαια!

Αγάπη, ΥΓΕΙΑ και πολλά πολλά χαμόγελα!!! Όλα τα άλλα νομίζω πως θα βρεθούν! Κλισέ; Μπααα ... ΟΥΣΙΑ!!:-)
Πολύ πολύ ΚΑΛΗ χρονιά να έχουμε!:-)
'Many many wishes to eeeeveryone for the new year (and all next ones!!) with beautiful intentions that become deeds, (positive) thoughts and ideas that become deeds too, the wish for all of us to know/learn what we want and how to defend it correctly, to have [our] brain inside our head [be prudent, sagacious] and our heart open and not blocked! Have I forgotten anything? Oh, of course!
Love, HEALTH and many many smiles!!! All the rest will be found I think! Cliché? Naaah ... GIST!!:-)
Very HAPPY New Year to us!:-)'
18 people like this

Alkis via his fervent wishes taps into a fantasized future we-inclusive identity (*we should be* in example 5.9, *will express all of us* in example 5.10, *the wish for all of us to know/learn, inside our head and our heart open*, and *Very HAPPY New Year to us!:-*) in example 5.11 defined by optimism, euphoria, love, health, happiness, positivity and action. Future here is constructed as fortune (i.e. an abstract, empty and quantifiable entity available for unrestricted use and free exploitation on the basis of past facts), as a hopeful expectation of action potential – it 'becomes ours to shape, make and take' (Adam 2009). Through his long, personal, emotionally laden wishes, Alkis places special value on a selected audience, which more or less already knows him (cf. the effect would not be the same on Twitter, for example, in which users do not necessarily know who is 'following' them).

The next sections explore a different way of perceiving time, more complex, subjective and emotionally loaded than what has been discussed so far: age.

Age and lifespan

Harking back to Evans's (2005) agentive sense of time above, time appears to bring about certain effects, one of which is age. Age identity is a product 'of the evaluative component of our life narratives, the cumulative assessment of where we stand, developmentally – as individuals and in relation to our social environments' (Coupland 2001: 203). Thus, apart from a chronological matter, age is also a developmental, psychological and social process best understood in terms of cultural definition and interactional accomplishment (Boden and Bielby 1986). Age categorization is something we do in discourse, so its analysis can disclose how cultural meanings of age are enacted, experienced and reproduced in interaction, that is, how age acquires meaning through discourse.

According to Coupland et al. (1991), older age identities in discourse are constructed in terms of two fundamental processes: age-categorization processes and temporal framing processes. The former processes include:

- **disclosing chronological age**
  (e.g., I'm not very well these days too. I'm seventy last October.)

- **age-related categories/role references**
  (e.g., I'll have to pay for that myself and I'm a pensioner.)

- **age-related experiences of illness and decline**
  (e.g., I pray I'll keep my faculties until I go.)

(Original examples from Coupland et al. 1991: 92–4)

Temporal framing, on the other hand, deals with:

- **adding time-past perspective to current or recent events and topics**
  (e.g., I've been going there for eleven years.)

- **associating the self with the past**
  (e.g., I wouldn't recognise the place (.) it's years since I've been up this part of the city … years ago I used to come up here scrubbing floors.)

- **recognizing historical, cultural and social change**
  (e.g., But times are so different aren't they? … Everything's fast isn't. You've got to sort of run with it.).

(Original examples from Coupland et al. 1991: 94–6)

While the Coupland et al. (1991) taxonomy is grounded in the talk of the elderly, it can be adapted for other age categories as well as for different communicative settings such as Facebook. Guided by Coupland et al. (1991) and being consistent with the purposes of this book and the nature and content of my data, the analysis in the remainder of the chapter addresses the following issues: disclosing chronological age, attributing age-related categories, celebrating birthdays, adding past perspective to current states, recalling the past, recognizing change and Facebook as a record of changes.

Disclosing chronological age

Revealing one's age is the most crystal clear means of self-identifying in terms of time (Coupland et al. 1991). Following Facebook's profile information format, Carla writes she was born on 21 December 1975; Helen on 16 March 1979; Romanos on 18 February 1989; and Gabriel on 9 August 1990. Alkis, however, as I discuss in more detail in Chapter 8, viewing age as a vital piece of personal data, has chosen to camouflage it from other users, at least at first sight. Based on repeated views of his profile I deduced that he was born on 1 March 1981, which was later confirmed by Alkis himself after reading drafts of my analysis. Startlingly, despite his privacy concerns, he is the only one out of the five informants who has made explicit references to his age in individual posts as shown in Examples 5.12 and 5.13.

5.12

Alkis

28 January 2011 at 16:58

Πα μαλ … Λίγο Λαμπαντέ βέβαια – αλλά μας αρέσουν τα ρετρό τώρα που τριανταρίζουμε …!!;-)
'Pas mal … A bit Lambada of course – but we like retro things now that we are getting into our thirties..!!;-)'
1 person likes this

5.13

Alkis

2 March 2011 at 11:28

Ααα, κι αυτό κι αυτό!!
Ρε παιδιά, στα 30 μου θα γίνω μέταλλο! (οκ, υπό προϋποθέσεις!!)
'Aah, and this one and this one!!
Hey guys, in my 30s I will become a fan of metal music! (ok, under conditions!!)'
3 people like this

Example 5.12 was Alkis's opening comment in uploading Jennifer Lopez's song 'On The Floor', while *this one* in Example 5.13 refers to Lady Gaga's song 'Born This Way' for which she has produced a metal version as well.[9] Alkis here touches on two cultural stereotypes germane to what is acceptable for one's age. The first stereotype is that as people grow older, they tend to resist modernity showing preference towards old – *retro* as Alkis writes – things. The hype with Lambada, a Brazilian dance, started in 1989, when Alkis was a primary school student. Lopez's song pays homage to Lambada including recurrent elements from the original composition. Alkis does not seem fully satisfied with the song, tactfully evaluating it as *pas mal* (meaning 'not bad' in French) and *a bit Lambada*; yet, he still enjoys it. Interestingly, he does not write 'I like (but rather: "we like") retro things now that I'm getting into my thirties' (compare with the first person pronoun in Example 5.13). This *we* (*we like*, *we are getting*) pronominal reference could be seen as creating a certain feeling of shared identity with his peers through shared points of reference, in this case music. With the blinking **smiley** ;-) and the two exclamation marks, Alkis wishes to further emphasize that 'getting into our thirties' is important to him.

Example 5.13 fuels the stereotype that when older adults share with younger adults the same enthusiasm for a music genre, metal in the case at hand, they are likely to be treated as distanced and in some cases derogated outgroups. Alkis appears to acknowledge that pure metal bands (i.e. those using loud and distorted guitars, powerful drum and bass sound and vigorous vocals) are not that appropriate for his age choosing to share – one day after his birthday – the pop and metal mashup 'Born This Way', which could mildly initiate him into the metal genre (*under conditions*). One could suggest that by making known his foray into metal in his 30s, Alkis attempts to show that he is not somebody who does the 'done' thing; he is different and distinctive.

What we are facing in the above examples, besides the explicit disclosure of age, is that Facebook participants can take expressive stances towards their age and the experiences of people of a certain age by more implicit means such as music or TV shows, as we will see in the next section.

Attributing age-related categories

A significant age-categorization process refers to the assigning of nominal or attributive category labels to individuals or groups (Coupland et al. 1991) such as 'young', 'old' or 'our/their age'. Example 5.14 offers a vivid picture of such labelling. FBU1 has tagged Gabriel in a photo which depicts him together with her, three other girls (FBU2, FBU3 and FBU4) and two boys, all of them international students around their early twenties, sitting on a dinner table during a summer school in Brussels.

5.14

1. FBU1 [female]: we all look so young in here :))))
15 February 2012 at 03:33

2. FBU2 [female]: :)) it sounds like we are really old now!
15 February 2012 at 11:09

3. FBU1: hihihi
well, to make myself clear, my point was the following: even though the picture was taken in summer 2010 (so not that long time ago) we look very young in it if I saw this as an independent observer I would say there are kids under 18 but it's a compliment! we probably were just soooo happy at the summer school! and happy people look younger hihi
15 February 2012 at 12:10 · Like · 3

4. Gabriel: though i <u>still</u> feel <u>young</u>!!;-)
15 February 2012 at 17:26 · Like · 2

5. FBU3 [female]: When we were young, we had fun. Always, always!
15 February 2012 at 17:26 · Like · 2

6. Gabriel: http://www.youtube.com/watch?v=E1nbvplgElw (now i'm messing the picture sorry!)
[He embeds from YouTube the song *Young Forever* by the American rapper Jay-Z and the British R&B and pop singer Mr. Hudson.]
16 February 2012 at 02:00 · Like · 3

7. FBU4 [female]: bien joue [it plays well] gabbrieeeeel;)
16 February 2012 at 02:02 · Like · 1

8. FBU1: yes! still feeling <u>young</u> but year by year getting <u>wiser</u> and <u>wiser</u> :))
16 February 2012 at 02:04 · Like · 1

9. Gabriel: double like!
16 February 2012 at 02:05

10. FBU1: ☺
16 February 2012 at 02:06

FBU1 yields the category of youth by attaching the labels *so young* (comment 1), *very young* and *kids under 18* (comment 3) to all seven depicted actors. FBU2 jokingly replies that if these labels hold for a picture taken two years before the interaction at hand, then the label *really old* should be assigned to them now (comment 2). Youth as life position is also invoked in *happy people look younger* (comment 3) and *When we were young, we had fun* (comment 5). Not only does Gabriel identify with the label for the present (comment 4: *i still feel young*) but also for the future attaching a YouTube link which leads to the rap song 'Young Forever' (comment 6). FBU1 adds to Gabriel's identity claim via the label *wiser and wiser* despite the oxymoron of his feeling young (comment 8).

On Alkis's birthday, FBU1 posted on his Wall (Example 5.15) the Greek song *Δεν Φταίω εγώ που μεγαλώνω* ('It's not my fault if I grow older').[10] Here are the comments that accompanied FBU1's post:

5.15

FBU1 [female]: <u>μεγαλώνεις</u> και <u>ομορφαίνεις</u>!!!
'you <u>get older</u> and <u>more beautiful</u>!!!'
1 March 2011 at 13:02

... εμ, μεγαλώνεις και <u>ωριμάζεις σαν το καλό φρούτο</u>!
'you get older and <u>mature like a good fruit</u>!'
1 March 2011 at 13:07 · Like · 1

Although FBU1 assigns Alkis the label of *growing old*, she associates it with the positive attributes of beauty and maturity (via the simile *mature like a good fruit*).

The interaction in Example 5.16 was sparked after Carla's posting of the song 'Epic' by the American rock band Faith No More on her personal profile.

5.16

1. FBU1 [male]: Τι έγινε, ροκέψαμε;
'What's going on, have we turned to rock?'
17 April 2012 at 00:48

2. Carla: είδες τι παθαίνει ο άνθρωπος στα <u>γεράματα</u>;
'you see what happens to people in <u>old age</u>?'
18 April 2012 at 20:21

3. FBU1: Σου προτείνω τους Rolling Stones. Ελπιδοφόροι και σε ηλικία γάμου ...
'I recommend Rolling Stones to you. Promising and in marriageable age ...'
19 April 2012 at 02:34

Carla humorously self-selects the category *old* (comment 2) to justify her sudden change in the genre of the songs she uploads (compare to Example 5.6) as she usually prefers ethnic or indie rock songs. Notice that her question *'you see what happens to people in old age?'* is expressed in a generic way; she does not say, for instance, *'you see what happens to me in old age?'* In a similar amusing tone, FBU1 faces Carla as someone who has not been exposed to rock music and therefore she should listen to Rolling Stones for a start (compare with the case of Alkis and metal performed by Lady Gaga in Example 5.13).

The thread in Example 5.17 below was unfolded when Alkis posted the theme song – performed by the American jazz singer Al Jarreau – of the American TV series *Moonlighting* (1985–9; screened in Greek TV in early 1990s) in which a former model (Cybill Shepherd) and a detective (Bruce Willis) collaborate to solve various cases. In comment 1, FBU1 mentions another character of the show, Herbert Viola (Curtis Armstrong).

5.17

Alkis
6 April 2012 at 23:11
Τι όμορφο κομμάτι και τι ωραία σειρά!! :-)

'What a beautiful track and what a beautiful series!! :-)'
[He embeds from YouTube the video Al Jarreau – *Moonlighting* (Pilot Theme).]
4 people like this

1. FBU1 [male]: Τι να κάνει άραγε ο Χέρμπερτ Βαϊόλα;
'What is Herbert Viola doing?'
7 April 2012 at 00:55 · Like · 2

2. Alkis: Χαχαχαχχαχαα!! ΔΕΝ υπάρχεις!!!
Υ.Γ. Ελπίζω να έχει κουρευτεί! Lol
'Hahahahhahaa!! I DON'T believe it!!!
P.S. I hope he has his hair cut! Lol'
7 April 2012 at 00:57

3. FBU2 [female]: αxxxxxxxxxxx <u>ta niata mas</u>!
'ahhhhhhhhhhh <u>our youth</u>!'
7 April 2012 at 01:48

4. FBU3 [female]: Πραγματικά!! Μπράβο Άλκη!!
'Indeed!! Well done Alkis!!'
7 April 2012 at 03:31 · Like · 1

[Another 9 comments with FBU3 and Alkis talking about a Greek TV series which was inspired by *Moonlighting*.]

5. FBU4 [female]: ναι τετοια κανεις και διαπιστωνουμε πόσο <u>εχουμε...</u>
<u>ωριμασει</u>!!! ...
'yes you're doing such things and we realize how much <u>we have...</u>
<u>matured</u>!!! ...'
7 April 2012 at 09:37 · Like · 1

Seeing *Moonlighting* standing metonymically for a whole period of life, FBU2 uses the collective *our youth* (comment 3) to point to a shared age category membership among viewers of the show, emitting a feeling of nostalgia. FBU3, in comment 4, provides 'generational alignment' (Coupland et al. 1991) with the categorization by writing *Indeed* peppered with expressive punctuation. FBU4, on the other hand, jokingly reprimands Alkis for *doing such things* (comment 5), that is, posting old resources (songs), which make his audience realize the lapse of time and the fact that they have come into maturity, a label she likewise attaches collectively (*we have... matured*). The three dots before *matured* might suggest that FBU4 was tempted to say *έχουμε... γεράσει* (*we have... grown old*), but she eventually selected a more appropriate and self-praising verb. Anyhow, the dots do draw attention to the issue of ageing and the users' feelings about it.

In all, age categorization in the preceding examples was rendered by means of nominals (young, old, old age, youth), verbal clusters (get older and mature, we have matured), intensifiers (*so* young, *very* young), comparative morphology (younger, older, wiser, more beautiful), **circumlocution** (kids under 18) and commonplaces (happy people look younger). Apart from Carla's *in old age*, the rest of the age labels were attributed by the profile hosts' Facebook friends. In Example 5.17, we saw that Alkis's opening comment to the music clip was one of aesthetic appreciation virtually extraneous to ageing: *What a beautiful track and what a beautiful series!! :-)*. His posting triggers a feeling of nostalgia among his friends, which in turn triggers the age labelling. The point I wish to establish here is that although it may not have been the poster's original aim at all (Alkis does not seem to participate in this reminiscence; he just shared and evaluated a song he liked), identity constructions can be initiated by Facebook friends, who in their exchanges pick up certain aspects of age identity (e.g. youth, maturity) and play with them.

A crucial issue, then, that emerges is whether my informants accept the assigned age label. Revisiting Example 5.14, Gabriel approved of the label *young* through the time adverbial *still* plus the Jay-Z song. Moreover, to his friend's remark (comment 8) he replied *double like* having already clicked 'Like' on it to further enforce his alignment. In like manner, in Example 5.15, Alkis has clicked 'Like' on his friend's likening him to a good fruit as well on his other friend's comment on maturity in Example 5.17 (comment 5). What we witness in these instances is that the 'Like' button serves the 'pragmatic function' (Barton and Lee 2013: 88) of ratifying age identity categorization. However, in Example 5.17 again, unlike FBU3, Alkis passes by FBU2's label *our youth*, providing neither comment nor 'Like', perhaps due to the fact that FBU2 is six years older than him, excluding thus himself from the particular collective.

Age categorization can also be indirectly endorsed, as shown in Example 5.18.

5.18

FBU1 [female]: Χαχαχαχα!!! Μαλλον και μεις γερασαμε σαν τη Καρει!!!! Χαχαχαχα!!!!
'Hahahaha!!! Perhaps we've grown old too like Carey!!!! Hahahaha!!!!'
7 April 2012 at 02:45

Alkis: ΣΣΣΣΤ! Μας διαβάζουν!!
'SHUSH! They're reading us [our thread]!!'
7 April 2012 at 02:47 · Like · 1

A friend has posted on Alkis's Wall a music video with the American pop singer and dancer Paula Abdul performing 'Straight Up' in response to an Alkis's earlier post with the American pop/soul singer and actress Mariah

Carey singing, hence FBU1's *we've grown old too like Carey*. Alkis both tacitly and humorously aligns with the simile via *SHUSH!* to prevent the viewing audience from learning more details with respect to their age.

Another point that should be underscored with respect to age categorization is the hyperbole in label projection. When Carla writes *in old age* in Example 5.16, she is just 37, while the participants in Example 5.14 were still very young when they exchanged their comments. Such exaggerations are seen as having a justifying effect: Carla, on the one hand, rationalizes her veering towards rock music. FBU1, on the other, in Example 5.14, reinforces her observation on the temporariness of youth even within two years' time.

Celebrating birthdays

Birthday, the annual upgrading of chronological age, is a key element in the self- and other concept of the ageing individual (Bytheway 2005). Among others, Facebook functions as a birthday reminder (i.e. it tells you when someone's birthday is), provided that the user has filled in their date of birth and made it visible to their audience, facilitating thus the renewal or sustainment of relationships in view of distance and neglect. The next two examples look at how birthdays are sieved through wishes both by my participants and their Facebook friends. What is exceptional with Facebook – contrary to birthday cards or wishes over the phone or SMS – is that we have a persistent written record of how the birthday person responds to the wish (and a persistent record of all of the birthday wishes on their Wall, not just one's own), unless they choose to answer with a private message, delete the wishes from their Timeline, not respond to the wishes at all, or not allow anybody to write on their Timeline.

Example 5.19 is a wish[11] on Alkis's Wall by his sister. Alkis appears to resist time and, therefore, the grown up label, with two tropes: the oxymoron *I'm growing younger instead of older* and the simile *as they do to small kids*.

5.19

Alkis's sister: χρόνια πολλά αδερφάκι μου <3 θα σε ζουπήξω αύριο γτ μου φαίνεσαι λίγο περίεργα. <3 <3 <3
'happy birthday my little brother <3 I'll squeeze you tomorrow cause you seem a bit strange to me. <3 <3 <3'
1 March 2013 at 21:21

Alkis: Είναι που <u>μικαρίνω αντί να μεγαλώνω</u> και μου φαίνεται περίεργο!! :) <3 <3 <3
Να με ζουπήξεις όπως κάνουν στα μικρά! Χαχα

'It's because <u>I'm growing younger instead of older</u> and it seems strange to
me!! <3 <3 <3
Squeeze me as they do to small kids! Haha'
1 March 2013 at 21:24

In Example 5.20, FBU1 jokingly points to the fact that Carla's birthday on
21 December 2012 coincided with the Mayan calendar world end-date,
reproducing the song lyric 'you were born for disaster' :).[12] Carla picks her
friend's joke and offers her own reflection on the coincidence in the same
spirit (*I was ready for the rendezvous with disaster anyway!*) identifying it as
a steady feature of her attitude (*I'm always ready!*).

5.20

FBU1 [male]: Χρόνια πολλά Κάρλα. 21 Δεκέμβρη, γεννήθηκες για την καταστροφή:)
'Happy birthday Carla. 21 December, <u>you were born for disaster</u>:)'
21 December 2012 at 11:09 · Like · 1

Carla: χαχαχαχαχαχαχαχαχαχαχαχα! τέλειο!!!! εγώ ήμουν έτοιμη για το ραντεβού
με την καταστροφή πάντως! <u>πάντα</u> είμαι!
'hahahahahahahahahahahaha! perfect!!!! I was ready for the rendezvous
with disaster anyway! I'm <u>always</u> ready!'
21 December 2012 at 18:08 · Like · 1

But users do not content themselves in publicly commenting each individual
wish written on their Walls. They also post on their birthday to thank massively
their contacts for their wishes, to remind their audience of their birthday, in
case they have overlooked Facebook's reminder, or to make some age-related
identity claim as I will immediately show.

Decade boundaries, that is, turning 20, 30, 40, 50 or 60 years old and so on,
are considered special milestones that call for equivalently special interactional
marking (cf. Nikander 2009) such as that in Figure 5.4, which Alkis uploaded as
a profile picture the day he turned 30.

Alkis, instead of worrying for leaving his 20s, resting on the double meaning
of the symbol XXX, as the number 30 in Roman numerals and as a kind of
rating applied to pornographic films, jocularly evokes connotations of hotness
and sexiness as well as connotations of being a consumer of porn.

Romanos, in Example 5.21, does not seem to share a similar enthusiasm
two days after his birthday. His status update is in fact a song title by the
American hard rock musician Meat Loaf. This is a quite pessimistic song
about ageing; the narrative persona of the song is someone who does not
want the future (the song ends with the lyric 'I wish it wouldn't come but it
always does…'). Perhaps Romanos experiences melancholy or some kind of

FIGURE 5.4 *Alkis's profile picture on his 30th birthday (1 March 2011).*

disappointment and frustration, and sees Facebook as a medium to give a public, intertextual, yet discreet, vent to his feelings.

5.21

Romanos
20 February 2011 at 00:09
The future ain't what it used to be...
1 person likes this

The celebration of birthdays conveys to people a sense of identity continuity and an indication of change (Bytheway 2005). The users above saw birthdays in positive ways: an opportunity to express love and affection (Alkis's sister in Example 5.19); to sustain friendship and have fun (Example 5.20); and to feast (Figure 5.4). Romanos, on the other hand, downplayed the significance of his birthday, marking indirectly the passage of time and probably a change in his life. These findings correlate fairly well with Stæhr (2015a) and further support the argument that birthday posts on Facebook are a good place to look for identity (co)construction, identification practices and discursive creativity.

Adding past perspective to current states

In discourse management, the past can be reshaped, discovered, rediscovered, remembered, forgotten and invented by virtue of temporal framing processes (cf. Coupland et al. 1991; Jenkins 2002). Two essential ingredients of identification across time are 1) consciousness, the 'active focusing on a small part of the conscious being's self-centered model of the surrounding world' (Chafe 1994: 28) and 2) memory, the 'capacity to have personal and collective pasts' (Jenkins 2002: 268). This section describes how the users make their consciousness visible and sharable on Facebook through chronological shifting into the past, whereas the next one deals with the overall theme of memory as expressed in Facebook contributions and exchanges.

As we saw in Example 5.14, FBU1 reports that *the picture was taken in summer 2010*, providing a time-past frame within which age identities are inscribed. Weaving present states, activities and events with the past involves numerical markers of time past that enable inferential work to age categorization (Coupland et al. 1991). The examples that follow illuminate how music can provide key temporal benchmarks that allow the users to intermingle the past with the present.

In posting Madonna's[13] 'Hung Up' and alluding to the song lyric 'Time goes by so slowly', Alkis – realizing that seven years have elapsed since the particular song's release – commented:

5.22

ΕΦΤΑ χρόνια κιόλας... Time DOES NOT go by so slowly!!!
'It's been SEVEN years already... Time DOES NOT go by so slowly!!!'
4 April 2012 at 12:33 · Like · 1

In Example 5.23, posted twelve minutes later, he voices a similar surprise as regards Madonna's song *Music* this time.

5.23

Alkis
4 April 2012 at 12:45
Ή πιστεύει κανείς πως έχουν περάσει σχεδόν 12 χρόνια από αυτό;;!!!
'Or does anyone believe that nearly 12 years have passed since this??!!!'
[He embeds from YouTube the song *Music* by Madonna.]
2 people like this

The interaction in Example 5.24 took place underneath Carla's post (on her personal profile) of the song *I Love The Way You Dream*, by the British electronic music duo 1 Giant Leap, for which she offered no opening comments.

5.24

FBU1 [female]: Εκεί γνωριστήκαμε! Πέρασαν 9 χρόνια;;;
'There we met each other for the first time! Have 9 years passed???'
11 October 2011 at 00:13

Carla: wow!!!! έτσι φαίνεται!!
'wow!!!! It seems so!!'
12 October 2011 at 10:37

With *there*, FBU1 recalls the day she first met Carla during a concert celebrating the European Music Day in Athens where the music project *1 Giant Leap* was run. The time frame is articulated in the form of a rhetorical question (*Have 9 years passed???*).

When Alkis uploaded 'You Are My Sunshine', covered by Anne Murray, a friend responded to him with a reggae version of the same song performed by Papa Winnie.[14] Example 5.25 is Alkis's follow-up comment in which he frames his past entertainment experience after being prompted by his Facebook contact.

5.25

Η κλασική εκτέλεση! Ε ρε χορό που έχω ρίξει στα 90's με αυτό ☺
'The classic version! Re[15] how much have I danced to this in the 90's ☺'
16 May 2012 at 13:25 · Like · 1

An intriguing commonality in the examples quoted above is the element of unexpectedness as my participants become conscious of the amount of time elapsing. Their surprise is realized via multiple interrobangs (??!!!), multiple exclamation marks (!!!!), multiple question marks (???), interjections (*wow*), capitalization (SEVEN, DOES NOT) and pragmatic markers that signal remarkable piece of information (*re*) and exclamative structures (*How much have I danced*). Recognizing the passage of time and framing particular life stages, such as the initiation of a friendship (Example 5.24) or rejoicing in adolescence (Example 5.25), in the present are tasks performed in unison after having been informed and triggered by particular musical tracks.

Recalling the past

It has been argued that reminiscence talk can renew senses of identity and belonging that individuals have jointly experienced in the past (Buchanan and Middleton 1995). This issue is addressed in the following four posts by Alkis and Carla.

5.26

Alkis
4 April 2012 at 23:53

Δύο πολύ ξεχωριστές φωνές σε ένα πολύ όμορφο τραγούδι ...
'Two very special voices in a very beautiful song...'
[He embeds from YouTube the song *Sous Le Vent* (Downwind) by the Canadian singers Garou and Céline Dion.]

Alkis: Από μια <u>περίοδο</u> με πολύ όμορφες <u>αναμνήσεις</u>...
'From a <u>period</u> with very beautiful <u>memories</u>...'
[he tags names of 5 friends]
4 April 2012 at 23:55

5.27

Carla
13 January 2011 at 01:16
έτσι μπράβο, ρίξε βροχούλα να μπαίνουμε σε κερκυραϊκό mood σιγά σιγά ...
'that's it well done, pour rain so as we can slowly get into a Corfu mood ...'
4 people like this
[another 3 comments]

FBU1 [male]: ..πωπω <u>τι μου θύμισες</u> τώρα. Λιακάδα στην Κέρκυρα μετά από
10 μέρες βροχής. Bliss.
'..gee <u>what you reminded me of</u> now. Sunshine in Corfu after 10 days of
rain. Bliss.'
19 January 2011 at 11:42

5.28

Alkis
18 December 2011 at 11:36

Τώρα, ΓΙΑΤΙ μου ήρθε αυτό το κομμάτι όταν είδα τον καιρό που έχει έξω ... Τι να πω ...
Πλάκα είχε αυτό το <u>flashback</u> πάντως!!
'Now, WHY did I remember this song when I saw the weather outside...
What can I say... This <u>flashback</u> was fun anyway!!'
[He embeds from YouTube the song *Blue Da Ba Dee* by the Italian dance
group Eiffel 65.]
5 people like this

Alkis: Χορό που <u>είχαμε ρίξει τότε</u> ...
(<u>εποχή πανεπιστημίου</u> για όσους – κάνουν πως – <u>δεν θυμούνται</u>!)
'How much <u>we had danced then</u> ...
(<u>university era</u> for those who – pretend that they – <u>don't remember</u>!)'
18 December 2011 at 11:37 · Like · 3

5.29

Alkis
2 April 2012 at 20:41

Ένα κομμάτι που <u>είχα ξεχάσει</u> πόσο μου αρέσει!
Thanx [όνομα φίλης]!

'A track that I had forgotten how much I like!
Thanx [name of friend]!'
[He embeds from YouTube the song *Golden Brown* by the English punk rock group The Stranglers.]
8 people like this

The participants do not use the word *past* (*παρελθόν* or *παλιά* in Greek) to refer to the past. In its place, we encounter the items *period* (Example 5.26), *then* (Example 5.28) and *university era* (Example 5.28). Buchanan and Middleton (1995: 480) reason that such kind of terms 'constitute discontinuities between past and present, in ways that the term "the past" does not'. Appeals to memory are expressed by means of phrases like *very beautiful memories* (Example 5.26) and *this flashback was fun* (Example 5.28) as well as cognitive verbs of reminiscence: *what you reminded me of now* (Example 5.27), *those who don't remember* (Example 5.28) and *I had forgotten* (Example 5.29). Collective pasts are mobilized by Facebook's facility of tagging particular names of contacts (Example 5.26) and the inclusive pronoun *we* (*we had danced*) (Example 5.28).

A few points deserve our attention at this juncture. First, as exemplified in 5.26, common past does not have to be precisely specified in terms of dates (cf. Examples 5.22–5.25) or phases (e.g. student years as in Example 28). We do not know exactly to which period Alkis is referring, yet his five tagged 'in the know' recipients have got his message retrieving the respective memories. This evocation of and summoning to past experiences could be conceptualized here as a resource for constructing a collective identity in the present. Second, in Example 5.27, it is Carla who rekindles the memory to her friend, albeit her initial status update was not past-oriented (see also Example 5.17). This kind of individual memory arousal is a recurrent phenomenon in Facebook, at least among Greek users, cued with the discourse marker *τι μου θύμισες τώρα* (*what you reminded me of now*).

In Example 5.27 above, we observe that memory is bound to a specific place, Corfu. Boden and Bielby (1986: 77) have powerfully argued that 'places are full of memory' and their invocation in discourse 'can achieve immediate interactional currency through related memories of public people or events' (see also Chapter 4, Example 4.5 with Papiris tavern). Example 5.30 is a paragon of how time and place can be mutually 'constructed, contested, negotiated and/or re-set' (Georgakopoulou 2003: 420) in the course of providing comments.

5.30

Alkis: If no one reads my wall, this should be a short experiment. If you read this, leave one word on how we met. Only one word, then copy this

to your wall so I can leave a word for you. Please don't add your word and then not bother to copy...you'll spoil the fun.
13 January 2013 at 00:24 · Like · 7

1. FBU1 [female]: ένα ονομα μία ιστορία: ΟΠΕ! :p
'one name a whole history: HEPO! :p'
13 January 2013 at 00:29 · Like · 2

2. FBU2 [female]: Pappas!!
13 January 2013 at 00:30 · Like · 1

3. FBU3 [female]: χαχαχα... Η κα FBU1 έχει δικιο... ΟΠΕ και πάσης Ελλάδος ;)
'hahaha... Ms FBU1 is right... HEPO and all Greece ;)'
13 January 2013 at 00:30 · Like · 2

4. FBU4 [female]: ΑΣΟΕΕ!
'AUEB!'
13 January 2013 at 00:30 · Like · 1

5. Alkis: Όμορφες εποχές! :)
'Beautiful times! :)'
13 January 2013 at 00:30 · Like · 3

6. Alkis: ΚΑΙ ο ΟΠΕ ΚΑΙ η ΑΣΟΕΕ!! :D
'BOTH HEPO AND AUEB!! :D'
13 January 2013 at 00:31 · Like · 4

7. FBU5 [male]: cosmopolitan!!! :p
13 January 2013 at 00:31 · Like · 2

8. Alkis: ;)
13 January 2013 at 00:31

9. Alkis: *Cosmo the Gym, not the cocktail ...
13 January 2013 at 00:32 · Like · 2

10. FBU2: polu omorfes omws!!!ante pote 8a ta poyme??? ...
'very beautiful indeed!!!come on when shall we meet??? ...'
13 January 2013 at 00:33 · Like · 1

11. Alkis: Σταμάτα να τρολάρεις στον τοίχο μου – εδώ είναι τοίχος αναμνήσεων, όχι agenda :D :-*
'Stop trolling on my wall – this is a wall of memories, not an agenda :D :-*'
13 January 2013 at 00:34
[another 4 comments with puns on a Greek song]

12. FBU6 [female]: Αμαρυλλιδα
'Amaryllis'
13 January 2013 at 00:42 · Like · 1

13. Alkis: ΕΔΩ παει και το γνωστό άσμα, "θέλω να γυρίσω στα παλιά, εδώ και τώρα"!!!!!!!!!!!!
'THERE goes the well-known song "I want to go back to the old times, right now"!!!!!!!!!!!!'
13 January 2013 at 00:43 · Like · 1

14. FBU6: Εντελως ομως …
'Absolutely…'
13 January 2013 at 00:43

15. Alkis: :-D
13 January 2013 at 00:44 · Like · 1

16. FBU7 [female]: MSM#ΟΠΑ#
'MSM#AUEB#'
13 January 2013 at 00:49 · Like · 1

17. FBU8 [female]: αλκη εχεις αποτρελαθει!!
'alkis you have gone totally mad!!'
13 January 2013 at 08:09 · Like · 1

18. FBU9 [female]: Ελαφακιαααα!!!!!!!!!
'Little deeeer!!!!!!!!!'
13 January 2013 at 10:12 · Like · 1

19. FBU10 [male]: ΟΠΕ
'HEPO'
13 January 2013 at 10:33 · Like · 1

20. Alkis: FBU8 είναι η έλλειψή σου που με απο-τρέλλανε! :-P
'FBU8 it's your absence that has driven me totally mad! :-P'
13 January 2013 at 12:09

21. FBU11 [male]: Kreontas-show
13 January 2013 at 13:29 · Like · 2

22. Alkis: Χμμμ…
Με τέτοιες απαντήσεις, μια η Αμαρυλλίδα, μια τα ελάφια, μια ο Κρέοντας, θα αρχίσει να πλέκεται ένα πέπλο μυστηρίου γύρω από το όνομά μου! Χαχα
'Hmmm…

With such answers, Amaryllis on the one hand, deer, on the other, Kreontas, a veil of mystery will start being folded around my name! Haha'
13 January 2013 at 13:33 · Like · 1

23. FBU12 [female]: ΟΠΕ ΟΛΕ!!!
'HEPO OLÉ!!!'
13 January 2013 at 22:07 · Like · 1

24. FBU13 [female]: Αεροδρόμιο :)
'Airport :)'
13 January 2013 at 22:35 · Like · 1

25. Alkis::-* +:-*, για τις δυο από πάνω φίλες μου!;)
':-* +:-*, for my two friends above!;)'
13 January 2013 at 22:35 · Like · 1
[another 4 comments with puns on a Greek song]

26. FBU14 [female]: Πανεπιστήμιο (αλλά πώς;).
'University (but how?).'
14 January 2013 at 01:00 · Like · 1

27. Alkis: Δεν θυμάσαι ή μου κάνεις κουίζ;:)
'Don't you remember or are you quizzing me?:)'
14 January 2013 at 01:01

28. FBU14: Δεν θυμάμαι. :) Εσύ θυμάσαι;
'I don't remember. :) Do you remember?'
14 January 2013 at 01:24

29. Alkis: Σίγουρα στο Μέγαρο! :)
'Surely at Megaron! :)'
14 January 2013 at 01:24

30. FBU14: Είναι μετρημένες στα δάκτυλα (του ενός χεριού) οι φορές που θυμάμαι πώς γνώρισα τους φίλους μου. Εδώ σε θέλω, τώρα... Στο Μέγαρο ή στον Αρίωνα;
'In very rare occasions do I remember how I met my friends. Beat that, now... Megaron or Arion?'
14 January 2013 at 01:25

31. Alkis: Τώρα κόλλησα! Χαχα
'I'm stuck now! Haha'
14 January 2013 at 01:26

32. FBU14: Και ενώ δεν θυμάμαι πώς γνωριστήκαμε, θυμάμαι ότι το δωμάτιό σου στον Αρίωνα ήταν στον τρίτο όροφο και, κατά πάσα πιθανότητα, ήταν το 322. 'And although I don't remember how we met, I remember that your room in Arion was on the third floor and, in all likelihood, it was number 322.' 14 January 2013 at 01:27

33. Alkis: Κι εγώ έτσι νομίζω!! Χαχαχα 'I think so!! Hahaha' 14 January 2013 at 01:30 · Like · 1

[Another three comments between Alkis and FBU14 on whether the room was 321 or 322.]

Alkis posts a chain message, that is, a message which is passed from user to user through social media with a view to being noticed, liked, commented on and shared anew. Although these messages are prepackaged, extensively copied and pasted and, sometimes, considered annoying by Facebook audiences (Livingstone 2008), here Alkis and his friends reformulate this kind of status update in a number of ways. On the one hand, with the exception of proper names, all of the participants provide their comments in Greek even though Alkis's status update is written in English. On the other hand, most of them answer where they met Alkis not how, as also pointed out by FBU14 in comment 26 (*but how?*). What is more, contrary to what the initial status asks, they use more than one word while Alkis constantly intervenes in the interaction. By stretching the possibilities of chain messaging affordances to their own ends, the participants make meaning and shape their identities probably in ways the first creator of the message had not even thought of.

Within the thread, three types of collective past identities are simultaneously recalled and activated, principally through proper names of social places (van Dijk 2009): professional, educational and recreational. Starting with professional pasts, four friends (comments 1, 3, 19 and 23) refer to *HEPO*, the Hellenic Foreign Trade Board, where they used to work with Alkis. With regard to educational pasts, Alkis's former MSM (MSc in Services Management) fellow students mention *AUEB* (Athens University of Economics and Business) (comments 4 and 16). FBU14, on the other hand, in comment 26, appeals to their common undergraduate studies elucidated by Alkis via mentioning Megaro Kapodistria and Arion. Megaro Kapodistria (Kapodistrias Mansion) is a historical building in Corfu where courses of the Department of Foreign Languages, Translation and Interpreting of the Ionian University were taught whereas *Arion* is the name of students' residencies. Recreational pasts include meetings at the gym (*Cosmopolitan* in comment 7), live music venues (*Amaryllis* in comment 12 and *Kreontas-show* in comment 21) and the airport (comment 24). The references to *Pappas* (comment 2) and *little deer* (comment 18) remain opaque as they can be unpacked only by friends who share the same background.

Such articulations of place and time in Facebook interactions corroborate 'the salience of identities of friendship, familiarity and sharedness' (Georgakopoulou 2003: 425). Here we witness that the participants embrace Facebook and the affordance of commenting to display and enhance their connectedness and closeness. The collaborative construction of *a wall of memories*, as Alkis very successfully puts it in comment 11, titling the concluding section of the chapter further down, is achieved by

- **requests for ratification:** *but how?* (comment 26), *Don't you remember* (comment 27), *Do you remember?* (comment 28);

- **ratification:** *Ms FBU1 is right* (comment 3), *;)* (comment 8), *very beautiful indeed!!!* (comment 10), *Absolutely* (comment 14), *:-* + :-*, for my two friends above!* (comment 25), *surely at Megaron! :)* (comment 29), *I think so!!* (comment 33);

- **elaboration:** *I remember that your room in Arion was on the third floor and, in all likelihood, it was number 322* (comment 32);

- **allusion:** *the well-known song 'I want to go back to the old times, right now'!!!!!!!!!!!!* (comment 13);[16]

- **pun:** *HEPO and all Greece* (comment 3). The user here plays with the title given to Greek Orthodox archbishops, that is, archbishop of Athens and All Greece, to underline the significance of HEPO;

- **positive evaluation:** *a whole history* (comment 1), *Beautiful times!* (comment 5), *OLÉ* (comment 23).

Throughout the thread, different users give rise to different memories, thus providing different angles to Alkis's biography on the basis of what they have shared with him. To that end, different processes are at play:

- **reinterpretation of the present because of the past:** *alkis you have gone totally mad!!* (comment 17), *With such answers ... a veil of mystery will start being folded around my name!* (comment 22);

- **nostalgia**: *very beautiful indeed!!! come on when shall we meet???* (comment 10);

- **selective recall**: *Little deeeer!!!!!!!!!* (comment 18);

- **filling gaps**: *And although I don't remember how we met, I remember that ...* (comment 32).

This rich extract showcases two vital issues. First, it attests to the enhanced **reflexivity** that characterizes social media (Stæhr 2015b), given that it is unusual to ask a question like '*Where did we meet?*' in such a large group face-to-face interaction. Second, it dismisses the tendency of Facebook 'to concertina time into a relentless fixation with the present' (Miller 2011: 191). Previous scholarship (Page 2010; Georgakopoulou 2013c) has explored how 'recency is prized over retrospection' (Page 2010: 440) in Facebook posts, for example, via announcing and sharing breaking news. The analysis of the previous exchange has gone some way towards showing the vitality of reminiscing in social media identity construction (see also Georgalou 2015). Revitalizing the past in the now together with people from earlier parts of one's life, even through fragmented, one-worded comments (e.g. AUEB), turns out to be a valuable resource for situating and re-seeing the self in both personal and collective history as well as for cultivating and enforcing relationships.

Recognizing change

Change constitutes a common fact of human ageing (Nikander 2009). Facebook participants primarily talk about change while browsing, sharing and commenting upon resources, such as photos, that belong to their pasts, as is the case in Example 5.31.

5.31

1. FBU1 [female]: pou?
'where?'
23 June 2012 at 23:51

2. Gabriel: Ισπανία,Γρανάδα
'Spain, Granada'
23 June 2012 at 23:52 · Like · 3
[another two comments]

3. FBU2 [female]: Καλά ήταν να πας Alhambra και δε μου το είπες;; Είχα τόσα μέρη (bar με tapas) για την ακρίβεια στη Γρανάδα να σου προτείνω ...
'OK you were about to go to Alhambra and didn't tell me?? I had so many places (tapas bars) in Granada precisely to recommend to you ...'
24 June 2012 at 01:01

4. FBU3 [female]: em bebaia και σε εμενα δν ηρθες ... οκ θα τα πουμε
'well you didn't visit me either ... ok I'll tell you a thing or two'
24 June 2012 at 01:04

5. Gabriel: είχα πάει δευτέρα λυκείου! <u>Μα καλά δεν έχω αλλάξει καθόλου!!</u>
'I had been [there] in the second grade of Lyceum! <u>Oh well I haven't
changed at all!!!!</u>'
24 June 2012 at 02:00 · Like · 2

6. Gabriel:?
24 June 2012 at 02:00

7. FBU4 [female]: Katholou omws..
'Not at all..'
24 June 2012 at 02:01

8. Gabriel: καλό είναι αυτό??
'is this good??'
24 June 2012 at 02:03

9. FBU4: Opws to parei kaneis.Esy pes nai..!
'It depends. You should say yes..!'
24 June 2012 at 02:04

10. Gabriel: ναι
'yes'
24 June 2012 at 02:06 · Like · 1

This thread is unfolded underneath a Gabriel's profile picture shot in Alhambra
palace and fortress in Granada, Spain. Both FBU2 and FBU3 think that the
time of the post coincides with the time of Gabriel's trip. Gabriel clears up
their misunderstanding by specifying that he had been to Granada as a second
grade Lyceum student, namely when he was approximately 17 years old. His
astonishment in *Oh well I have not changed at all!* (comment 5) and the follow-up
question mark (comment 6) suggest that he himself recognizes change in his
external appearance and therefore it should have been obvious to his friends. To
FBU4's answer *Not at all* (comment 7), Gabriel seems dubious about whether this
is an asset. There are reasonable grounds for his self-denigration (*is this good??*
in comment 8) though. He was 22 years old at the time the above interaction
took place. This is a landmark age for youth adults as they have to take strategic
decisions for their future, for example, continue with postgraduate studies or pick
a career. Looking younger than 22 detracts from one's maturity and decisiveness
that go hand in hand when future plans are concerned.

Facebook as a record of changes

As was argued in Chapter 2, identity is not something fixed but in constant
flux, so change is quintessential in the process of becoming. Change does not

only occur in bodily but also in psychological and mental terms. It may involve change in habits, tastes and preferences (e.g. in clothing, music, food), the people we associate with, even the way we use Facebook. Wilson et al. (2012: 208) draw parallels between studying Facebook and studying culture over time:

> As with any culture (e.g., the culture of a neighborhood), an expectation that Facebook should consist of static demographic patterns and unchanging social processes neglects the element of change that is a core feature of the OSN [online social networks]. Culture shifts with time. Populations grow, laws are amended, and people's perceptions living in a culture change. Such change is also inherent in Facebook use [.]

While interviewing Helen, she aptly remarked that *Facebook is a record of changes as well* (*einai kai record ton allagon* in the original). To what extent are Facebook users cognizant of changes in the stories they present and what they do? Alkis has confessed that from time to time he deletes posts from his Wall because

> *some things may not express me anymore (rare reason but it has happened)*

Whenever he acknowledges undesirable change in beliefs or tastes, he opts for the practice of deletion (see also Chapter 8) as he disagrees with an old part of himself. But this is an isolated incident. My general feeling is that my informants do not fully realize change when they upload their stories on Facebook. This is what Alkis emailed me when I sent him an earlier draft of Chapter 6:

> *It's very interesting what 'written story' we create with Facebook and we have no idea, after some time, for what we have written where, when etc.!!!! You reminded me of my dissertation adventure too ...!!*

For an online ethnographer, who constantly goes back and forth to her subjects' profiles to reread, reflect upon and reinterpret their posts that expand over a considerable time span, change is more easily pinpointed. As a reader I could perceive an overall narrative that might not have been that clear to them. The Timeline structure proved to be of unaccountable assistance in my cycling back to their profiles. The argument, therefore, that I wish to put forth is that changes in one's life, both on an individual and a collective level, are highly likely to affect Facebook use. In particular, I observed changes in my participants':

- **language of posting**. For example, when Gabriel moved to the USA for his MA, and started living and studying in a multicultural environment, his posts in English were increased.

- **frequency of posting**. Romanos's posts and commenting activity were dramatically reduced when he joined the army.

- **content of posting**. All of my five participants, having been experiencing the socioeconomic and political change taking place in Greece because of the crisis, have superseded, to a greater or lesser degree, amusing statuses and sentimental songs with more crisis-oriented posts, articles and videos (indicative examples can be found in Chapters 4 and 7) in comparison to what they shared at the time they were first recruited.

Building a wall of memories

This chapter embarked on investigating how my participants construct time as well as how they construct themselves and others in time. The analysis revealed interesting aspects on how they time their past, present and future social activities; think and talk about time and age; and enact time in discourse. The findings suggest that Facebook can serve as an interactive, co-authored digital memory bank, as an online self-continuum in which these users could temporally position themselves taking up certain orientations to time that have particular meanings to them. Returning to Evans's (2005) senses of time, as outlined in the beginning of the chapter, my informants principally constructed time as duration (e.g. maintaining same preferences, forgetting things, planning a presentation, wishing for the future), moment (e.g. cooking, reminiscing about being fellow students), instance (e.g. meeting Psarantonis), event (e.g. birthdays, holidays, concerts), agentive (e.g. recognizing change and ageing) and measurement system (e.g. using numerical markers of time). Being involved in activities such as browsing and uploading older photographs or other visual imagery, sharing songs, copying lyrics, wishing, exchanging comments, liking and tagging, my participants

- appeal to shared experiences;
- recollect memories and indulge in nostalgia;
- recall past tastes and habits;
- generate collective past and future identities;
- evoke certain periods of life (e.g. puberty, student life) through a gamut of intertextual references;
- mark milestones;
- evaluate and express humorous or ironic attitudes towards present, past and future events.

With respect to the enactment of time in discourse and its relation to identity, I would like to zoom in on the prominent role of narratives and music. Although the small stories genre was discussed in Carla's encounter with Psarantonis (Example 5.2), more narratives of that kind are traced all through the chapter including

- Romanos's recounting of how he was going to spend New Year's Eve (Example 5.7);

- Alkis and his fellow student's hypothetical scenario of their upcoming presentation (Example 5.8);

- Alkis and his friends' recalling of how they first met each other (Example 5.30);

Such miniaturized life stories allow us to explore the modes in which temporality is reworked within the context of Facebook (Page 2010; Georgakopoulou 2014) often divorcing it from its orientation to the present. Moreover, they shed light upon different narrative styles and dimensions (Ochs and Capps 2001; Page 2012). Storytelling is not strictly restricted to linear, detailed textual descriptions, as was the case with Psarantonis and Alkis's presentation plan. It can alternatively acquire a bullet-like form (Example 5.7) or even be encapsulated in just one word such as *AUEB* (Example 5.30). **Tellership** can be single (stories told by my informants), and can also be multiple as members of the audience actively engage in and contribute to the storytelling via commenting. Lastly, structuring and playing with these small narratives is tantamount to playing with identity. The analysis suggests that the users are part of a story but also agents with a story, who are not just focusing on experiencing a narrative – they are equally eager to sense, explain, explore and modify who they are (Friedlander 2008: 187).

Turning to music, in addition to indicating individual dispositions, and facilitating in attaining and maintaining certain states of feeling (see also Chapter 7), it can be used for retrieving memories and therefore 'remembering/ constructing who one is' (DeNora 2000: 63). Sometimes, the users opt for the ad hoc posting of music that brings to their memory particular events and incidents like the summer or a students' party, constructing in this manner either an individualized or a collective time and age identity. At other times, they may post music just for the sake of it. Yet, this can function as a fuel to recycle memories, and awaken past tastes and habits among members of their audience, conducing to an unintentional, on my informants' part, crafting of other-time and age identity or even a 'we'-time and age identity (e.g. Example 5.17 with the *Moonlighting* theme song). In this fashion, Facebook, owing to its facility of music video sharing becomes a befitting platform to remember and remind, more than other social media technologies, mainly on account of its members' pre-existing ties.

A notable aspect that the data brought to the fore was the interactional and collaborative character of time and age identities, concurring in this way with previous research in different settings, including everyday conversations, TV interviews and reality shows (e.g. Antaki and Widdicombe 1998; Nikander 2002; Poulios 2011). On Facebook, time and age identities are projected, credited, challenged, endorsed, negotiated and collaboratively constructed in front of a viewing audience consisting of friends and acquaintances from different slices of one's life, different shared pasts and presents, and different kinds of shared knowledge. Through the use of temporality the poster and their audience can display and enhance their mutual ties. Facebook interaction is, hence, not just about staying connected here and now via the medium. It is about staying connected via indications of shared experiences, feelings, activities, ideas, values, things, events and situations that were there in the past, but are also given prominence now through Facebook. The types of time and age reference reported in this chapter had a central, reuniting, function: they invited participation which in turn enhanced sociality and solidified relationships among friends that have known each other from the past and perhaps 'meet' more regularly now on Facebook rather than offline.

This chapter presented a multifaceted take on time, temporality and identity on Facebook. Among other things, the analysis addressed the ways in which shared professional and educational pasts and futures can be co-constructed in Facebook threads. The next chapter will delve deeper into professional and educational identity matters.

Time and age identity: Why and how

The theme of time and identity rose to the surface after various and careful readings and comparisons of the data, as it was not that transparent from the beginning. My examples in this chapter were coded in terms of

- verbs that refer to change and ageing (e.g. *change, get old*)
- reminiscence verbs (e.g. *remember, remind*)
- age-related adjectives (e.g. *young, old, mature, same*)
- temporal references by means of nouns (e.g. *time, years*)
- temporal adverbials (e.g. *since the old times, always*)

- temporal framings (e.g. *3 years ago*)

- personal/possessive pronouns indicating generational cohorts (e.g. *our youth*)

- references to past periods (e.g. *2nd grade of Lyceum*)

- future tenses

- anecdotes and narratives

- references to resources from shared cultural repertoires (e.g. songs, singers)

- birthday wishes/New Year wishes

ACTIVITY 5.1: ELDERLY IDENTITY ON FACEBOOK

Many studies have concentrated on the ways in which teens and undergraduate students construct their identities on Facebook and other social media (exemplary discussions can be found in boyd 2014). This chapter investigated enactments of subjects' age identity from 22 to 37 years old. Yet, what is the case of 'silver surfers', namely internet users who are more than 60 years old? How have they adopted Facebook? What aspects of their identity are observed in their Timelines? You could support your answers with interviews with elderly Facebook users you already know.

Useful resources

Print

For more insightful discussions of time within the realms of philosophy and sociology, see O'Rourke et al. (2009) and Adam (2004), respectively. On questions of time, narration and discourse, Chafe (1994) holds an in-depth discussion. For an all-embracing introduction to small stories research, see Georgakopoulou (2015b). An interesting analysis on the multiple discourses of age (as chronological, physical, experiential, and symbolic), can be found in Aapola (2002). Georgakopoulou and Charalambidou (2011) provide a meticulous overview of young-age and old-age identities in language studies.

For succinct information on synchronicity and asynchronicity in social media and CMC, see Page et al. (2014: 18–22). A valuable source on how new and existing narrative genres are being (re)shaped in different social media contexts is Page (2012). If you are especially interested in birthday greetings on Facebook, I recommend Stæhr (2015b) and Theodoropoulou (2015).

Regarding age identity in various types of digital communication, Lin et al. (2004) have studied online discussion forums for elderly people and showed that age identity can be bound up in negative themes such as physical decline, loss and resistance to ageing, as well as in positive ones like mind-over-body attitude, active engagement, wisdom and maturity, and the freedom of age. Adopting a corpus-assisted discourse analysis approach, Tommaso (2015) investigates how the participants in *Boomer Women Speak* discussion forums present and negotiate age identities seeing retirement as an opportunity to start a new phase in life. Nishimura (2017) explores how Japanese elderly bloggers skilfully construct their identities using role language (i.e. lexical and orthographical choices associated with particular character types) to create personae that they expect their audiences to recognize and to deal with age and ageing in a positive light. For other social media outlets, such as MySpace and Facebook, there has been an abundance of studies (e.g. Livingstone 2008; Androutsopoulos 2014; boyd 2014; Larsen 2016) on the sophisticated (and often playful) ways in which teens and young adults create and manage separate, narrow contexts tailoring their self-presentations in accordance with these contexts.

As key constituents of identity, place and time are often studied in parallel. Based on the Bakhtinian notion of 'chronotope' (the representation of time and space in language and discourse), Blommaert and De Fina (2016) discuss how identity work is organized in specific time-space configurations. The special issue edited by Georgakopoulou (2015a) wonderfully brings together emerging discourse and sociolinguistic perspectives on marking or evoking time and place in digital media including Facebook, YouTube, online review sites, diasporic online communities, Second Life and mobile applications.

Web

International Media and Nostalgia Network
https://medianostalgia.wordpress.com

6

Professional and educational identity on Facebook

Chapter overview

Professional and educational identity

For most people, work amounts to a pervasive life domain and a fundamental source of meaning which gives them focus and allows them to form, transform and modify how they define themselves and others within the framework of work-based situations and activities (Gini 1998; Dutton et al. 2010). The objective of this chapter is to identify and describe the ways in which Facebook functions as a significant basis and a conduit for displaying and constructing professional as well as educational identities. The decision to centre simultaneously on these two substantial interactional social identities was fuelled by three reasons.

First and foremost, both professional and educational identities are cemented around specific areas of knowledge – they hinge upon showing and acquiring learning and expertise. In public, especially, constructions of these two types of identities, as those occurring on Facebook, at least three interacting dimensions are at play: the individual, the domain (or domains) of knowledge and the audience (cf. Jacoby and Gonzales 1991).

Both professional and educational identity are institutional identities and as such, in consonance with Eckert and Wenger (1994), I see them not as mere labels or titles, but as constructed in the everyday practice of learning to function within the professional and/or educational institution as well as within local communities of practice characterized by mutual engagement; joint enterprise; and shared interpretative frameworks, practices and repertoires among colleagues and/or fellow students.

Lastly, the idea of this parallel examination stemmed from my own collected data. Initially, I was thinking of providing two separate chapters, but while coding the material that pertained to occupation and education, I discerned several common themes and discourse strategies that seemed to be worth synchronized comparing and contrasting. Henceforth, within this chapter, the word 'work' is understood as embracing both paid jobs and activities that involve – primarily – mental effort.

With this in mind, the questions that confront me are: What kinds of acts of identity do Facebook participants perform as professionals and/or as students? What are the meanings and functions of these acts? How are public professional and educational identities co-constructed and negotiated via a combination of relational content and social ties (cf. Gilpin 2010)? To answer these, we first need to define professional and educational identities.

Professional identity refers to the constellation of activities, tasks, roles, groups, memberships, interactions, motives, goals, orientations, attributes, beliefs, values and experiences in terms of which individuals define themselves in a professional role (Schein 1978; Drew and Heritage 1992; Dutton et al. 2010). As Achugar (2009: 65) argues, 'Becoming a professional means positioning oneself in relation to others by differentiating, affiliating, challenging, or accepting certain ways of constructing knowledge, being, and doing in the world.' It follows from this that the quintessence of professional identity lies in exhibiting a command of specific information and knowledge as well as in performing accordingly in specific work settings, conveying qualities such as judgement, acumen, competence, creativity and trustworthiness (Ibarra 1999). Professional identity is thus formed gradually on the basis of varied experiences and constructive feedback that enable people to gain insight about their potential, preferences, talents and values (Schein 1978).

Educational identity now is a social structure located within the student, as well as a social perception of what being a student implies, and is founded on the meanings shaped in the context of education (Moore 2006). Eckert and Wenger (1994) stress that educational identity 'is not part of the curriculum, and it need not be: it takes place as an apprenticeship in practice, whether the school wants it or not. It is part and parcel of the institutional package. It comes with the diploma, and without it'. Moreover, it should not be viewed as a provisionally assigned identity that expires after finishing one's studies but should be viewed as a process that can dynamically transcend time.

Given the demographics of my interviewees, the centre of my attention is exclusively on further and tertiary education. Heavily influenced by Goffman (1956), Kaufman and Feldman (2004) have found that educational identity in college revolves around three indispensable domains: intelligence and knowledgeability, occupation and career, and cosmopolitanism. To explicate each one in turn, students that attend university have a certain degree of intellectual competence and knowledge manifested through critical thinking and talking 'smart'.[1] The second domain, occupation and career, deals with how students view peer interactions and social networking in relation to their self-perceived future professional identities as well as how their participation in distinctive activities (e.g. listening to distinguished speakers, serving on committees, securing internships, participating in academic conferences) can help them shape these identities. The third domain of cosmopolitanism refers to acquiring more sophisticated cultural tastes and interests, engaging in new leisure activities and hobbies, and being exposed to cultural diversity (see Gabriel's case in Chapter 4).

Collision of personal and professional identities on Facebook

It is by now a truism that new technologies have reconfigured the relationship between the personal and the professional. As Miller (2011: 195) has pointed out:

> There seems to be no way to stop most people carrying on with their personal lives while in the workplace. The Trojan horse that led to the collapse of this wall from the inside is the personal computer. The computer has become vital to almost any and every kind of work but it remains a technology that is very difficult to keep focused entirely on the job in hand. ... Facebook doesn't just intrude into work; it swarms all over it.

The blurring of personal and professional domains is not unproblematic for Facebook participants as it can lead to **context collapse** (see also Chapter 8), namely the flattening of multiple diverse audiences into a single group under the generic name 'Friends', with possibly serious repercussions for their privacy and concurrently their career.

Ollier-Malaterre et al. (2013) have identified four sets of behaviours in which users engage to manage the boundaries between their personal and professional identities in SNS which are personal in nature, such as Facebook and Twitter: 1) open, 2) audience, 3) content and 4) hybrid behaviours. According to their framework, when users adopt open behaviours, they do not establish any boundaries to separate their professional and personal identities. Others, however, may opt for abiding by audience behaviours, maintaining a clear-cut boundary between their professional and personal contacts by setting up private profiles and ignoring or denying friend requests from certain professional contacts. For example, Carla has conceded that

> I avoid friending people if I don't want them to know e.g. whenever I am online (e.g. my employer).

Users characterized by content behaviours actively control the kind of information they share by opting for content they consider that it is interesting, appealing or helpful to their professional contacts or that it is indicative of their expertise. Regarding my informants' behaviour, Helen, Gabriel, Alkis and Romanos fall into this category. The simultaneous management of audience and content boundaries constitutes hybrid behaviour, with users, like Carla, splitting their professional and personal contacts into separate audiences and tailoring the content for each audience (see Chapter 8).

Profession and education
in profile information

The social identities of occupation and education are given prominence by Facebook's architecture as users are setting up their profiles. A substantial, though optional, part of completing the 'About' section in one's profile pertains to work (current and previous employers) and education (university, college, secondary school).

Table 6.1 displays what my informants[2] have filled in the 'Work and Education' entries in 'About', whereas Table 6.2 provides some samples of pages they have liked on Facebook that are pertinent to these two vital domains.

Enlightening as these pieces of information may be, professional and educational identities on Facebook cannot be compacted in mere lists and

TABLE 6.1 'About' – 'Work and Education' information

Informants	Work	Education
Carla (professional)	–	Ionian University, Department of Foreign Languages, Translation and Interpreting
Carla (personal)	–	–
Alkis	–	–
Romanos	Technical Support	• Akmi private institute of education • 3rd High School of N. Smirni
Gabriel	–	• Johns Hopkins SAIS [tertiary education] • Unipi [tertiary education] • PSPA [secondary education]
Helen	• Academic English lecturer • EAP Tutor • The Open University Researcher	Lancaster University MA, PhD Linguistics

TABLE 6.2 Samples of Work and Education 'Like' pages

School/University	*Carla* [professional profile]
	• meta|φραση School of Translation Studies
	• Ionian University Library and Information Center
	• Translation scholars
	Alkis
	• meta|φραση School of Translation Studies
	• Athens University of Econ and Bus
	• Master in Services Management (part time)/ASOEE
	• Translation scholars
	Gabriel
	• Bologna Institute for Policy Research
	• John Stuart Mill Research Group – Ερευνητικός Όμιλος 'John Stuart Mill'
	• Student Association for International Affairs, European Parliament Simulation (Euro.Pa.S) at University of Pireaus
	Helen
	• Linguistics and English Language, Lancaster University
	• Lancaster University
	• The Open University
	• Academic Earth
	• PhD (Piled Higher and Deeper) Comic strips
Professional tools	TheFreeDictionary (Alkis), SPSS (Alkis), LingEducator | linguistic resources for those who teach (Helen)
Professional websites	Lexilogia (Alkis), Bewords (Alkis), Translatum – Greek Translation Vortal (Alkis)
Professional services	Interpreting for Europe (Alkis), Corfu Translation Centre (Carla, professional profile), onlinetranslators.gr (Carla, professional profile)

Media	Babel: The Language Magazine (Helen), Foreign Policy Magazine (Gabriel), International Journal of Young Leadership (Gabriel)
Experts	Terry Eagleton (Helen), John Searle (Helen)
Recruitment	EU Careers (Alkis), TheLAMP.gr (Learning About My Potentials) (Romanos)

frozen CV versions, but are in effect unravelled in individual posts and/or in subsequent comments. This will be the focus of the sections that follow.

Being involved in actions and activities

Doing work

My informants use Facebook to talk about practical, goal-oriented operations (cf. Fasulo and Zucchermaglio 2002: 1129), that is to say, tasks in which they are currently involved or are preparing for the future. To illustrate this point, I will take my examples from Helen and Alkis.

In Figure 6.1, Helen's announcement is accompanied by the Monty Python humorous sketch video *Argument Clinic* in which a man knocks on a door and says 'I came here for an argument' while another man, sitting at a desk in the room, says 'No you didn't.' 'Yes I did', the first man answers and they keep

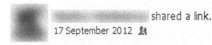

17 September 2012

teaching argumentation tomorrow:-)

Argument Clinic
www.youtube.com

Monty Python's Flying Circus http://www.amazon.com/Complete-Monty-Pythons-Flying-Circus/dp/B001E77XNA/ref=sr_1_1?ie=UTF8& s=dvd&qid=1226597796&sr=1-1

Like · Comment · Share   3

FIGURE 6.1 *Helen posts about her professional activity.*

on arguing on what constitutes an argument. In this post, therefore, we are informed in a pleasant and witty manner about Helen's professional activity, that is, her forthcoming lecture.

In Example 6.1, Alkis makes known that he has to study:

6.1

Alkis

19 December 2011 at 13:16

Μου αρέσει ο ήχος της βροχής στο παράθυρο, ωραίο και το χουχούλιασμα στο σπίτι (το ένα καλό της <u>ανεργίας</u>) αλλά να πρέπει να ανάβω τα φώτα του δωματίου <u>για να μελετήσω</u>, λες και είναι βράδυ, ε, όχι... Γι' αυτό είμαι υπέρμαχος της λιακάδας κι όχι της <u>μουντάδας</u>... Ακούς εκεί, φωταψίες πρωινιάτικο.... Πφφ....

'I like the sound of the rain on the window, it's nice to be warm under the duvet at home (one of the advantages of <u>unemployment</u>) but the fact that I must turn on the lights of the room <u>in order to study</u>, as if it was night, eh, no... that's why I'm a proponent of sunshine and not of <u>dull weather</u>... Gosh, what illumination so early in the morning.... Pff....'

3 people like this

Here are some of the comments underneath the above status:

1. Alkis: ... όταν είμαι <u>καλά</u> ή δεν έχω <u>σκοτούρες</u> (πού το θυμήθηκα αυτό, πόσα χρόνια έχει να συμβεί!) ή έστω υπάρχει κινητικότητα, άρα <u>είμαι σε γραφείο</u> <u>(δουλειά)</u> κ.λπ. δεν με νοιάζει, αλλά <u>όταν έχω (καλή ώρα) να μελετήσω όλη μέρα</u>, το να είμαι από το πρωί με τη λάμπα σαν το <u>κρυφό σχολειό</u> ΜΑΛΛΟΝ με νοιάζει και με κόφτει...!!!!

'When I'm <u>fine</u> or I don't have <u>hassles</u> (how did I remember this, it's been years since it has happened to me!) or even when there is mobility, which means that <u>I'm at an office (job)</u> etc. I don't care, but <u>when I have (like now)</u> <u>to study all day</u>, being from the morning with the lamp as if I'm in the <u>secret school</u>[3] PROBABLY makes me care deeply...!!!!'

19 December 2011 at 13:21

2. FBU1 [female]: ... dear alkis..... uparxei mia eukolh k volikh lush! MHN DIAVASEIS!!! Uparxei panta k to aurio! shmera vges na kaneis mia volta na goustareis!

'dear alkis..... there is an easy n convenient solution! DON'T STUDY!!! there is always tomorrow! today go out for a walk and enjoy!'

19 December 2011 at 13:24 · Like · 1

3. Alkis: ΑΧΑΧΑΧΑΑ!!! Μην ανησυχείς, το έκανα και με το παραπάνω, γι' αυτό διαβάζω ΑΚΟΜΑ! Χαχαχα

'ΑΗΑΗΑΗΑΑ!!! Don't worry, I have overdone it [with walks], that's why I'm STILL studying! Hahaha'

19 December 2011 at 13:25 · Like · 1

What is interesting here is that Alkis's study announcement comes up against the backdrop of different contexts: the weather (*I'm a proponent of sunshine and not of dull weather*), unemployment (*one of the advantages of unemployment*),[4] employability (*I'm at an office (job)*), moods and feelings (*When I'm fine or I don't have hassles*), Greek history (*secret school*), leisure (walks) and time management (*study all day, I have overdone it, I'm STILL studying*).

Example 6.2 contains a comment Alkis wrote when a fellow student posted on his Timeline the video 'Crazy Singing Bird – Billie Jean (Drums)', which features a cartoon bird playing drums and singing in a high-pitched voice Michael Jackson's 'Billie Jean'.

6.2

Alkis: ΑΧΑΧΑΧΧΑΑΑ!!!

Έτσι αισθάνομαι τώρα! ΠΤΥΧΙΑΚΗ ΤΕΛΟΟΟΣΣΣ!!

PDFάκι έτοιμο, πάμε για ppt αύριο και ΠΑΠΑΛΑΑΑ!!:D

'ΑΗΑΗΑΗΗΑΑΑ!!!

That's how I'm feeling now! EEEND OF DISSERTATION!!

PDF+DIM is ready, ppt tomorrow and FINISSSHED!!:D'

11 January 2012 at 01:42

Not only does Alkis proclaim the end of writing his thesis, but he also projects the immediate future event of preparing the PowerPoint slides for his defence presentation. It is notable here how the educational meets the personal and affective, and how text, paratextual features (*AHAHAHHAAA*, capitalization, multiple letters and exclamation marks, smiley), video and music convey the intertwining of these two realms.

The next day, being punctual to his Facebook audience, as soon as he finished his dissertation, Alkis entextualized *Mission Impossible* theme (Figure 6.2), from the American spy film under the same title, to liken his thesis to a mission not impossible anymore but accomplished.

Recent, current or upcoming doings may also come to the fore even when the initial aim of the post is utterly different. At some point, Alkis had uploaded a funny video followed by a lengthy discussion on why film producers spend

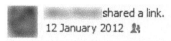

shared a link.
12 January 2012

Mission: Accomplished!!

AUEB Thesis Finale Theme !!
www.youtube.com

FIGURE 6.2 *Alkis's post after finishing his thesis.*

money on projects that are not worthwhile. These comments come after some teasing by FBU1:

6.3

1. Alkis: Θα σου έλεγα τώρα αλλά έχε χάρη που <u>έχω δουλειά!</u> χαχα

'I'd like to tell you a thing or two now but you're lucky <u>I've got work to do!</u> Haha'
7 February 2012 at 13:00

2. FBU1 [male]: ego apergo
'I'm on strike'
7 February 2012 at 13:03

3. Alkis: Εγώ, πάλι, ανεργώ!
'I'm unemployed!'
7 February 2012 at 13:12

4. FBU1: ke giati den katevikame sintagma?
'and why didn't we go to Syntagma?'
7 February 2012 at 13:31

5. Alkis: Γιατί <u>ετοιμάζω την υποστήριξη της διπλωματικής μου,</u> που είναι σε μερικές ώρες!;)
'Because <u>I'm getting ready to defend my thesis</u> in a few hours!;)'
7 February 2012 at 13:48

We learn that Alkis is rehearsing to defend his thesis because of his friend's question on why they did not go to Athens Syntagma Square on that day as a massive demonstration against austerity measures was held.

FIGURE 6.3 *Helen's marking post.*

Actions can also be stated in indirect and smart manners as it can be gleaned from Figure 6.3. The specific photo, shot by Helen herself (a couple of months prior to the post at hand), is posted at 2.00 am. The depicted Latin graffiti *carpe noctem* (seize the night), in equivalence to *carpe diem* (seize the day), together with the owl (a nocturnal bird which symbolizes learning and wisdom) suggest that night time should not go wasted by sleeping – one can work instead. Helen's comment *for all those still marking essays* creates a parallelism to the image's *for all those sleeping* underscoring her differentiation from them, encompassing perhaps any colleagues that are in the same position with her. Instead of writing a bland update of the type 'it's two in the morning and I'm still marking', Helen exploits the semiotics of the image to relay her message more forcefully.

Aside from individual posts, actions that are in progress and are expected to have certain duration can be communicated through the selection of marked profile pictures. Once Alkis became entangled in writing his thesis, he put Figure 6.4 as a profile picture, with the caption *Μέχρι τις 16/12…* (Until 16/12…), appearing to his network as an old wise man drowned in books and papers burning the midnight oil. The same motif occurs in Figure 6.5, the profile picture that he had chosen during the period he was garnering his data.

In the comments that accompanied Figure 6.4, one of Alkis's female friends (in Example 6.4) maps the depicted old man's qualities (*wiser, more mature, more settled*) onto him characterizing the process of working on his dissertation as a *story*:

FIGURE 6.4   *Alkis's profile picture from 29 September to 10 October 2011.*

FIGURE 6.5   *Alkis's profile picture from 4 to 9 November 2011.*

6.4

από <u>όλη αυτή την ιστορία</u> θα βγεις <u>πιο σοφός</u>, <u>πιο ώριμος</u>, <u>πιο κατασταλαγμένος</u> .... φαίνεται από τη φωτογραφία! θα σε αγαπάμε κι έτσι όμως!

'after <u>this whole story</u> you will become <u>wiser, more mature, more settled</u> … it is shown in the photograph! we will love you anyway!' · Like · 1

By uploading this image, Alkis apart from implying the situation he is into, typified by intense workload, deadlines, pressure, sleeplessness, he also sets in motion a collective graduate student identity as expressed by another female fellow student:

6.5

nomizw   oti   kapws   etsi   <u>eimaste   oloi</u>   ....   den   mporw varethkaaaaaa!!!!!!!!!!!!!!!!!!!!!!!!!!!!

'i think that <u>all of us</u> are somehow like this …. i can't i'm boooooooor ed!!!!!!!!!!!!!!!!!!!!!!!!!!!!!'

To sum up, references to actions can be direct, latent, supported by multimodal material or arise in the course of interaction with peers. Notably, throughout the preceding examples, there was a deluge of time expressions: *tomorrow, all day, still, end, finished, accomplished, in a few hours, until.* It is within these time bounds that an activity is invested with meaning and acquires its status as scheduled, exigent, in progress or completed, constructing at one go its doer as committed and diligent. But this is not always the case. The next section takes up references of not doing or refusing to do work.

Not doing work

A very typical response to work is that of denial, especially on Mondays or after vacations, as well as in cases of fatigue, sleepiness or boredom. A crucial factor to take into consideration is the degree to which it is acceptable for Facebook posters to discuss publicly such subtle issues in front of an audience consisting of workmates, managers, students or teachers. Most of the times, the informants appear to be aware of this fact expressing their denial in manners which soften the negation.

In Example 6.6, the denial is not stated straightforwardly in the status update but arises while exchanging comments. It is FBU2 who first admits that he is not in the mood of working, and Carla agrees with him specifying that she feels *sleepy* (*κάνει νύστα* is slangy in Greek).

6.6
Carla [personal profile]
6 August 2012 at 15:18
λουλουδομπόρα-μπόρα
'flowerbora-bora'

1. FBU1 [female]: se gamo eisai?
'are you at a wedding?'
6 August 2012 at 15:25

2. Carla: όχι στο γραφείο
'no at the office'
6 August 2012 at 15:27 · Like · 1

3. FBU2 [male]: skeftomoun pws ean prosthetes ena komma, oli i protasi
tha allaze noima – 'se gamo,[5] eisai?' – (nai, bariemai na doulepsw)
'I was thinking that if you added a comma, the whole sentence would
change meaning – "I'm fucking you, are you in?" – (yes, I'm bored with
working)'
6 August 2012 at 15:34 · Like · 1

4. Carla: κι εγώ σκεφτόμουν την πρόταση αλλιώς, αλλά θα στο πω από κοντά
'I was too thinking the sentence differently, but I'll tell you face-to-face'
6 August 2012 at 15:42

5. Carla: (κι εγώ βαριέμαι, κάνει νύστα... αλλά η λουλουδομπόρα-μπόρα να είναι
καλά... σύντομα στα Sims
'I'm bored too, feel sleepy... but bless flowerbora-bora... coming soon to
Sims'
6 August 2012 at 15:43 · Like · 2

As I also discuss in Chapter 8, Carla started at some point being involved
in an association of professional translators. Several members of the
association sent Facebook requests to her personal profile. Carla then
decided to create a Facebook profile strictly for professional purposes to
put translation queries, suggest translation tools, announce conferences,
promote her and her colleagues' work, advertise book launches and
translation events, curate interesting quotes and aggregate pictures with
funny translation mistakes, among others. We will see relevant examples
of these activities of hers in the course of this chapter. Note that Example
6.6 above appeared on Carla's personal and not professional profile.
Making sexual innuendo (*I was too thinking the sentence differently*) and
admitting she feels bored and sleepy while working would detract from the

seriousness of her professional profile and damage the decent professional and intellectual image she crafts there.

Figure 6.6 is an internet meme from 9GAG posted by Romanos on a Sunday night. He was returning to his office after the Christmas break. The communicative function in the figure is emotive, that is to say, it is oriented towards Romanos's unwillingness as physically incarnated through an image that has humorous overtones.

Apart from bad temper and fatigue, a basic culprit in procrastinating work seems to be Facebook itself. The following string of comments occurred when Alkis uploaded the song 'My Number One' by the Swedish heavy metal band Dream Evil:[6]

6.7

1. FBU1 [female]: kaneis dialleima apo to diavasma????????????
'are you having a break from studying????????????'
17 October 2011 at 12:57 · Like · 1

2. Alkis: Ωπ, να και η Study Police!!! ☺ Yes Ma'am!

FIGURE 6.6   *Romanos's post to express denial of work.*

'Oops, here comes the Study Police!!! ☺ Yes Ma'am!'
17 October 2011 at 13:01

3. FBU1: xaxaxxxxax
axx!!!!!!ela!!!mprossssss!!!!!anoikse ta vivlia!!!!!mani mani ....
'hahahhhhahahh!!!!!! come on!!! coooooome on!!!!! open the books!!!!!
chop-chop....'
17 October 2011 at 13:06

4. Alkis: Μα η πλάκα είναι πως τα βιβλία μου ΕΙΝΑΙ το λαπιτόπι!!!!
Τώρα, πώς τρύπωσε ο <u>σατανάς το fb</u> εδωμέσα, μη με ρωτάς!!!!
'But the funny thing is that the laptop IS my books!!!!
Don't ask me now how <u>the devil of fb</u> has holed up in here!!!!'
17 October 2011 at 13:09

FBU1 points to the contradiction: Alkis, instead of studying for his dissertation, is posting music videos on Facebook. Alkis, on his part, humorously calls her *study police*, signifying that she controls when he studies or not. FBU1 accepts the label and jocularly addresses him in a tone respective to that of a study police officer by employing **directives** (*come on*, *open*). Nonetheless, Alkis's reading material exists in a computer with internet connection and therefore browsing on Facebook, especially for him who is an avid user of the platform, seems to be irresistible, confirming in this way Miller's (2011) claim, cited earlier, that Facebook swarms all over work. Flouting Grice's **maxim of quality**, Alkis pleads ignorance of how Facebook was found open in his computer personifying it as a perfidious entity who opposed him. Contrary to Carla, Helen and Romanos above, who openly articulate their resistance to work, Alkis here does not explicitly state right from the outset that he refrains (or would like to refrain) from studying even for a while. It is his friend who deduces that Alkis is not studying because a) she knows him well so as to be aware that he is supposed to study at the given moment, and b) she observes his Facebook activity on her News Feed.

The examples in this section attest to kinds of tensions encountered in professional and student identities. What is noteworthy is that these tensions are brought out in the form of complaints that are audience-designed and lodged in a non-entirely serious way, drawing on colloquialisms, tropes and humorous visual resources. Moreover, references to 'not working' seem to be an essential aspect of working – they show just how central work is to the discussion of everything else (e.g. weather, friendships and so on).

I now turn to instances of doing work for work, that is to say, using Facebook to publicize and promote one's work, efforts and achievements.

Doing work for work

As Fairclough (1995: 140) has asserted, in contemporary societies self-commodification is becoming part and parcel of our identity. Facebook provides users a speedy and cost-effective way to do so, enabling them to advertise and disseminate their work to multiple and heterogeneous audiences. Consider Figure 6.7 by way of exemplification. It is an invitation to the launch of a book that Carla co-translated.

This is the thread of comments below the invitation:

6.8

1. Carla: θα γελάσετε, θα κλάψετε (από τα γέλια), θα συγκινηθείτε

'You'll laugh, you'll cry (from laughing), you'll get moved'

30 November 2012 at 11:10

2. FBU1 [male]: Γμτ, θα δουλεύουμε επίσης

'Fck, we'll be working too'

30 November 2012 at 11:12

3. Carla: (μετά από απαίτηση πολλών αναγνωστών, <u>μπορεί και να το επαναλάβουμε, i will keep you posted</u>. κατά τα άλλα, <u>κυκλοφορούμε</u> στα βιβλιοπωλεία από την περασμένη βδομάδα. και <u>η αυτοδιαφήμιση πάει σύννεφο</u>

FIGURE 6.7 *Carla's invitation to a book launch on her personal profile.*

'(at the request of many readers, <u>we may repeat</u> it [the event], <u>i will keep</u> <u>you posted</u>. in other respects, <u>we have been released</u> in bookstores since last week. and <u>self-advertising runs rampant</u>'

30 November 2012 at 13:03 · Like · 1

4. Carla: επίσης, λόγω περιορισμένων θέσεων, όσοι έχετε σκοπό να κοπιάσετε, <u>ελάτε</u> και λίγο νωρίτερα. οι καλοί παντού χωράνε μεν, αλλά δεν υπάρχει λόγος για έξτρα ταλαιπωρία.

'moreover, because of limited seats, those of you who intend to come, <u>come</u> a bit earlier. all good folks are welcome of course, but there is no reason for extra trouble.'

30 November 2012 at 17:31

Carla adopts the promotional language of advertising afforded by the parallelism of the pronoun *you*, which directly addresses the audience, plus verbs that promise emotional outpourings (*laugh, cry, get moved*). To reassure her friend who is unable to attend, she says that *we may repeat* the event. By means of this inclusive plural, Carla identifies herself as a member of the team who translated the book and is involved in its presentation. The **decisional utterance** (Fasulo and Zucchermaglio 2002) *i will keep you posted* indexes her commitment to a given line of action. The fact that the professional effort was a result of synergy is highlighted by the metonymic replacement *we have been released* whereby the product is substituted by its creators (in lieu of saying 'the book has been released'). The self-referential phrase *self-advertising runs rampant* is a humorous acknowledgement on her part. By advising the guests through the directive *come a bit earlier*, she appears to care about the smooth staging of the event and their best possible enjoyment. The most striking observation to emerge from this example is that Carla self-promotes and mocks self-promotion at the same time. One reasonable guess this happens is because her invitation, similarly to her comment in Example 6.6, appears on her personal profile in which she adopts a more flexible way of addressing her (close) friends.

Facebook affords the means to self-advertise in even more intricate and innovative ways. As a real estate agent, one of Alkis's principal duties is the marketing and promoting of properties for sale via advertising and open houses. Figure 6.8 is an interesting hybrid, multimodal and multilingual ad he shared, which consists of a Facebook event to join, a detailed invitation text given in both Greek and English and a link to a YouTube video which shows the apartment for sale. Moreover, Alkis has added the feature of highlight (the star in the upper right corner; available on Facebook till 2015) to the post to signal the importance of the event to him and his company as well as to absorb members of his audience interested in the service he is about to offer.

This post seems like straight advertising, and is thus possibly over the boundary (and a bit out of place) within a stream of updates from one's friends and family. Alkis realized that and as he revealed to me in a follow-up interview, he proceeded to create a separate professional Facebook profile,[7] just like Carla, so as to promote there anything pertinent to estate agency (ads of houses that he and his colleague sell, some interesting articles and so on).

As pointed out in the beginning of this chapter, students have the unique opportunity to be involved in university activities that will boost their future professional career. Among the range of such opportunities that Gabriel had

FIGURE 6.8 *Alkis's promotion of his work.*

seized, he had also served as one of the organizers of EURO.PA.S. (European Parliament Simulation) at his university. The organization of the event and its promotion so as to reach and attract all students who might wish to participate constituted a recurrent theme in Gabriel's Timeline from October 2011 to

FIGURE 6.9   *Gabriel's repetitive posts on EURO.PA.S event.*

January 2012. He started with the status update in Example 6.9, writing on behalf of the committee:

6.9

Gabriel

3 October 2011 at 11:00

Είμαστε στην εξαιρετικά ευχάριστη θέση να σας ανακοινώσουμε την έναρξη των δ ιαδικασιών του EUROPAS 2012!!!

Η οργανωτική Επιτροπή της φετινής εκδήλωσης σας προσκαλεί να υποβάλλετε τις αιτήσεις σας για την επιλογή των προεδρείων των επίτροπων μέχρι και 31/10/2011.

Καθώς στην παρούσα φάση η ιστοσελίδα του EUROPAS τελεί υπό κατασκευή οσοι ενδιαφέρονται, παρακαλούνται να αποστείλουν email που να δηλώνουν το ενδιαφέρον τους στο mail: [διεύθυνση email]

'We are in the very pleasant position to announce the opening of EUROPAS 2012!!!

The organising committee of this year's event invites you to apply for selecting the chairs of the parliamentary committees until 31/10/2011.

As the website of EUROPAS is under construction at the moment if you are interested, please send an email to express your interest at [email address]'

25 people like this

Gabriel then adopted the practice of the repetitive uploading of a relevant link with a view to inviting more participants to register to the event. A general flavour can be captured through Figure 6.9 where I have included screenshots of exactly the same post from different time spans. By dint of this constant reminder, Gabriel appears involved, committed, methodical and genuinely concerned about the success of the event he has undertaken to co-organize.

While working on his dissertation, Alkis created a Facebook event (Figure 6.10) not just to trumpet that he was conducting research but to recruit subjects for his survey on sea tourism and ask his Facebook friends to share his event to that purpose. Indeed, this kind of promotion proved to be very helpful and effective to Alkis's research as 190 people completed his questionnaire in just 24 hours.

What we observe in the examples of this section is that the users' purpose is not just to communicate 'here I am and this is what I have done/am doing' but to go a step further (in most cases they may have already done what was required). For instance, they may want their Facebook audience to do something with their publicizing apart from being informed: buy the product (e.g. book), give feedback (I expand on this later on), come to offline events

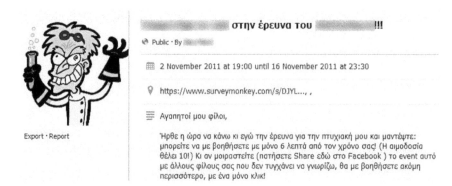

FIGURE 6.10 *Alkis's data collection event.*

[Translation: It's about time for me too I did my research for my dissertation and guess what: you can help me by devoting 6 minutes from your time! (Blood donation needs 10 minutes!) And if you share (Click Share here on Facebook) this event to other friends of yours that I happen not to know, you will help me even more, with just one click!]

to offer support, promote the work anew, assist in research or participate in projects that will lead to the accomplishment of a collaborative piece of work.

Constructing and advancing knowledge

Claiming expertise

A hallmark in the public construction of both professional and educational identities is the choices that participants make to demonstrate their depth and breadth of knowledge on a topic as well as their entitlement to speak on this topic in particular contexts, namely their expertise (Myers 2004: 177). Social media, in general, and Facebook, in particular, can function as ideal instruments for displaying knowledgeability, disseminating links and information and suggesting tools that people believe to be valuable and relevant to work mates and fellow students. As Gabriel has confided:

> I use [Facebook] exclusively as a means of projecting a particular image of myself (mainly 'scholarly') to others and as a channel of communicating topics of this kind.

Example 6.10 will give us a taste of how showing expertise might work:

6.10

Carla [personal profile]

24 February 2012 at 21:40

η λέξη της ημέρας: serendipity

'word of the day: serendipity'

3 people like this

1. Carla: meaning: The faculty of making fortunate discoveries by accident.
24 February 2012 at 21:40 · Like · 3

2. Carla: πείτε μου ότι την ξέρατε τη λέξη να με στείλετε βραδιάτικα...

'tell me you knew this word because you've got me there this time late at night...'
24 February 2012 at 21:42 · Like · 1

3. FBU1 [female]: but of course...
24 February 2012 at 21:43

4. FBU1: to eixa dei se mia tainia kai to eixa psaksei!

'I'd seen it in a film and I'd searched for it'
24 February 2012 at 21:43 · Like · 1

5. Carla: εύγε!

'well done!'
24 February 2012 at 21:44

[another 4 comments of small talk on another colleague's behaviour at the office]

6. Carla: τώρα είδα ότι δεν δημοσιεύτηκε η ετυμολογία-που έχει την πιο πολλή πλάκα ...

'I've just seen that the etymology was not posted – which has more fun'
[she copies word history]
http://www.answers.com/topic/serendipity#ixzz1nKWiZ1pR
serendipity
24 February 2012 at 21:50

Carla offers a piece of knowledge she has discovered and thinks it would be worth distributing. In the subsequent comments, she gives the dictionary meaning of the word followed by the directive *tell me* (comment 2) which is intended to enact conversational interaction (Myers 2010b: 84) with those who are also in the know. Indeed, a friend responds to Carla's call by providing the context of how she became familiar with the word *serendipity*. In comment 6, Carla realizes that the etymology of *serendipity* was not posted so she copies and pastes it again. For her, it is not only the meaning but the history of the word that will arouse her audience's interest. Notice also the professional practice of including the source where she copies from.

Example 6.11 introduces a creative way of feeding an audience with new information. Helen, imitating the structure of an email sent to her students, as if addressing someone other than her Facebook friends (*Dear students*, *Please find attached* ...), lists some pinnacles of contemporary digital education (interactive activities, YouTube video, photos from Flickr, journal articles, colleagues' personal websites, Linux operated pc, academic earth, forum discussions) only to conclude that these are at stake because of SOPA (Stop Online Piracy Act bill). Note that this status update was originally conceived by Helen – it is not a standard message circulated as part of the anti-SOPA campaign.

6.11

Helen
18 January 2012 at 21:57

Dear students,
Please find attached this week's pp presentation, which includes interactive activities based on a youtube video, photos from flickr, journal articles uploaded by my colleagues on their personal websites (since I am based outside the academic centre and I don't necessarily have access to every single journal paper) and finally created on my Linux operated pc. It has been inspired by presentations posted on academic earth and forum discussions. <u>Imagine</u> how this presentation would look like without the above and <u>read</u> more about SOPA here:

https://en.wikipedia.org/wiki/Stop_Online_Piracy_Act
4 people like this

As we can see, she does not explain what SOPA exactly is; she delivers the directives *imagine* to alert her recipients and *read* to invite them to take action and follow the relevant Wikipedia link in order to be fully informed.

A similar pattern, with the directive *read* preceded by *please*, to appeal to the readership, plus a link, occurs in Example 6.12:

6.12

Carla [professional profile]
29 October 2010 at 03:10
<u>Αναρωτιέστε</u> πώς μπορεί να προφέρεται το όνομα Quetzalcoatl;
<u>Ιδού η απάντηση</u>:
'<u>Are you wondering</u> how the name Quetzalcoatl may be pronounced?
<u>Here's the answer:</u>'
quetzalcoatl pronunciation: How to pronounce quetzalcoatl in Nahuatl
www.forvo.com
1 person likes this

1. FBU1 [male]: Πάρα πολύ χρήσιμο! Thx!
'So much useful! Thx!'
29 October 2010 at 03:21

2. Carla: Ε, δεν είναι;;; Έπαθα πλάκα! Να ναι καλά ο φίλος [όνομα]!
'Eh, isn't it??? I was surprised! Bless my friend [name]!'
29 October 2010 at 03:31

The audience's attention is captured first by the device of the question (*Are you wondering*), which opens the status update, and second by Carla's choice of the rather weird name *Quetzalcoatl* (a deity in the Mesoamerican civilization). Based on the presupposition that readers are unaware of its pronunciation, Carla comes to offer the solution (*here's the answer*) by attaching a link to *forvo* (www.forvo.com), a free online pronunciation dictionary including sound clips in almost 300 different languages. As can be read in the comments, one of her friends recognizes and ratifies Carla's recommendation of this tool (*So much useful! Thx!*). Carla, however, does not present herself as the absolute bearer of knowledge; she shifts her expertise by disclosing that this discovery was courtesy of another friend (*Bless my friend*).

Thus far we have witnessed that expertise is offered by directly addressing the audience through second person plural references, directives and questions. Another – subtler yet equally engaging – way of advising on sources of knowledge is to evaluate the information that you introduce to your recipients. As displayed in Figure 6.11, Helen attaches to the video, entitled 'Killing us softly 4: Advertising's image of women', the labels *well known*

 shared a link.
8 March 2012

Well known video, excellent for language and gender modules

 **Killing Us Softly 4: Advertising's Image of Women [Trailer] - Available on DVD**
www.youtube.com

Available on DVD - April 2010
http://www.mediaed.org In this new,

Like · Comment · Share   👍 2

FIGURE 6.11 *Helen's video suggestion for teaching.*

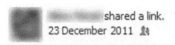

Like · Comment · Share   👍 1 💬 2

FIGURE 6.12 *Alkis's link on translation questions.*

and *excellent*, having watched it herself, and perhaps already incorporated it successfully in one of her lectures. Apart from academic expertise, she also conveys a broader sense of knowing things (Jacoby and Gonzales 1991: 152) and feeling sensitized, seeing she chose to share the particular post on 8 March, the International Women's Day.

Propagating knowledge on Facebook is not always attained directly. Figure 6.12 is an example of a link shared by Alkis and is related to one of his fields of expertise, translation. The link is stripped of any expert or authoritarian voice on Alkis's part, in the form of a comment or a piece of advice on what to do with it, which entails that readers get the gist from the text that appears in the thumbnail of the post and then decide whether to follow it up and get the benefit of the recommended source (Myers 2010b: 28).

The last example in this section concerns job advertising as a means of sharing knowledge from the inside. A large percentage of job posts are never advertised anywhere – it is through network contacts that many positions become known to the public. Example 6.13 contains such an informal job ad posted as a status update by Alkis. It is not targeted at particular individuals but *anyone interested* (notice the political correctness in Greek *όποια* – anyone female and *όποιος* – anyone male), willing and qualified to fill in the position, whether they are translators or experts in constructions with good command of English:

6.13

Alkis

31 May 2012 at 14:48

Όποια/ος ενδιαφέρεται να κάνει την ερχόμενη εβδομάδα διαδοχική διερμηνεία (αγγλικά προς ελληνικά κι ενδεχομένως για κάποιες ερωτήσεις να κάνει κι αντίστροφη) για περίπου 3 ώρες σε μια εκδήλωση με θέμα τα δομικά υλικά, ας επικοινωνήσει μαζί μου στο inbox για λεπτομέρειες.

Ευχαριστώ!

'Anyone interested in doing consecutive interpreting next week (from English to Greek and maybe vice versa for some questions) for approximately 3 hours in an event for building materials, can contact me in the inbox for details.

Thanks!'

2 people like this

Alkis here crafts a double work-related identity: on the one hand, as an insider of job information, willing to provide more details via inbox messaging and, on the other, as a concerned professional who wishes to help his peers. Several comparable job ads are scattered around his updates. Taking into consideration that (1) Alkis himself had been unemployed for 9 months, and (2) the unemployment rate in Greece has been sky-high since 2011, I see this job posting on Facebook as a fully conscious practice on his part. Not only has he been in jobless people's shoes, but also he recognizes Facebook's immediacy in circulating such type of information to friends and acquaintances who may sorely need it. Moreover, it displays that he is well connected himself.

To wrap up, examples in this section identified that being an expert in your domain involves the display of command of specific information mainly in the form of links and/or personal comments that aim at engaging the audience. As Miller (1995) has appositely described it: 'Show me what your links are, and I'll tell you what kind of person you are.' Through their links my participants are constructed as cognizant, involved, and ethical, mastering special knowledge with eagerness to share it.

Joint production of expertise

Becoming an expert can involve drawing on other experts, which in turn leads to collaborative creation of knowledge. The extended example below will be used to explicate this point within the context of Facebook.

6.14

Carla [professional profile]
3 February 2013 at 20:25

Περί μεταγραφής κύριων ονομάτων
Abu Simbel.
Εμείς παραδοσιακά το λέμε Αμπού Σιμπέλ. Είναι το 'σωστό' ή φταίει η 'εξ Αιγύπτου γαλλική μας παιδεία';
Το βρίσκω και ως Άμπου Σίμπελ.
Εσείς, τι λέτε;
'On transliterating proper names

Abu Simbel.

We traditionally say Ambú Simbél. Is it "correct" or is "our French education from Egypt" to blame?

I have also found it as Ámbu Símbel.

What do you reckon?'

1. FBU1 [female]: Δεδομένου ότι δεν πρόκειται για εξελληνισμένη λέξη (όπως το 'Λονδίνο') και βάσει της φωνητικής γραφής του, το σωστό είναι Άμπου Σίμπελ, μη χέσω τη γαλλική μας παιδεία.

'Given that it is not a word incorporated into the Modern Greek declension system (like 'λονδίνο')[8] and on the basis of its phonetic transcription, the correct is Ámbu Símbel, fuck our French education.'

3 February 2013 at 20:31 · Like · 1

2. FBU1: Για την ακρίβεια, Άμπου Σίμ-μπελ!

'More precisely, Ámbu Sím-mbel!'

3 February 2013 at 20:33 · Like · 1

3. Carla: Ναι ρε συ, αλλά και τον Γράχαμ Γκρην δεν τολμάω να τον γράψω Γκρέιαμ Γκρην.

'Yes, but I don't dare to write Graham Greene as Greɪəm Greene.

3 February 2013 at 20:33

4. FBU1: Κακώς! Ευτυχώς, πολλοί τον λένε πλέον σωστά. Όπως έγινε σταδιακά και η αλλαγή του Σιν σε Σον Κόνερι.

'Wrongly! Fortunately, many people now pronounce his name correctly. As was the gradual change from ʃɪn to ʃɔːn Connery.'

3 February 2013 at 20:34

5. FBU1: Δυστυχώς, τον Τσάρλτον Χέστον, λίγοι τολμούν να τον πουν σωστά (που του αρμόζει και καλύτερα, λόγω της οπλοφιλίας του).

'Unfortunately, few people dare to pronounce Charlton Heston[9] correctly (it suits him better, because of his love for guns).'

3 February 2013 at 20:35 · Like · 2

6. FBU1: Επίσης, οι καφροαθλητικογράφοι ποτέ δεν είπαν λάθος τον Γκρέιαμ Σούνες.

'In addition, the lout sportscasters have never pronounced wrongly Graham [transliterates Greɪəm] Souness.'

3 February 2013 at 20:36

7. FBU1: Αλλά, θα μου πεις, είμαστε στη χώρα που μιλάει ακόμη για τον Χένρι ΚίσινΓΚερ!

'But, we are in the country that is still talking about Henry Kissiŋger!'

3 February 2013 at 20:38

8. Carla: Point taken (into consideration)
3 February 2013 at 20:39

9. FBU2 [female]: ΑΜΠΟΥ ΣΙΜΠΕΛ
'ÁMBU SIMBEL'
3 February 2013 at 20:44

10. FBU3 [male]: Μακάρι να μπορούσαμε να γράψουμε Άμπου Σίμμπελ (2μ) για να αποδοθεί τελείως, αλλά σίγουρα Αμπού Σιμπέλ είναι λάθος... Αχ Γαλλία, πόσο μας επηρεάζεις :)
'Wish we could write Ámbu Símmbel (2m) to render it entirely, but surely Ambú Simbél is wrong... Oh France, how much you influence us :)'
3 February 2013 at 20:45

11. Carla: lol ;) Is THAT your PROFESSIONAL opinion?
3 February 2013 at 20:45 · Like · 2

12. FBU2: Αν είναι σε κείμενο όχι, αν είναι σε έγγραφο του ΑΜΠΟΥ, ναι!
'If it's in a text no, if it's in one of AMBU'S documents, yes!'
3 February 2013 at 20:47

13. FBU2: :)
3 February 2013 at 20:49 · Like · 1

14. FBU3: Μίλησα με ομιλητές της Αραβικής και με διαβεβαίωσαν πως η σωστή προφορά είναι Άμπου Σίμπελ.
Ξέρεις, νομίζω, πόσο αξιόπιστες είναι οι πηγές μου!;)
'I talked to speakers of Arabic and they assured me that the correct pronunciation is Ámbu Símbel.
You know, I think, how reliable my sources are!;)'
3 February 2013 at 20:50

15. Carla: ευχαριστώ τις εξ Αιγύπτου πηγές σου που παραμέρισαν τη γαλλική τους παιδεία για να σε/με διαφωτίσουν. Ο Μεγάλος Ραμσής Β να σας έχει όλους καλά!
'thanks to your sources from Egypt who ignored their French education to enlighten you/me. May Ramesses II the Great bless all of you!'
3 February 2013 at 20:52 · Like · 1
[Another 31 comments follow on the proper names *Nefertiti* and *Nefertari* followed by some bantering between FBU1, FBU3 and Carla.]

The extract is built upon Carla's interacting questions *Is it 'correct' or is 'our French education from Egypt' to blame?* and *What do you reckon?*, which aim at eliciting expert opinions on which is the correct way to stress the proper name *Abu Simbel*[10] while transliterating it into Greek. My starting point in discussing this thread is the usage of pronouns. With *we* and *our* Carla expresses generic reference to Greek speakers who, being heavily influenced by French, have the tendency to stress all Arabic words on the final syllable. In contrast, *you* is used to refer to the professionals who are in the know and therefore are in a position to provide a responsible and respectable answer. What is striking in the original Greek status update is that *Εμείς* (*We*) and *Εσείς* (*you*) are given special prominence by being placed in initial thematic position. On account of a highly developed inflectional system, word order in Greek is relatively more flexible than in English. This means that the use of the pronoun as a theme is largely unnecessary since it is signalled by the inflection of the verb. That is, if Carla had written *παραδοσιακά το λέμε Αμπού Σιμπέλ. ... τι λέτε;*, the meaning would still be the same. By thematizing the two pronouns, she seems to mark a stark contrast between the common belief held among speakers regarding pronunciation, including herself and recognizing its falseness (accentuated by the double quotation marks in '*correct*' and '*our ... Egypt*'), and the professional expertise. Notably, before she formulates her question to her expert audience, she records her own discovery (*I have also found it as Ámbu Símbel*), manifesting that she has done some relevant research beforehand and does not demand an answer handed to her on a plate.

To her request, Carla receives five opinions from three translators. First, the correct stress is Ámbu Símbel following its phonetic transcription and because the name has not acquired Greek morphology (comment 1). FBU1 draws on logic and professional experience to provide the answer listing some additional examples of proper names. Carla understands and accepts the explanation (comment 8). Second, the capitalized form ABU SIMBEL is presented as the correct one (comment 9). FBU2 is joking as in writing in capitals you do not have to stress words in Greek so you do not have to worry about such issues. Carla replies in the same humorous tone capitalizing the word *PROFESSIONAL* insinuating that capitalization is not a proper answer. Third, both FBU1 and FBU3 are in favour of *Símmbel* (comments 2, 10), yet such a choice would be unacceptable in Greek orthography. Fourth, both FBU1 and FBU3 recognize the bad influence from French including themselves into Carla's generic *we* (comment 1: *our French education*, comment 10: *Oh France, how much you influence us*). Fifth, the right choice is Ábu Símbel (comment 14). FBU3 invokes expertise, that is, speakers of Arabic, boasting for its reliability.

Eventually, and within 25 minutes, Carla has got the answer she wanted. She thanks FBU3's sources for enlightening him and concomitantly her (comment 15) and closes playfully with a humorous wish to those who contributed to her query appealing to Ramesses II, the Egyptian pharaoh who erected Abu Sibel temples.

The above thread shows vividly how Facebook can function as a fruitful medium for the synergetic construction and organization of expertise via commentary. The most conspicuous feature in the interaction was the careful balance of display of expertise with jokey undercutting of that display. Such expertise no longer builds on rational argumentation exclusively, but vitally, is framed in informal, interpersonal discourse styles (e.g. swearing and humour) that enhance and smooth out collaboration.

Working and studying are not solitary quests but joint negotiated enterprises of mutual engagement (Wenger 1998: 73). The next section will focus on how this mutuality can be discursively realized on Facebook.

Building rapport with peers

Reciprocal conventions

Revisiting the Facebook public event of Alkis's data collection for his dissertation (Figure 6.10), we will see that he had asked his friends to promote his venture:

6.15

Κι <u>αν μοιραστείτε</u> (πατήσετε Share εδώ στο Facebook) το event αυτό με άλλους φίλους σας που δεν τυγχάνει να γνωρίζω, <u>θα με βοηθήσετε</u> ακόμη περισσότερο, με ένα μόνο κλικ!

'And <u>if you share</u> (click Share here on Facebook) this event to other friends of yours that I don't have the chance to know, <u>you will help me</u> even more, with just one click!'

Indeed, two of his friends forwarded the event to assist and support him. One wrote a short introduction as a status update followed by a comment in which she copied and pasted Alkis's text from the first page of his survey. The other friend opted for a more humorous update (Example 6.16):

6.16

My beloved fcb Friends ... I would appreciate to take part in this survey!!!! Its for a gooood cause!!!!!!SurveyMonkey [a free online survey software and questionnaire tool] .Alkis is The Monkey!!!!!

Building and preserving rapport online between researcher-informant is a reciprocal process. As Alkis contributed considerably to my research, I helped him with his own. What follows is our interaction that took place in the Facebook page of his dissertation public event right after I completed his survey:

6.17

1. Mariza: OK! Καλή επιτυχία, Άλκη! Πολύ ενδιαφέρον το θέμα.
'OK! Good luck, Alkis! Your topic is very interesting.'
4 November 2011 at 00:24

2. Alkis: Πράγματι! Σ' ευχαριστώ πολύ Μαρίζα! Ελπίζω να πηγαίνει και η δική σου καλά! <u>Είμαι σε ετοιμότητα</u> για νέο ερωτηματολόγιο <u>όποτε χρειαστείς, ε;!</u>
'Indeed! Thank you very much Mariza! I hope [your research] goes well too! <u>I'm ready</u> for a new questionnaire <u>whenever you need, ok?!</u>'
4 November 2011 at 00:25

3. Mariza: καλά πάει, σ' ευχαριστώ! αλήθεια, είσαι σε ετοιμότητα? όποτε μπορείς έχω κάνα-δυο πράγματα που θα ήθελα να σε ρωτήσω :)
'it goes well, thank you! really, are you ready? I have a couple of things that I'd like to ask you whenever you can :)'
4 November 2011 at 00:28

4. Alkis: Και το ρωτάς; <u>Ρώτα!!</u> χεχε
'You bet. <u>Ask!!</u> hehe'
4 November 2011 at 00:29

5. Mariza: θα σου στείλω μέιλ άμεσα
'I'll send you an email soon'
4 November 2011 at 00:35

6. Alkis: Οκ, αν το στείλεις άμεσα άμεσα μπορεί να στο απαντήσω <u>τώρα</u> μιας και θα είμαι online για λίγη ώρα ακόμη!
'Ok, if you send it right away I may answer it <u>now</u> as I will be online for a little while!'
4 November 2011 at 00:42

Interestingly, by means of the decisional utterances *I'm ready for a new questionnaire whenever you need* and *I may answer it now* as well as the imperative *ask*, Alkis further enhances this mutuality constructing himself as a committed informant willing to take practical action.

Alkis's genuine interest in and encouragement to other people's work is also featured in Example 6.18 where he advertises his fellow student's research by mentioning her name and characterizing her questionnaire as *interesting* in order to attract respondents. Instead of challenging FBU1's – potentially humorous – downscaling assessment of his research (*your friend has a nicer research topic than you!!!*), he aligns with it (*I couldn't agree more!!!*) recognizing his friend's research innovativeness and appearing eager to read her findings.

6.18

Alkis

1 December 2011 at 12:30

Όποιος έχει 5-10 max λεπτάκια ας βοηθήσει τη φίλη μου [όνομα] με την έρευνα για την πτυχιακή της! Έχει <u>ενδιαφέρον</u> το ερωτηματολόγιο!!
"Η συναισθηματική νοημοσύνη ως παράγοντας επιτυχίας στη σύγχρονη επιχείρηση" www.surveymonkey.com ...
'Whoever has 5-10 minutes max to help my friend [name] with the research for her dissertation! The questionnaire is <u>interesting</u>!! "Emotional intelligence as a factor of success in contemporary business" www.surveymonkey.com ...'

1. FBU1 [female]**:** done! ΥΓ:η φιλη [όνομα] εχει <u>πιο ωραιο</u> θεμα ερευνας από <u>σενα</u>!!!
'done! PS:your friend [name] has a <u>nicer</u> research topic <u>than you</u>!!!'
1 December 2011 at 13:22

2. Alkis: <u>Συμφωνώ κι επαυξάνω</u>!!! <u>Ανυπομονώ</u> να δω τα αποτελέσματά της ...!
'<u>I couldn't agree more</u>!!! <u>Can't wait</u> to see her results ...!'
1 December 2011 at 13:22

The same rationale is echoed in posts where users promote and recommend a colleague's work. For instance, in one of her statuses, Carla had written a catchy quotation and then provided the name of her colleague that had translated into Greek the book from which the quotation came along with the publisher's name.

Praising achievements

One of the most significant social lubricants in the bolstering of camaraderie is providing positive and encouraging feedback on someone's performance in the form of compliments. The following thread is extracted from Carla's professional profile.

6.19

1. FBU1 [female]: Κάρλα, διάβασα τον [τίτλος βιβλίου] (κάλλιο αργά ...). <u>Θερμά</u> <u>συγχαρητήρια</u>. Σε περίμενα στη γωνία για 'κανα λαθάκι (επαγγελματική διαστροφή, γαρ) αλλά βαρέθηκα να περιμένω κι έφυγα. <u>Μπράβο σου! Κιπαδεγκουντγουέρκ!</u>
'Carla, I read [title of the book that Carla has translated] (better late ...). <u>Warm congratulations</u>. I was waiting in the corner for any mistake+DIM

(due to professional perversion) but I was bored with waiting and left. <u>Well done to you!</u>
<u>Keepathegoodwerk!</u>'
29 October 2010 at 21:27

2. Carla: <u>κοκκινίζω</u>!!!! <u>ευχαριστώ πολύ πολύ</u>!!!!!:-)
(<u>κάτι θα υπάρχει, δεν μπορεί</u>, αλλά άμα είναι καλοπροαίρετη η αναγνώστρια, δεν πέφτει το μάτι!)
πάντως, άμα θες <u>ΛΑΘΑΡΑ</u> -όχι απλώς λαθάκι- <u>έχω μια ξεγυρισμένη</u> στην [τίτλος βιβλίου]! Αλλά ξεγυρισμένη, λαθάρα με τα όλα της, <u>μ' αυτή έχω καθαρίσει</u> για μια δεκαετία και βάλε, <u>δε μου επιτρέπεται</u> άλλο τέτοιο!
<u>'i'm blushing</u>!!!! <u>thank you very very much</u>!!!!!:-)
(<u>something may exist, it can't be the case</u>, but if the reader is well-intentioned, the eye doesn't see it!)
however, if you want a <u>MISTAKE+AUG</u> -not just a mistake+DIM- <u>I have a whacking one</u> in [title of book]! But whacking, MISTAKE+AUG with its everything, <u>i'm done with this</u> for more than a decade, <u>i'm not allowed</u> to make another one like this!'
30 October 2010 at 01:51

3. FBU1: Got it! You wanna trick me into reading it... Το πέτυχες. Άρα, I'll get back to you in a couple of months on that. Μη μου πεις, όμως, θα το βρω μόνη μου (καμία πιθανότητα, όμως...). Ωστόσο, <u>οι κριτικές είναι διθυραμβικές και πάλι.</u> Θα κρίνω και θα σου πω. ΧΟΧΟ
'Got it! You wanna trick me into reading it... You did it. So, I'll get back to you in a couple of months on that. But don't tell me, I'll find it alone (no chance, though...). However, <u>the reviews are dithyrambic again.</u> I'll judge and I'll tell you. ΗΟΗΟ'
30 October 2010 at 12:40

4. Carla: πιάνει το κόλπο! χεχεχε! <u>να κρίνεις</u> και <u>να με κρίνεις</u>. <u>μ' αρέσουν οι παρατηρήσεις! διορθώνομαι!</u>
'the trick works! hehehe! <u>judge</u> and <u>judge me</u>. <u>I like remarks! I get improved</u>!'
31 October 2010 at 22:49

5. FBU1: Αυτή είναι σωστή αντιμετώπιση! (Νά επρόκειταο και για 'κανα λάθος της προκοπής... Κανένα ορθογραφικό θα είναι από τον δαίμονα του τυπογραφείου. Στο λέω από τώρα: <u>δεν πιάνεται.</u>)
'That's the right attitude! (if it was for an important mistake... It will be a typographic one. I'm telling you by now: <u>it doesn't count</u>.)'
1 November 2010 at 18:43

6. Carla: Δεν είναι τόσο απλό. Είναι <u>πατάτα ολκής</u>! Πίστεψέ με!
'It's not so simple. It's a <u>terrible blunder</u>! Believe me!'
2 November 2010 at 12:43

7. FBU1: Χμμμ... Ακόμα κι έτσι νά 'ναι, <u>σταγόνα στον ωκεανό...</u> Θα επανέλθω όμως, μην επαναπαύεσαι. ΤΟ (ΜΙΣΟ-)ΑΓΡΥΠΝΟ ΜΑΤΙ :)
'Hmmm... Even if it is so, <u>a drop in the ocean</u>... I'll come back though, don't feel complacent. THE (HALF-) ALERT EYE :)'
2 November 2010 at 22:07

Carla's colleague commends her on a book she has translated (comment 1: *Warm congratulations, Well done to you! Keepathegoodwerk!*, comment 3: *the reviews are dithyrambic*), sculpting her thus as a competent, infallible professional (comment 5: *it doesn't count*, comment 7: *a drop in the ocean*). Notably, *again* in the *reviews are dithyrambic again* presupposes that Carla has also done excellent job in the past. Carla, on her part, appears tremendously self-effacing. She offers an appreciation token (comment 2: *thank you very very much!!!!!*) scaling down at the same time the complimentary **force** (*i'm blushing!!!!*), pointing persistently to flaws in her work (comment 2: *something may exist, it can't be the case, I have a whacking one, i'm done with this, i'm not allowed to make another one like this!*, comment 6: *a terrible blunder*). What she asks for is not praise but advice on how to become a better professional (*judge and judge me. I like remarks! I get improved!*).

Another instance of praising the work of another is found in Example 6.20. FBU1 expresses her gratitude (*thank you*) towards Helen for her outstanding performance as an EAP tutor (*EAP star*). Identically to the previous example (comment 3), *again* secures Helen as a competent professional over time.

6.20
1. FBU1 [female; foreigner]: We'll miss you. <u>Thank you for being such an EAP star again</u> this year. x
2 October 2011 at 20:02

2. FBU2 [male; foreigner]: We gonna miss you~ See you next year~
3 October 2011 at 19:13

3. Helen: I'll miss you too so much and I hope I'll see you next year!!!! <u>that's all thanks to the star coordinators:-)</u>
4 October 2011 at 23:01

Compared to Carla's downgrading, Helen redirects FBU1's praise to the EAP coordinators. By confessing mistakes (Carla) and shifting credit to colleagues (Helen), both Carla and Helen appear to 'democratise' their expertise by publicly performing 'a delicate balancing act between the status-conscious professional and the ordinary modest [person] going about [their] everyday business' (Dyer and Keller-Cohen 2000: 298–99).

In Examples 6.19 and 6.20 alike, there was no particular summons (e.g. a photograph or a status by Carla and Helen) that invited a response. It was my informants' friends who initiated the supportive action of complimenting by writing first on Carla's and Helen's Walls. The context is slightly different in Example 6.21. The commentary is triggered by a Gabriel's photo, which depicts him as a valedictorian reading the graduation oath to his fellow students during the ceremony for receiving their degrees.[11] It should be noted that the particular photo was not uploaded by Gabriel himself (he did not post any photo at all from this red-letter day) but by his mother. She then tagged him and as a result (and in accordance with Gabriel's profile settings on what content he has allowed to be visible) the photo became available to his friends' News Feeds. In total, the particular photo received the striking number of 124 'Likes', which encode the intended meaning of congratulating.

6.21

1. FBU1 [male]: brings back memories
1 November 2012 at 21:49 · Like · 1

2. FBU2 [female]: sugxarhthria Gavriil!!!!
'congratulations Gabriel!!!!'
1 November 2012 at 22:14 · Like · 2

3. FBU3 [female; foreigner]: Bravo Gavriil! Congrats!
1 November 2012 at 22:27 · Like · 1

4. FBU4 [female; foreigner]: congrats!
1 November 2012 at 22:38 · Like · 1

5. FBU5 [female]: sunxarhthria gavriil... k eis anwtera..
'congratulations gabriel... way to go.'
1 November 2012 at 22:41 · Like · 1

6. FBU6 [female]: Συγχαρητήρια!! Πάντα επιτυχίες!
'Congratulations!! Always successes!'
1 November 2012 at 22:47 · Like · 1

7. FBU7 [female]: sygxaritiria gavriilako!!k eis anwtera..mono ta kalytera!!
'congratulations gabriel+DIM!!way to go..only the best!!'
2 November 2012 at 01:48 · Like · 1

8. FBU8 [female]: Μπράβο!!!!!!!!!!!!!!!!!
'Bravo!!!!!!!!!!!!!!!!!'
2 November 2012 at 11:40 · Like · 1

9. FBU9 [female]: ΣΥΓΧΑΡΗΤΗΡΙΑ!!!!!!!!!!!!!!!!!
'CONGRATULATIONS!!!!!!!!!!!!!!!'
2 November 2012 at 15:24 · Like · 1

10. FBU10 [female]: agori mu gliko... poso perifanus mas kaneis!!
ftu ftu... SIgxaritiriaaaa!!!
'my sweet boy... how proud you've made us!!... Congratulatioooons!!!'
2 November 2012 at 16:23 · Like · 1

11. FBU11 [female]: Μπράβο...πολλά, πολλά συγχαρητήρια! Καλές επόμενες
επιτυχίες! Το ταξίδι που ξεκινάει τώρα είναι το καλλίτερο και εύχομαι
να ανταποδώσει τα μέγιστα των κόπων που προϋποθέτει!!
'Bravo...many, many congratulations! Good luck in your future endeavour!
The journey that is now starting is the best and I wish it will compensate
the greatest of the efforts it requires!!'
4 November 2012 at 20:22

12. FBU12 [female; foreigner]: very well done dear xDD
8 November 2012 at 19:13

The thread is replete with praising lexical items in both Greek and English
(*congratulations, Bravo, Congrats, way to go, CONGRATULATIONS!!!!!!!!*
*!!!!!!!!!, Congratulatioooons!!!, Bravo ... many, many congratulations, very
well done*), abundant exclamation marks, an exclamative fronting structure
(*how proud you've made us!!*), wishes and encouragement (*only the best,
Always successes, Good luck in your future endeavour, I wish it will compensate the greatest of the efforts it requires!!*) and endearments (*my sweet
boy, gabriel+DIM, dear*). If the valedictory photo constitutes powerful evidence of Gabriel's intellectual competence (see definition of educational
identity in the beginning of the chapter), his friends' emotionally laden comments publicly corroborate this competence of his. Notice that, instead of
thanking every friend individually, Gabriel accepts the complimentary force of
their utterances by clicking the 'Like' button next to each comment. That the
latter two comments were not 'liked' could be attributed to the fact that they
were posted at a later time and thus lost in the sea of 'Likes' that the picture
collected.

Gabriel was also tagged in photos of the party that followed the graduation
ceremony. In one of them a friend wrote him *Bravo*. Akin to Helen, he opted
for reassigning the complimentary force to his teachers:

6.22

Πάντως για να τα λέμε όλα η ορκομωσία είναι ημέρα χαράς και συγκομιδής <u>και για
τους καθηγητές</u>!<u>δεν διδαχτήκαμε μόνοι μας</u>!
'Yet to tell the truth the graduation ceremony is a day of joy and harvest <u>for
teachers too! we weren't self-taught</u>!'
2 November 2012 at 17:54 · Like · 4

In much the same spirit, in the follow-up comments under her tacit self-promotion (mentioned earlier towards the end of the section *Doing work for work*), included in Example 6.23 below, Carla has a personal interaction with her Spanish teacher and gives her credit for what she has attained professionally (*dear professor, thank you very much!!!*). See also how the use of Spanish ratifies Carla's expertise in the language.

6.23

1. FBU1 [Greek female]: felicitaciones Carla. Por qué será que yo también me siento orgullosa??!!
'Carla congratulations. Why do I also feel proud??!!'
15 March 2011 at 02:23 · Like · 1

2. Carla: asi debe ser querida profesora por que gran parte de esto comenzo con aquellas lecturas de los cuentos de eva luna y de cortazar en corfu en aquel entonces! te lo agradezco muchisimo!!!
'It must be so dear professor because much of this started with those readings of the stories of eva luna [novel written by Chilean writer Isabel Allende] and of cortazar's (stories) [Argentine writer] in corfu back then! thank you very much!!!'
15 March 2011 at 02:25 · Like · 1

3. FBU1: humildemente ... de nada!
'humbly ... you're welcome!'
15 March 2011 at 02:56

Praising one's professional and educational achievements can occur in combination with other speech events like birthday and name day wishes, which by default enforce solidarity. Example 6.24 was written by a male friend on Carla's birthday:

6.24

NA ZHSEIS CARLOYLA KAI XRONIA POLLA, MEGALH MH GINEIS ME ASPRA MALLIA. PANDOU NA SKORPIZEIS METAFRASHS FWS KAI OLOI NA LENE 'CARLOULA EINAI MIA, SAFWS'
'LONG MAY YOU LIVE CARLA+DIM AND HAPPY BIRTHDAY, DON'T GROW OLD WITH WHITE HAIR, MAY YOU SPREAD OUT EVERYWHERE THE LIGHT OF TRANSLATION AND MAY EVERYBODY SAY "CARLA+DIM IS ONE, OF COURSE"'
21 December 2010 at 1:18 · Like · 1

The particular piece alludes to the Greek birthday song,[12] mimicking its grammar and phrasing but not its words. What is exceptional in this case is that Carla's friend has substituted the *give to everyone the light of youth/ knowledge* bit with *give to everyone the light of translation*. The friend's presupposition here is that Carla is a translation expert and as such she can infuse her professional knowledge and wisdom to other people.

Correspondingly, in Example 6.25, we have the presupposition that Gabriel is an excellent student (*excelling*) so his friend wishes him for his name day to continue being so.

6.25

xronia polla file gavriil! o,ti epi8umeis!!! euxomai n eisai panta ugihs, eutixismenos k <u>na sunexiseis na diaprepeis st tmhma!</u> :)

'happy name day Gabriel mate! may all your wishes come true!!! wish you're always healthy, happy and <u>keep on excelling in the department!</u> :)'

Constructing membership categories

We saw earlier how the participants in Example 6.14 presented themselves as a group of translators. In this section, I put more flesh on the issue looking at instances of identification and solidarity with a particular group.

Example 6.26 is the caption of a photo of a badly translated text (from English to Greek) that Carla uploaded on the International Translation Day (30 September) while Alkis in 6.27 dedicated the soundtrack *The Lion King – Orpheus in the Underworld Overture* to his fellow students as at that time they were finishing off writing their MSc dissertations.

6.26

Carla [personal profile]
30 September 2010 at 03:19

αφιερωμένο στους <u>μεταφραστές</u>. χρόνια <u>μας</u> πολλά;-)
'dedicated to <u>translators</u>. many happy returns to <u>us</u>;-)'

6.27

Alkis
6 January 2012 at 21:43
Αφιερωμένο στα <u>msmpartάλια</u>!!
Επειδή κάπως έτσι <u>τρέχουμε όλοι</u> αυτές τις μέρες ...;-)
'Dedicated to <u>msmwrecks</u>!
Because <u>we are all running</u> like this [refers to a scene in "Lion King" animation film] these days ...;-)'

In order to fortify fellowship, both Carla and Alkis employ constructive strategies realized in two ways. First, through 'functionalization' (van Leeuwen 1996), namely by referring to their peers in terms of their occupation or role: *translators* in Carla's case and *msmpartάλια* (msmwrecks) in Alkis's. This is a term that he has coined himself: *msm* stands for MSc in Services Management (the degree he was studying for) plus the Greek slang word *παρτάλι* (partáli) which can be rendered as *wreck*, someone in a bad physical or mental condition. Apart from joking on his and his fellow students' tiredness because of their intensive study, Alkis also chooses the word *partali* to pun on the fact that they were studying part-time for their degree. Second, via the 'we' inclusive pronouns (*many happy returns to us* and *we are all running*), Carla and Alkis refer to other translators and fellow MSc students as a generally conceived group with which they are affiliated in terms of common activities.

Membership can also be evoked using Facebook software facilities such as tagging and photo sharing. Starting with tagging, Figure 6.13 represents a lifetime event, that is to say Alkis's graduation day, as created by one of his fellow students who tagged him together with sixteen other people writing *And history repeats itself... We were grumbling, we didn't have time, we were shouting, we just wanted it to end and now... :(Love you, let's move on to new things :)*. Alkis's friend here, in juxtaposition with Examples 6.26 and 6.27, makes an individuated use of inclusive 'we', as she refers to specific tagged individuals to report their common experience as postgraduates.

My final example treats membership on the basis of sharing visuals. Figure 6.14 is posted to Helen's Wall by an EAP colleague from the UK and portrays a placard-waving demonstrator. His message is in Spanish and is translated as: 'Being a professor and not supporting students is a pedagogical contradiction.' The colleague anchors in his background knowledge of Helen participating

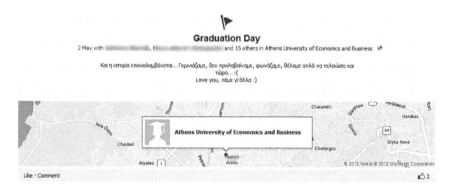

Graduation Day
2 May with ▬▬▬▬, ▬▬▬▬▬▬▬ and 15 others in Athens University of Economics and Business

Και η ιστορία επαναλαμβάνεται... Γκρινιάζαμε, δεν προλαβαίναμε, φωνάζαμε, θέλαμε απλά να τελειώσει και
τώρα...:(
Love you, πάμε γι'άλλα :)

FIGURE 6.13 *Alkis tagged on his graduation day event with other fellow students (2 May 2012).*

in demonstrations in Athens (see Chapter 4). He does not straightforwardly assign her a label but rather combines the picture with the simile *como tú* (*like you*), to communicate – as becomes apparent in his subsequent comment – that the depicted professor is like Helen, and not the other way round, framing her as an absolute archetype of teacher-fighter.

Belonging to a specific professional and/or educational group can be expressed via an abundance of discourse means including pronouns (we, you), tropes (rhetorical questions, similes), and functionalization references, either formal (e.g. translators) or informal and amusing (msmwrecks). Facebook brings the novelty of nominating members of these groups through the facility of tagging. Image sharing, on the other hand, complements and augments membership evocation.

FIGURE 6.14 *Post to Helen's Wall by a colleague.*

Projecting professional and scholarly images on Facebook

According to Gini (1998: 708), 'We are known and we know ourselves by the work we do.' This chapter documented and interpreted a multitude of different modes in which Facebook participants can be defined by their work in relation to their professional and educational settings and backgrounds. These modes were identified as formal or informal, serious or humorous, conscious or unconscious, meticulous or spontaneous, promotional or discreet, occurring at any time of the day and more often than not without the user being physically located within the institution. The analysis focused on three core facets of professional and educational identities: (1) actions and activities, (2) knowledge and (3) relations. More specifically, it was shown how my informants utilize Facebook to

- announce and inform about accomplished, current or upcoming actions and undertaken tasks;

- complain about work;

- chat about work and study topics;

- promulgate their work;

- publicize their achievements;

- organize and promote events;

- inspire their network with interesting posts;

- share knowledge;

- gain new cognitive capacity;

- ask for information;

- buttress solidarity and collegiality through endorsing, extolling, giving credit and constructing collectives.

Depending on contexts and audiences, the participants appear as doers, advisers, advertisers, experts, learners, supporters, unfolding the attributes of being involved, committed, hard-working, knowledgeable, cooperative, ethical and modest.

Three key points emerge from the examples discussed in this chapter. First, Facebook provides a space for various confluences of personal, with the professional and educational identities. Carla's, Helen's and Alkis's cases corroborate this point. Although Carla has set up a profile exclusively for professional reasons, her professional identity is so powerful that it permeates her personal profile as well. That Helen works in an educational institution, teaching and researching what she has studied, namely linguistics, results in an intermingling of her professional and educational identities in her posts. Alkis, on the one hand, has accumulated valuable expertise both from his BA in translation and his MSc in management. On the other hand, working full-time during the first year of his MSc studies meant that he had 'simultaneously two social identities (or two social roles) in relation to work society: one of an employee and the other of a university student' (Moore 2006: 156). Alkis's composite identification with many roles is uniquely brought out and reflected in his postings.

Second, Facebook, by virtue of its architecture, functions as a crucial forum to display, monitor, co-construct, gain and mediate expertise. By exploring its affordances (e.g. links, images, events), users create new and versatile possibilities for collaborative knowledge creation and learning in 'a friendly, supportive, and relatively safe environment' (Barton and Lee 2013: 130–1). The kind of learning that takes place on Facebook is informal and unfettered. As such, it enables and invites participants' socialization in the learning process and the acquisition of new identities. Such an observation has implications of paramount importance for research too. Facebook is not only a research site but also a research tool in itself. Consider, for instance, the inventive way in which Alkis utilized Facebook to find participants for his research (Figure 6.10). Facebook also allows more types of learning among informants themselves. After reading an earlier incarnation of this chapter, Alkis wrote me back that he found Romanos's liked page TheLAMP.gr (mentioned in Table 6.2) very interesting, and clicked 'Like' on the page as well.

Lastly, apart from an interactive inventory of activities and a dynamic knowledge depository, we saw that Facebook can function as a gateway for self-expression in cases of heavy workload or unwillingness to work. In the following chapter, I focus on Facebook as a venue for stance-taking, that is, expressing emotions, thoughts, opinions and assessments.

Professional and educational identity: Why and how

The fact that Carla maintained a separate profile for professional reasons turned my attention to professional identity. Alkis and Gabriel often shared experiences and views in relation to higher education studies, so I could not disregard educational identity. The examples chosen for this chapter were coded on the basis of

- operative verbs (e.g. *study, teach*);

- decisional utterances (e.g. *I'll keep you posted*);

- nouns specific to profession and education (e.g. *book, dissertation, presentation, research, office, graduation, university*);

- references to bodily aspects related to work (e.g. *I'm bored, I'm sleepy*);

- role categorization (e.g. *translators, all those still marking essays*);

- questions (e.g. *What do you reckon?*);

- imperatives (e.g. *read this*);

- presuppositions (e.g. *the reviews are dithyrambic again*);

- assessments on one's work (e.g. *congratulations*);

- wishes that refer to professional/academic success;

- inclusive pronouns (e.g. *we are all running like this these days*);

- URLs related to users' fields of expertise;

- (visual) promotional content (e.g. invitations to events).

ACTIVITY 6.1: BIRTHDAY/NAME DAY WISHES AND IDENTITY

In this chapter as well as in Chapter 5, we saw how birthday wishes can be related to place, age and professional/educational identity. Wishes via Facebook constitute an important genre for the co-construction of identity as, apart from the wish per se, we typically have access to the wished person's response. Collect from your Timeline examples of birthday and/or name day wishes that you have received together with your responses to these wishes.

1 What is the content of these wishes?

2 Do they express solidarity? Are they potentially intrusive (e.g. revealing information about you that you did not wish to be there)?

3   Do your friends construct particular images of you within their
    wishes?

4   How do you respond to wishes that refer to other matters related
    to you other than your birthday or name day?

5   Do you think that wishing ties Facebook to a long tradition of
    social practices?

ACTIVITY 6.2: COMPLIMENTING AND MODESTY

Facebook is often seen as a scene of boasting and narcissism. This chapter has gone some way towards showing how modesty is instrumental in praising and building rapport online. Collect examples of complimenting behaviour from different Timelines (e.g. yours, your friends', celebrities') and examine whether there are any instances of modesty.

1   How do users accept, mitigate or deny compliments in front
    of their audience? How can this be linked to their identity?

2   Do you think modesty is an idiosyncratic discourse feature of
    particular users or a type of norm owed to the public nature
    of Facebook and the existence of a viewing audience?

Useful resources

Print

For an overall literature review of discourse in the workplace, see Holmes (2009). Gunnarsson (2009) and Schnurr (2012) offer thorough linguistic analyses of authentic data within different work environments.

Jones and Hafner (2012; Chapter 12) consider how people use digital tools to support teamwork, and how social media can be used for creating a sense of belonging and community in large organizations as well as for career advancement and professional development. Darics's (2015) volume casts light on how CMC technologies (email, IM, blogs, Twitter, online reviews) affect institutional discourse practices and meaning-making in the professional workplace. Papacharissi (2009) examines LinkedIn as the predominant social network service with 'professional taste ethos', while van Dijck (2013) provides a comparative interface analysis between Facebook and LinkedIn concerning online self-presentation affordances. Gillen (2014; Chapter 6) gives a systematic account of how a sports journalist constructs his professional identity on Twitter. Mak and Chui (2014) address how colleagues make use of Facebook status updates to perform workplace talk and negotiate power outside the workplace and afterwork hours from the perspective of impoliteness. Interesting insights on the Group function of Facebook in facilitating learning can be found in Barton and Lee (2013: 158–9, 186–9).

Web

Language in the Workplace Project
www.vuw.ac.nz/lals/lwp/

Tips and resources to take advantage of social media for professional purposes
http://wersm.com/

7

Stance-taking and identity on Facebook

A few preliminaries

ΔΕΝ ΑΝΤΕΧΩ ΑΛΛΟ ΤΑ ΔΙΕΘΝΗ ΛΟΓΙΣΤΙΚΑ ΠΡΟΤΥΠΑ ΛΕΜΕ
'I SAY I CAN'T STAND ANYMORE THE INTERNATIONAL
ACCOUNTING STANDARDS!!!!'

ααα, τον είπα κι εδώ τον πόνο μου!
'aaah, I confessed my pain here too!'

The example above gives a fine foretaste of what is to come in this chapter. Carla, in one of her posts, is referring to accountancy issues (e.g. bookkeeping and VAT) that impinge on all Greek translators who work as freelancers. Apart from the phrases *I can't stand anymore* and *my pain*, her frustration is also fortified by capitalization. Notably, Carla's *here too* suggests that she views Facebook as a meta-friend. The feeling that Facebook becomes a 'witness' to her suffering turns out to be alleviating and cathartic in its own right (see also Miller 2011: 172).

The value of Facebook as a platform to communicate stances, that is, feelings, thoughts, opinions and evaluations, is also pointed up in the interviews by Alkis and Helen:

> *I feel that [on Facebook] I have many ways to express many things for which I'm not probably given the chance or the stimuli to express in the rest of my daily life.*

(Alkis)

> *Facebook has many functions for me*
> *you get a picture of what is going on in the world – which is not filtered by the official media*
> *or some people's personal opinion*
> *some postings are food for thought*
> *you read extreme opinions which in other circumstances you would never hear*
> *and you exercise in argumentation even if you don't do it explicitly*

(Helen)

Alkis believes that Facebook encourages self-expression in miscellaneous ways outclassing other domains of externalization in his daily life. Another major asset of Facebook, as is suggested by Helen, is that it offers the unique opportunity not only to encounter and access others' personal opinions, be that interesting, alternative, or provocative, but also to engage in the process of structuring and developing arguments.

In the contemporary social media landscape, with the perpetual user-produced and user-consumed content, stances have found fertile soil to thrive. They are articulated in status updates, comments, tweets, retweets, and in patchworks of texts, video and images. They are unbridled, public or semi-public, innovative, and for the most part uncensored; yet they can now and then be hazardous having serious consequences on one's reputation and hence their life leading to breaches in personal relations or even costing them their career.

This chapter addresses one main question: What can stance-taking on Facebook tell us about identity? Here I perceive the term 'stance-taking' as suggesting that stances are something that people actively engage in. Let me provide a substantial caveat before beginning my discussion. Jaworski and Thurlow (2009b: 197) have argued that 'the stance evaluation nexus appears to permeate all aspects of meaning making, all communicative functions, and all levels of linguistic production'. In tune with them, I see stance as a thread that runs through nearly every segment in this book. From this perspective, a great proportion – if not all – of the data at hand could have been distilled through a stance filter.

Stance is pervasive in my informants' Timelines. First and foremost, the act of posting something onto Facebook is in itself already an act of stance-taking (cf. Barton and Lee 2013: 91). For example, posting photos from demonstrations in Athens indexes a political stance; sharing songs one used to listen in their adolescence indexes a nostalgic stance; reproducing a meme related to denial of work indexes a humorous stance and so on. Moreover, the language in which users choose to post constitutes an important indication of stance-marking. That Helen's status updates are written almost exclusively in English is a deliberate act of stance-taking, which involves a relation between one subject and another (see also next section), as she explains:

I'm consciously addressing an audience that doesn't necessarily know Greek or doesn't have knowledge of the Greek context

In the same vein, she opts for exchanging comments with Greeks in English because

someone who doesn't speak Greek may want to intervene
neither do I nor do [my other Greek friends] want to exclude them
... the purpose is to keep the discussion open for non-Greek speakers as well

Stances are also taken through **script-switching** (see also Androutsopoulos 2013a). For instance, in Carla's posts we can encounter different script varieties, including Engreek (English transliterated in the Greek alphabet) and Spangreek (Spanish transliterated in the Greek alphabet) as in ϑενκς (thanks) and μούτσας γράσιας (muchas gracias – thank you very much), respectively. Such blending of language and orthography is a conscious choice to create or elicit pragmatic meaning (Androutsopoulos 2013a). For instance, in transliterating *gracias* as γράσιας ('grasjas'), that is, with Latin American pronunciation, and not γράϑιας ('graϑjas'), which is the Castilian pronunciation, Carla in a way pays homage to the variety of language spoken by the authors whose literary works she translates.

Furthermore, emotional stances are continuously indexed and pushed forward by elements of typography. My participants', as well as their friends', posts and comments overflow with written signals of laughter (χαχα, haha), smileys, letter capitalizations, vowel and consonant lengthening, and exaggerated or random use of punctuation.

Lastly, my respondents repeatedly produce pastiches of prior texts and discourses. Intertextuality and interdiscursivity (see Chapter 3) are both significant resources for stance-taking with stance being centrally implicated in the creation of intertextual and interdiscursive links (Jaffe 2009: 20) (see further down, the section on cross-modal stance-taking).

It is not then overstatement to assert that the whole edifice of Facebook communication is founded upon acts of stance-taking. My decision to single out stance for this chapter was taken for purposes of conducting a more systematic and fine-grained analysis of how users express their feelings and thoughts, which are substantial parts of one's identity, zooming in on different facets of stance within Facebook's 'stance-rich' environment (Barton and Lee 2013: 31). In this endeavour, many of the examples I have selected for the present chapter refer to the Greek crisis (see Appendix). Occurring both at a sociopolitical and a personal level since 2009, the crisis and its concomitants – austerity, unemployment, political instability, rise of fascism, violence, and generally uncertainty and insecurity – heavily clouded my informants' daily life. As a result, individual stances (i.e. evaluation and expressiveness) as well as sociocultural stances (i.e. general beliefs and knowledge they shared as members of the Greek community) (see Scheibman 2007: 113) about the crisis were ubiquitous in their Facebook posts, illustrating a wide range of stance-taking modes. That said, let's start by exploring the concept of stance.

Stance

One of the most vital things people do with words is taking a stance (Du Bois 2007). The term 'stance' refers to the expression, whether by overt assertion or by inference, of a writer's or speaker's personal attitudes, feelings, beliefs, evaluations, judgements or commitment towards a precise target (Biber and Finegan 1989; Du Bois 2007; Englebretson 2007; Du Bois and Karkkainen 2012). This target can be an interlocutor, a person represented in the discourse, ideas represented in the discourse or other texts (Kiesling 2011). Stance, therefore, is an umbrella term underneath which various linguistic features can be gathered like modality, evaluation, **evidentiality**, **hedging**, politeness, appraisal and **metadiscourse** (Lampropoulou and Myers 2012). Yet, stance, as Du Bois (2007: 163) has pithily remarked, is not only a linguistic act but also a social act:

> Stance is a public act by a social actor, achieved dialogically through overt communicative means, of simultaneously evaluating objects, positioning subjects (self and others), and aligning with other subjects, with respect to any salient dimension of the sociocultural field.

So, in any given stance statement, there are four major components: (1) the person expressing the stance (the stance-taker); (2) the topic under discussion (the stance object); (3) the resources being drawn upon (e.g. evaluative lexis, modal verbs, punctuation, typography, different languages) and (4) the addressee (the reader or the hearer in any stance-taking situation) (Barton and Lee 2013: 87).

A central notion pertinent to stance-taking is that of alignment (or disalignment) (Du Bois 2007), namely our lining up (or not lining up) with others' attitudinal assessments, beliefs and assumptions. As Martin and White (2005: 95) have contended, when people take stances,

> they not only self-expressively 'speak their own mind', but simultaneously invite others to endorse and to share with them the feelings, tastes or normative assessments they are announcing. Thus declarations of attitude are dialogically directed towards aligning the addressee into a community of shared value and belief.

Stance thus is always an act of self-presentation and social judgement via which we express something not only about ourselves but also about others (as being or not being like us), and in this fashion we inevitably say something about our view of the world (Thurlow and Jaworski 2011: 245).

The springboard for my discussion is Jaffe's (2009: 10) argument that 'linguistic stance can be read as a more or less direct sign of a position, identity, or role with which an individual wishes to be associated'. Being an advocate of stance as a performative notion, I concur with Jaffe that from a stance-based angle identity is seen 'as discursively constructed rather than fixed' (ibid.: 11). Understanding stance-taking acts is vital in understanding how identities are constructed on Facebook (see also Barton and Lee 2013: 31). But before that step, it is indispensable to explore the facilities that Facebook offers to that purpose.

Facebook affordances and stance-taking

'What's on your mind', comments, 'Like'

The mobilization of stances on Facebook is triggered by its built-in features: (1) the prompt 'What's on your mind', (2) the system of comments and (3) the 'Like' button. The vast majority of stance instances is obviously found in the user's status update, that is, their answer to 'What's on your mind'. The removal of the original prompt 'What are you doing right now?' and the obligatory 'is', and its replacement by 'What's on your mind' in July 2008 has allowed greater linguistic flexibility to the participants as the sentence structures became much more varied, longer and creative (Lee 2011). So, Facebook itself urges users to write about, reflect upon and share their intimate feelings, responses to their life experiences and/or views of the world and the very fact that they decide on doing it, as previously pointed out, is a matter of taking a stance.

Apart from the prompt modification, the whole Facebook experience was further enhanced by the addition of the comment function and the 'Like' button, in February 2009. These changes in template have been conducive to the evolution of attitudinal styles in Facebook establishing it as a site for fostering 'affective talk' and hypersociality, enunciating views, emotions and projecting social connections (Page 2012: 66ff). Commenting is a major site for stance-taking since stances are not only taken by a single user, but are constantly created, expressed, discussed, negotiated and renegotiated collaboratively by a networked public (Barton and Lee 2013: 31, 88) (I will go into this in the section *Intersubjective stance-taking* further down). It is these shared evaluations that bring Facebook posters and audiences together. Clicking the 'Like' button, on the other hand, is a social activity which indicates alignment with views and preferences among Facebook friends.

For my informants, commenting and 'Like' affordances are (dis)alignment builders which can cement affiliation, confirmation, commonality, even difference:

> By clicking Like, you affiliate with (others') content

> (Helen)

> I find this whole interactivity offered by Facebook very pleasant and interesting! ... Depending on how many and who will click like or will positively comment etc. I will confirm for some of them or discover for others that we have similar tastes.

> (Alkis)

[Comments and likes] confirm what I have in common with my friends – or state our differences

(Carla)

[I use Facebook] to express what I want, not to trigger comments
I take them into account only if they come from people who know me offline

(Romanos)

Romanos underscores self-expression attaching significance only to comments offered by offline acquaintances. This is a crucial parameter for the nature of stance-taking on Facebook in comparison to other social media platforms that are wholly public and users remain anonymous or they do not know each other personally even if their full names appear in their profiles. Shared background knowledge and experiences influence profoundly how participants take stances and form their alignment and/or disalignment on certain issues.[1]

Embedding music

One significant affordance of personal expression on Facebook is the ability to embed and share music links. For DeNora (2000), music adds to our agency and enhances our everyday lives: by way of music we can indicate certain dispositions as well as attain and maintain states of feeling (what interests us in this chapter), be aided in our concentration, retrieve memories and therefore reconstitute ourselves (as demonstrated in Chapter 5). Music has come to be linked – perhaps more than any other cultural form – with the emotional dimensions of our selves (Hesmondhalgh 2008) constituting an 'authentic expression of the soul' (Machin 2010: 26). The discourses that dominate how we think and talk about music have a double mission: (1) they shape how we assess what is good and bad music, and (2) they influence the way we think about our own musical tastes and knowledge telling us something about our identity (ibid.: 13).

My respondents upload music videos on their Walls abiding by stance-driven criteria:

According to my mood and my beliefs

(Alkis)

if I listen to music (I have several songs in the pc and I don't remember them all) and there's one that I like very much maybe I'll post it

(Romanos)

Something that I listened to, something I remembered, a favourite song. It can also be something like a 'response' to a song that a friend has uploaded.

(Carla)

The mere choice and uploading of a particular song is an act of stance-taking related to users' moods, personal beliefs and tastes (*I like very much, a favourite song*) involving also alignment/disalignment with their Facebook friends (*response to a song*). As it will be immediately shown, this stance-taking becomes even clearer when users accompany the songs of their preference with comments or lyrics.

Altogether, Facebook gives rise to dynamic, composite, interactive and cross-modal forms of stance-taking (see also Barton and Lee 2013: 89). The next section starts unpacking these forms.

Modes of stance-taking on Facebook

The examples in my data set teem with two types of stance: attitudinal and epistemic. Attitudinal stance is a broad category of stance concerned with affect, judgements and personal aesthetic preferences (Biber et al. 1999: 974–75; Martin and White 2005: 42–69). Affect deals with registering positive and negative feelings. Lemke (2013) classifies feelings into three general groups. The first group refers to the somatic aspect of how we feel, what he calls 'bodily feelings' (e.g. sleepy, hungry, nauseous, energized). The second group pertains to the traditional, canonical feelings that are responsive to a specific external trigger (e.g. angry at something, afraid of something). The last group of feelings includes evaluations of the self or self-of-the-moment (e.g. proud, expectant, noble, hesitant, mystified, lonely). Judgements refer to attitudes towards people and their behaviour, which we admire or criticize, praise or condemn (Martin and White 2005: 42). Aesthetic preferences involve evaluations of semiotic phenomena and concern our 'reactions' to these phenomena (do they catch our attention? do they please us?), their 'composition' (balance and complexity), and their 'value' (how innovative, authentic, timely, etc.) (ibid.: 56). Epistemic stance, on the other hand, signals knowledge, facts, certainty, doubt, beliefs, actuality, precision or limitation; or it can indicate the source of knowledge or the perspective from which the information is given (Biber et al. 1999: 972).

More often than not, my examples do not fit neatly into just one type of stance but can construe, for instance, affect, judgement and epistemicity within the same Facebook post. So, instead of grouping them in terms of types of stance, I focus on modes of doing stance that go from the more obvious stance-marking (e.g. via verbs, adverbs, adjectives, nouns) to less obvious realizations (e.g. via rhetorical questions, irony), from verbal to visual, and from autonomous to interactive ones.

Direct stance-taking

In order to show how much is covered by direct stance-taking, I examine a series of aesthetic appreciations of music posts. Out of my five participants, the most active in posting music videos is Alkis (with Carla following), who every now and then acts like a kind of Facebook DJ uploading songs back-to-back usually in terms of genre, artist or chronological period. In Table 7.1, I have randomly selected some of Alkis's music posts just to indicate the wealth of stance devices he draws on to talk about and appreciate the emotional impact of the songs on him.

In song 1, Alkis employs appreciative lexis (*best, unearthly, wandering*), metaphor (*speaks to the soul*), and a generic 'you' pronoun (*it lifts you up*).

TABLE 7.1 Aesthetic appreciation of music and expression of emotions

Song	Artist	Alkis's stance	Translation
1. *Χρυσαλλίδα*	Mikro	Από τις <u>καλύτερες</u> στιγμές των Μίκρο. <u>Υπερκόσμιο, ταξιδιάρικο, μιλάει στην ψυχή</u>... ΚΑΙ <u>σε</u> ξεσηκώνει! :)	One of Mikro's <u>best</u> moments. <u>Unearthly, wandering, it speaks to the soul</u>... AND it lifts <u>you</u> up! :)
2. *Γέφυρα*	Mikro	Από τα <u>ΠΛΕΟΝ</u> αγαπημένα μου...	One of my <u>MOST</u> favourite...
3. *Now that I found you*	Sundayman	<u>Υπέροχη</u>, ελληνική ηλεκτρονική μουσική!	<u>Amazing</u>, Greek electronic music!
4. *Two directions*	Konstantinos B	<u>Αριστουργηματικό</u>. Κι αφιερωμένο.	<u>Masterpiece</u>. And dedicated.
5. *Μένω εκτός*	Eleftheria Arvanitaki	<u>Πόσο όμορφη</u>, <u>πόσο μαγευτική</u>, <u>πόσο ταξιδιάρικη</u> μπορεί να είναι μια μελωδία;	<u>How beautiful</u>, <u>how magical</u>, <u>how wandering</u> can a melody be?
6. *Midnight City*	M83	Lllllllove it!	

In song 2, he opts for **graduation** (Martin and White 2005) in the form of the capitalized superlative *MOST*. In songs 3 and 4, Alkis's stance is worded in terms of appreciative lexis (*amazing, masterpiece*). Song 5 includes a rhetorical question in exclamative fronting structure (*how ...*) rife with evaluative adjectives (*beautiful, magical, wandering*). Lastly, for song 6, Alkis selects the affective mental process verb *love* intensified by multiple *I*'s.

In his aesthetic appreciation of music, Alkis also takes up the affordances of the multiple languages he speaks (Greek, English, French) and devises phrases of his own verifying Thurlow's (2011) claim on the playful discursive creativity spurred by social media. Some of his representative **neologisms** are provided in Table 7.2.

Summerικο (song 1) and *dansάτο* (song 3) are cases of morphological blendings/intra-lexical switchings which consist of the English noun *summer* and the Greek adjective suffix *-ικός* to give the meaning of *summery*. Respectively, compounded of *dance* and the Greek adjective suffix *-άτος*, *dansάτο* denotes something that can be danced. In *tres xesiquotique* (song 2), he transliterates the Greek adjective *ξεσηκωτικός* (ksesikotikos), meaning uplifting, into French by adding the French suffix *-que* and the French pre-modification *très* (very). While uploading two songs, the one right after the other, Alkis wrote *wow* for the first song (song 4) and then *wower* (song 5) for the second, inventing a comparative for the exclamation. The addition of *sic* in the parenthesis is an instance of adjusted stance where Alkis constructs a humorous internal dialogue for the purposes of stance-taking creating

TABLE 7.2 Linguistic creativity in evaluations

Song	Artist	Alkis's stance	Translation
1. *Summer's All Around*	Shaya, HouseTwins & Slick Beats	Πολύ summerικο!!!	Very summery!!!
2. *Played-A-Live*	Safri Duo	Και κάτι très xesiquotique από τα παλιά!!	And something very uplifting from the past!!
3. *Είσαι Αλλού*	Goin Through Ft. Z-Batist	Πολύ dansάτο!:-)	Very danceable!:-)
4. *Dia Europeo de la Opera en Pamplona*	Coro 'Premier Ensemble' De Agao	Wow	
5. *We No Speak Americano*	Cleary & Harding	And WOW-ER!!!! (sic!!)	

resonance between the two stances, 'even if the alignment being created is primarily disalignment' (Damari 2010: 621). All the aforementioned evaluations are upscaled (*very*, *très*, comparative morphology *-er*).

As DeNora (2000: 74) has succinctly put it, 'Music is a material that actors use to elaborate, to fill out and fill in, to themselves and to others, modes of aesthetic agency and, with it, subjective stances and identities.' By such stances of appreciation, Alkis reworks his feelings[2] as propositions about the value of music (see also Martin and White 2005: 45) regulating himself as an 'aesthetic agent' and a 'feeling being' (DeNora 2000: 62).

Narrative stance-taking

This section offers a brief insight into how small stories (see Chapter 5) in status updates can be fortified and livened up by stance-taking. Narrative stance-taking has been defined by Georgakopoulou (2013b: 22) as

> a moment of position taking where a speaker more or less reflexively mobilizes more or less conventionalized communicative means to signal that the activity to follow, the activity underway or the activity that is indexed, alluded to, deferred, silenced is a story.

Example 7.1 treats an elaborate hilarious narrative anecdote by Carla on her sister's wedding that took place in France.

7.1
Carla [personal profile]
20 February 2011 at 16:07

όλα του γάμου δύσκολα(*) κι η νύφη γκαστρωμένη:-)[3]

(*) τρύπα στο καλσόν της νύφης την παραμονή – η τιτάνια δανεική καφετιέρα δεν δούλεψε ανήμερα – τελείωσαν τα φίλτρα της οικιακής καφετιέρας – ξεχάσαμε το γαμήλιο μπουκέτο και τη μπουτουνιέρα!!!! ΑΛΛΑ το ελληνικό δαιμόνιο έσωσε την παράσταση στη γαλλική επικράτεια! γελάσαμε, κλάψαμε, συγκινηθήκαμε. άντε με το καλό και ο απόγονος της αυτοκρατορίας!

'there's nothing easy(*) in this affair:-)

(*) hole on bride's tights the previous day – the titanic borrowed coffee pot didn't work on the wedding day – we ran off filters for the domestic coffee pot – we forgot the wedding bouquet and the boutonnière!!!! BUT the Greek flair saved the show in the French territory! we laughed, we cried, we were moved. may the empire's descendant [be born]!'
13 people like this

Carla here inhabits the discourse identities of both a teller of the story and an assessor or evaluator (Georgakopoulou 2007) of the reported events, who is concerned with their point. She mobilizes the asterisk, which alludes to the typographic convention used in books for explanatory reasons, to send readers to the story that is about to follow. All her narrative comes as a footnote on *nothing easy*. Carla provides a list of events with a gloss already given to her readership on how to interpret them. She then takes up a powerful attitudinal stance offering a positive judgement on the Greek guests' capacity to save the situation augmented by the capitalized *BUT* and the metonymy the *Greek flair*. Her canonical feelings, in Lemke's (2013) terms, are then crystallized into the three mental verbs *laughed*, *cried*, *were moved* in a 'we-inclusive' form. Additional warm feelings are encoded in her wish regarding the forthcoming childbirth in which she likens the family to an empire connoting strength and robustness.

CMC-specific stance-taking

As noted in the introduction of this chapter, one stylistic device that is used over and over again in computer-mediated environments and can mark a stance is the smiley or the most recent **emoji**. Figure 7.1 presents a post by Alkis. He has uploaded another user's amateur video which shows clashes among Greek protesters and riot police on 29 June 2011, as the Greek parliament was voting to accept the European Union's austerity measures. Alkis's abhorrence, disappointment and sadness, namely his affective stance, because of the Greek police violence are condensed into the naked, self-contained sad smiley:-(.

Figure 7.2 depicts one of Helen's posts which links to a BBC article on how the Spanish village of Rasquera decided to germinate cannabis in an

FIGURE 7.1 *Affective stance inscribed in a smiley.*

effort to clear its 1.3 million euros debt. Compared to the previous example, the smiley here does not signal an emotional reaction to a specific trigger. It is rather used as an indication of the force of the textual utterance that it accompanies (Dresner and Herring 2010). Helen is not serious about the content of the message *the Spanish showing us the way out of the crisis*. It is the tongue-hanging smiley:p which indicates that the force of her words is sarcastic.

Stance-taking with audience in mind

I mentioned earlier that stance-taking on Facebook can have a detrimental impact on one's impression formation as posts are a persistent written record in (semi)public view. In this section I am looking at how Helen's hedging evinces that she is well aware of her audience's existence.

The previous chapter defined professional identity as a constellation of values, motives and experiences. Nevertheless, within an era of deep crisis and high unemployment, such a constellation can be neither stable nor enduring for Greeks. The impact of losing one's job is financial (inability to cope with austerity and taxation) and psychological (insecurity and fear for the future). Helen, in Examples 7.2 and 7.3, tackles the fragility of professional identities activating the mechanism of epistemic stance.

7.2

[Context: This is part of Helen's comment from the interaction that followed her status update *have stayed too long in this country*, discussed in Chapter 4 – Example 4.7.]

unknown whether I'll get a salary next month.. I guess I should consider myself lucky I still have one
25 May 2012 at 20:31

the Spanish showing us the way out of the crisis:p

BBC News - Spanish town to grow cannabis to pay debt
www.bbc.co.uk
The Spanish town of Rasquera has leased land to grow cannabis in order to pay its 1.3 million euros debt.

Like · Comment · 8 March at 01:04 via the BBC website ·

FIGURE 7.2 *Smiley adds sarcasm to the proposition.*

7.3

[Context: FBU1 and Helen's comments below – in English, although they are both Greeks – are sparked by an article from *The New York Times*, entitled *Greek Unemployed Cut Off From Medical Treatment*, which Helen had posted.]

FBU1 [female; Greek]: This is truly sad. Beginning to think there's no hope for our country any more.
29 October 2012 at 00:14

Helen: This was news for me too. If <u>you</u> have a job, insurance etc. <u>you</u> don't experience the full extent of this <u>destruction</u>..

'The development is new for Greeks – and perhaps for Europe, too. "We are moving to the same situation that the United States has been in, where <u>when you lose your job and you are uninsured, you aren't covered</u>," Dr. Syrigos said.' This part is <u>so scary</u>. <u>don't know</u> if there is hope, but <u>can't accept</u> that this is the future of Greece and the rest of (southern) Europe.
29 October 2012 at 00:28 · Like · 1

In Example 7.2, Helen refers to one of the fundamental benefits that a job guarantees, namely receiving a salary. Her stance seesaws from uncertainty (*unknown, I guess*) to recognition of obligation (the deontic modal verb phrase *I should consider*). In the same tone, in Example 7.3, she is concerned with the benefit of medical and health insurance. She shifts from a specific (*for me*) to a general stance (*you have, you don't experience*) to invoke a shared perception (Myers and Lampropoulou 2012) but not a shared experience as she is still a member of the workforce. Her attitudinal stance is compacted in the noun *destruction*. Grounded then on Syrigos's (Head of Greece's largest oncology department) voice, directly quoting him from the *New York Times* article, she takes an affective stance follow (Du Bois 2007: 161) to his statement (i.e. she takes a stance on his stance): *so scary*. Once more she appears uncertain (*don't know*), yet at the same time assertive (through the dynamic modal verb *can't accept*). The stance-taking devices she employs in both examples suggest that she stands in an adversarial position: on the one hand, she provisionally feels secure because she has a job with a salary and an insurance; on the other, she sees a bleak future for both employed – including herself – and unemployed Greeks.

The next examples refer to politics. Helen in Example 7.4 refers to Alexis Tsipras's, president of SYRIZA (Coalition of the Radical Left – Unitary Social Front), interview at CNN before the Greek elections in June 2012 during which he called Angela Merkel, the German chancellor, *Madam* instead of *Mrs*. At that time many people criticized his word choice pointing either to the fact that his English is somewhat poor or that he did it on purpose to indirectly insult the chancellor likening Europe to a brothel for which she is responsible. Helen seems to lean towards the second scenario.

7.4
Helen
19 May 2012 at 16:06

Not a <u>bad</u> idea at all to refer to Merkel as a Madam (aka brothel keeper) (the <u>most amusing</u> part in Tsipras CNN interview, <u>I thought</u>)
2 people like this

Not a bad idea is case of disclaim (Martin and White 2005), that is to say, negation which, from a dialogistic perspective, introduces in an alternative manner her positive positioning and thus ratification towards the event: it is a good idea to refer to Merkel as Madam. Helen here voices Tsipras's stance to take a stance follow, in other words, to align with his negative connotations regarding Merkel. The cognitive verb *thought*, on the other hand, functions as a hedge that mitigates the force of her utterance: something was amusing in Tsipras's interview (his English or his arguments perhaps) out of which the label attached to Merkel was the most amusing of all.

In Example 7.5, Helen expresses a series of judgements. First, she addresses in a generic way (*you*) the affective position of Greek voters (*shocked*). Second, she condemns the fascist political party, Golden Dawn, calling them *thugs* while she challenges other parties' and politicians' tenets with the pre-modifying adverb *supposedly*, implying that their moderation is nothing but a smokescreen. Her belief that there were serious problems in the Greek political scene (rendered through the iceberg metaphor) prior to Golden Dawn's rise is softened with the hedge *I'm afraid* via which she does not wish to impose her opinion on her audience.

7.5
Helen
7 May 2012 at 22:52

Those of you who are <u>shocked</u> with the entrance of the far right fascist <u>thugs</u> in the Greek parliament, please check again the racist, xenophobic, nationalistic discourse of <u>supposedly</u> more moderate parties and politicians. <u>I'm afraid</u> these neo Nazis are just the tip of the iceberg. ...
4 people like this

While interviewing Helen, I was taken by surprise when she posed the following question:

can I ask you something that puzzles me
do you believe that the political part appears in my profile
in an explicit or implicit way

Her posts abound in obvious sociopolitical content, so she should not need to ask if it is implicit. What matters is that she is very careful with how she commits herself to this content. As the previous examples indicated, she tends to downgrade the certainty of her statements via low modality choices (e.g. *I guess, I don't know, I'm afraid*), which 'can be seen as part of the process of texturing self identity' (Fairclough 2003: 166). With this texturing, she also textures her uptake of an audience comprised of colleagues, friends and even students of hers (see also Chapter 8).

Indirect stance-taking

Thus far stances were actualized by means of particular lexical items (verbs, adjectives, nouns, pronouns), stylistic choices (smileys, capitalization, asterisk), grammatical structure (exclamative fronting structure), tropes (metaphor, metonymy) and morphological formations (comparatives, superlatives, word blendings and intra-lexical switchings). This section probes into ways of taking stances that move beyond the word and sentence level, and rely on how Facebook users perceive language use in context. Consider Example 7.6.

7.6

Helen

22 April 2012 at 01:04

Who attends these pre-election speeches in Greece? Are these real people?
2 people like this

According to Myers (2010b: 109), rhetorical questions always express a stance. Helen phrases two rhetorical questions as regards voters. In this manner, she directs readers to take up her view that since Greek people are disappointed by domestic policies, it is flagrant contradiction for them to attend political speeches. Her underlying implication in *real* is that either these people live in ivory towers, oddly detached from the ongoing plight, or that they serve clientelistic relationships.

The same device is deployed by Romanos:

7.7

Romanos

11 May 2011 at 11:13

Otan pas na trakareis tin mprostini sou mixani, epeidi afise to gkazi gia na kanei to stauro tou pernontas apo ekklisia, ti kantilia prepei na tou katevaso kai poso ta aksizei?

'When you are about to crash the motorcycle in front of you, because he left the accelerator to cross himself when passing outside a church, how much should I swear his head off and how much does he deserve it?'
4 people like this

His rhetorical question *how much should I swear his head off and how much does he deserve it?* conveys a stance of moral judgement which strengthens his point of view presenting it as obvious. Through the generic usage of *you* (*you are about to crash, the motorcycle in front of you*), Romanos constructs a relationship of alignment with his addressees inviting them to understand and agree with his implied proposition: 'Of course the other driver deserves strong swearing, otherwise they would have an accident.' His bad temper is indirectly encoded in the Greek lexical item *kantilia* (literally translated as *vigil lamps*, metaphorically equivalent to *colourful language*), a slangy term with religious connotations,[4] which refers to grossly offensive words uttered when someone is in sheer exasperation.

In addition to the rhetorical questions discussed above, another especially powerful rhetorical figure used by Facebook participants to flag their attitude (often used when talking about crisis issues) is irony. Example 7.8 is a comment extracted from a longer bantering interaction occurring in Alkis's profile. At some point, after writing that he is a *natural-born troller*, his sister commented that he is a *natural-born trolley* attaching him the photo of a trolleybus. This was Alkis's answer:

7.8

ΧΑΧΧΑΧΑ!!! Τώρα που είμαι στο <u>σταυροδρόμι</u> της επιλογής δουλειάς (από την <u>βεντάλια</u> των <u>επιλογών</u> που ανοίγονται μπροστά μου) μόλις με βοήθησες να επιλέξω το επάγγελμα του μέλλοντός (μου).

'HAHHAHA!!! Now that I'm at <u>crossroads</u> in choosing a job (from the <u>array of choices</u> that are open in front of me) you've just helped me choose the job of (my) future.'
8 February 2012 at 14:25

At the zenith of crisis, encapsulated in Alkis's *now*, offers of jobs are scarce and usually involve posts that have nothing to do with the candidates' prior experience or knowledge. Alkis, with a background in translation and marketing, self-mocks that he might work as a trolleybus driver. For many job seekers, choosing something simply to make a living may resemble a cul-de-sac. Alkis is cynically referring to this situation as a *crossroads* and as an *array of choices* while in reality new job opportunities are very limited.

In a similar fashion, Carla, in Example 7.9, incorporates in her storytelling irony together with swearing.

7.9
Carla [personal profile]
28 April 2012 at 03:33

κάτι μάθαμε και σήμερα: όταν το κλειδί ξαφνικά δεν μπαίνει στην κλειδαριά της πόρτας του οδηγού, σημαίνει ότι σου έχουν διαρρήξει το αυτοκίνητο:-)

[downtown, Εδουάρδου Λω και Σταδίου, παρασκευή βράδυ κάπου μεταξύ 21.30-23.00]

πι.ες. προς <u>διαρρήκτας</u>: ευχαριστώ που μου αφήσατε το ραδιο/cd-player ΚΑΙ τα cd μου!!! ελπίζω να <u>βρείτε</u> κάτι να κάνετε με τα λιγοστά άπλυτα ρούχα που <u>πήρατε</u>;-) <u>πόρκα μιζέρια</u>!

'we've learnt something today: when suddenly the key does not turn in the lock of the driver's door, it means that they have broken into your car:-)

[downtown, Edward Law and Stadiou St., Friday night between 21.30-23.00]

ps to <u>burglars</u>: thanks for leaving me the radio/cd-player AND my cds!!! I hope <u>you found</u> something to do with the few dirty clothes <u>you've taken</u>;-) <u>porca miseria</u>!'
6 people like this

Carla reports how, where and approximately at what time she found out that her car had been burgled. Her narrative ends with the Italian interjection *porca miseria*, transliterated in Greek, which is equivalent to *bloody hell*, *damn* or *blast it!*. Emotional outbursts in the form of swearing are hard to identify as affect or judgement on their own (Martin and White 2005: 68–9; Thelwall 2008: 88). *Porca miseria*, though, is preceded by another less transparent stance. Although Carla knows it is virtually impossible for the thieves to view her Facebook status, she addresses them in second person in her postscript (which functions similarly to the asterisk device in Example 7.1) calling them *διαρρήκτας* (diariktas) in lieu of *διαρρήκτες* (diariktes), a form of vocative address met in past formal Greek contexts. This stylistic marker is nowadays almost exclusively used by Greeks for mocking purposes. Carla, therefore, not only indexes her vexation as a victim of burglary but also a shard of irony towards the perpetrators' wretched condition (later on in the thread she speculates they were drug addicts) since they took her dirty clothes leaving intact other valuables in the car.

Cross-modal stance-taking

Facebook offers users the affordances to go beyond mere verbal statements and piece together different semiotic modes in communicating their stances. For instance, they can use visuals to enhance the intended meaning of their stance or they can draw on and experiment with stances already encapsulated in particular cultural items (e.g. memes and song lyrics/titles).

Complementing stances with visuals

Painter and Martin (2011) have proposed the term 'intermodal complementarity' to describe the degree to which the metafunctions and the affordances of each modality commit to the creation of meaning. In Example 7.10, Carla articulates a rather mundane state she is into: sleepiness. However, she opts for doing it in an unconventional and playful way by coalescing language with a URL. Carla's stance is taken through the vehicle of the URL, which functions as a kind of puzzle for the readers (Myers 2010b: 49). To fill in the missing information and decipher her state, they have to follow the link that leads to the image of a sleepy dwarf from the *Snow White and the Seven Dwarfs* animated film.

7.10
Carla [personal profile]
7 January 2011 at 16:24

feeling reaaally

http://1.bp.blogspot.com/_5BV_YADVD7o/RpOTrsopWDI/
AAAAAAAAAuM/5jspfDWcpug/s1600-h/sleepy.jpg
1 person likes this

Gabriel in Figure 7.3 devised an alternative way to announce his gratitude after the wishes he received on his 22nd birthday. He took a selfie smiling in front of his computer and wrote in his opening comment: *Εγώ πολύ χαρούμενος μετά από τόσες ευχές!* (*Me very happy after so many wishes!*).

His happiness is amplified with the quality booster *very* and of course by the visual proof of his mood, that is, his smile.

Recycling ready-made stances

Stances do not necessarily have to be one's own words. Stance-takers can rely entirely on intertextual materials to embrace a gamut of attitudes and beliefs, which even though they are not explicitly spelt out, they are relayed very

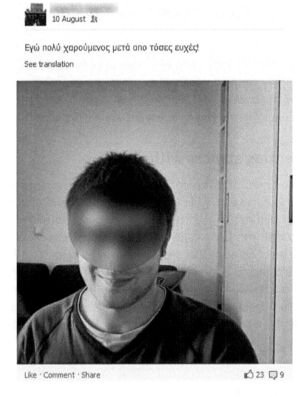

10 August

Εγώ πολύ χαρούμενος μετά απο τόσες ευχές!

See translation

Like · Comment · Share   23   9

FIGURE 7.3 *Gabriel responds to birthday wishes.*

forcefully. Helen, by way of illustration, shares an internet meme (Figure 7.4). Facebook is based to a great extent on such propagation and recirculation of content that is made by users for users. A meme conveys in itself certain ideas and ideologies. When reproducing a meme, users imitate[5] a certain position that they find appealing in order to show alignment (or disalignment) with the stance that is represented or implied.

Helen shares this meme to problematize the perception of what a Greek is thought to be (rioter for the police, lazy for other countries, vandal for the media, payer for banks, dreamer for him/herself, protester who stands up for basic goods in reality). Anchoring in my ethnographic observation, there are biographical snippets inscribed in this meme: Helen participates in demonstrations herself (see also Chapter 4); she holds a PhD and feels insecure as regards her professional future (as revealed earlier in Example 7.2).

Right after the election results in May 2012, according to which no party won an absolute majority, with Golden Dawn however entering the Greek parliament for the first time, also pointed out by Helen in Example 7.5. Romanos shared on Facebook Figure 7.5, while Alkis chose Figure 7.6 as a profile picture.

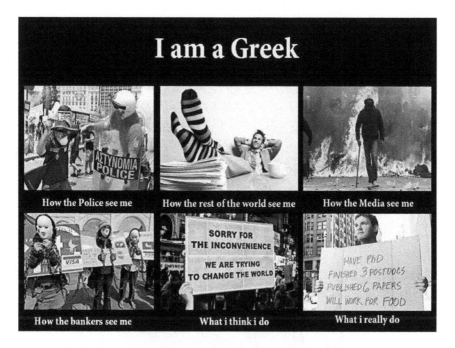

FIGURE 7.4 *Sharing a meme to show alignment.*

Figure 7.5 is a strip by Arkas, a renowned Greek comics artist, which reads: *It's great fortune to be born Greek and it's great fortune to die [being] Greek! ... The in-between, however, is great misfortune!* Aligning with the strip's punch line, Romanos shares this image to exude his frustration because of the election outcome. Alkis, on the other hand, with Figure 7.6, adopts a stance of aversion suggesting that Golden Dawn members should do what Hitler did, namely to kill themselves.

We saw previously how users take stances towards music. But they can also take stances through music, and particularly through lyrics, to evaluate a certain state of affairs. During times of economic hardship and threat (like the Greek crisis), individuals consume, listen to and share music to contemplate social issues (Pettijohn and Sacco 2009). Facebook is a venue to share music to that purpose.

As illustrated in Figure 7.7, Helen uploaded the Greek song Σιγά μην κλάψω (*I won't cry*) to embody her stance towards pre-election talks one day before the elections in Greece on 17 June 2012. The chorus lyrics[6] of the song talk about a person who is told by others that he is unable to change the prevailing situation. But this person says he will overcome the difficulties without crying and without being afraid. Combining Helen's comment, *dealing with pre-election terror talk*, with the lyrics, we can deduce that she draws a kind of parallelism between the song's others and the Greek politicians as well as

FIGURE 7.5   *Sharing a comic strip to show alignment.*

FIGURE 7.6   *Changing profile picture to show alignment.*

shared a link.
16 June

ΓΙΑΝΝΗΣ ΑΓΓΕΛΑΚΑΣ ΣΙΓΑ ΜΗΝ ΚΛΑΨΩ
www.youtube.com

ΓΙΑΝΝΗΣ ΑΓΓΕΛΑΚΑΣ ΣΙΓΑ ΜΗΝ ΚΛΑΨΩ

Θα πάω να χτίσω μια φωλιά στον ουρανό θα κατεβαίνω μόνο αν θέλω... γελάσω

Unlike · Comment · Share   👍 1 💬 1

👍 You like this.

dealing with pre-election terror talk
16 June at 14:07 · Like

FIGURE 7.7 *Lyrics do stance-taking in Helen's post.*

shared a link.
23 December 2012

Χίλια ευχαριστώ σε όλους τους φίλους για τις όμορφες ευχές που αφήσατε στον τοίχο μου! Να είστε όλοι καλά, γεροί και δυνατοί! Καλές γιορτές σε όλους και καλή ΔΥΝΑΜΗ για το 2013!!!!

See translation

Λουκιανός Κηλαηδόνης- Δεν μας τρομάζουν Τα νέα μέτρα...
www.youtube.com

Επίκαιρο, από το '79 έχουν περάσει παραπάνω από 30 χρόνια και ακόμα τα ίδια. Ουδέν μονιμότερο από τα

Like · Comment · Share   👍 5 💬 1

FIGURE 7.8 *Lyrics do stance-taking in Carla's post (from her professional profile).*

the song's narrative persona and herself as a conscious Greek citizen. It is as if the politicians threaten and warn people that they have no other choice of salvation but voting for them; the citizens are helpless without them and they are incapable of changing the situation on their own. Helen, though, chooses this song to yield a fearless stance towards the upcoming elections.

In Figure 7.8, Carla writes: *Thousand thanks to all my friends for the beautiful wishes you wrote on my wall! Wish health to all of you! Merry Christmas and be STRONG for 2013!!!!* The interesting bit in this post is the music link she attaches to which there is no reference at all in her opening. The title of the song is *Δε μας τρομάζουν τα νέα μέτρα* (*We are not scared of the new measures*).[7] Here it is the song title that does the stance-taking for Carla inviting her audience to collude in the co-construction of her understated stance: we are not afraid of austerity.

Intersubjective stance-taking

The true value of any stance is shaped 'by its framing through the collaborative acts of co-participants in dialogic interaction' (Du Bois 2007: 141). In order to explore deeper the intersubjective, that is, interactional and collaborative, nature of stance, I will lean on two different interactions. The first interaction (Example 7.11) is based on a humorous evaluation of the self. The second interaction (Example 7.12), lengthier and more elaborate, touches on mediating stance-taking towards crisis-related issues.

Humorous stance-taking

Romanos makes in his status a self-deprecating remark, a negative self-judgement of propriety that attends to how ethical someone is (Martin and White 2005: 52–3), horrible in this case.

7.11
Romanos
6 September 2011 at 13:55

I'm a <u>horrible</u> person....
1 person likes this

1. FBU1 [female]: Megalh idea exeis gia ton eauto sou!
'You have a big idea about yourself!'
6 September 2011 at 14:00

2. FBU2 [male; Greek]: we know hehhehe
6 September 2011 at 14:02

3. FBU3 [male; foreigner]: I thought you just look horrible.
6 September 2011 at 14:29

4. Romanos: No, I'm also <u>rotten</u> on the inside....
6 September 2011 at 14:31 · Like · 1

5. FBU4 [female; Greek]: And now you discovered it? apart from horrible u r also <u>idiot</u>!
6 September 2011 at 15:44

6. Romanos: Me krazeis opote vreis eukairia giati me zileueis. Eksalou, poios sou milise?
'You take a dig at me whenever you have the chance because you're jealous of me. Besides, who talked to you?'
6 September 2011 at 15:45

7. FBU2: htan na mhn to paradexteis,twra thn evapses lol
'It was not until you admitted it, now you'll suffer the consequences lol'
6 September 2011 at 15:46

8. FBU1: Όπως και να χει όμως παρ όλα αυτα εχεις εξαιρετικους φιλους που σε υποστηριζουν με γλυκες κ ειλικρινεις κουβεντες και σε βοηθουν να διατηρεις επαφη με την πραγματικοτητα.
'In any way, however, you have great friends that support you with sweet and honest words and they help you to stay in touch with reality.'
6 September 2011 at 15:46

9. Romanos: <u>Isxuei</u>, an kai den kserete tin aformi tis dilosis …
'<u>True</u>, although you don't know the reason behind the statement …'
6 September 2011 at 16:13

10. FBU5 [male]: xaxaxaxa … eisai <u>o pio teleiwmenos apesios</u> pou xerw kai gelaei me thn katantia ton allwn!!!!!!
'hahaha. … you're <u>the most hopeless awful person</u> I have known who laughs with others' predicament!!!!!!'
6 September 2011 at 17:39

FBU1, FBU2, FBU3 and FBU4 take Romanos's statement at face value and start offering their own judgement about him in a teasing manner: *you have a big idea about yourself!* (comment 1), *I thought you just look horrible* (comment 3), *u r also idiot!* (comment 5). Romanos banters with their bantering by adding that he does not just look horrible but his inside is also rotten (comment 4). By writing *true*, in comment 9, he endorses FBU1's ironic recognition, anchored to the ongoing interaction, that he has supportive friends (comment 8). In comment 9, though, he admits that *you don't know the reason behind the statement*. Romanos is an ardent gamer – bear also in mind that he has studied video game programming. The statement *I'm a horrible person* alludes to *Portal 2*, a first person puzzle game for PlayStation 3, Xbox 360 and PC platforms, in which GLaDOS, an artificially intelligent computer system, acts as a narrator and guide for players. However, she becomes very caustic and ironic towards them throughout the game. Romanos's status rests on the following GLaDOS's voice lines: 'Well done. Here come the test results: "You are a horrible person." That's what it says. "A horrible person." We weren't even testing for that.' FBU5 knows that Romanos is entranced[8] with the particular videogame and initiates a new round of pseudonegative judgements, characterizing him as *the most hopeless awful person* he has ever met because he makes fun of his friends' misunderstanding (comment 10).

Facebook interactions like this one indicate that sometimes participants do not entirely identify with the affective stances they take but rather over-perform, play with and ironicize them to test and spark their audience's reactions.

Mediating stance-taking

The second interaction I am going into is extracted from Alkis's profile:

7.12
Alkis

Καλό μήνα και με ΠΟΛΥ ΚΑΛΗ διάθεση συνέχεια!!!!!
'Have a nice month and a VERY GOOD mood all the time!!!!!'
1 September 2012 at 14:52
10 people like this

1. FBU1 [male]: ase mas ke si palioxroma ...:P
'Leave us alone ...:P'
1 September 2012 at 15:11 · Like · 1

2. FBU2 [male]: XAXAXAXAXAXA ΡΟΙΟ ΜΗΝΑ????????????
'HAHAHAHAHAHA WHAT MONTH????????????'
2 September 2012 at 18:52

3. Alkis: Τι παίρνεις; Τον Σεπτέμβριο ντε!!:-)
'Are you taking something? September of course:-)'
2 September 2012 at 18:52

4. FBU2: APO EW KAI PERA OLOI OI MHNES IDIOI THA EINAI!!!!!!!!!!!!!!!!!!!!
'FROM NOW ON ALL MONTHS WILL BE THE SAME!!!!!!!!!!!!!!!!!!!!'
2 September 2012 at 18:53

5. Alkis: Αν είναι καλοί κι έχουμε καλή διάθεση, ας είναι! :)
'If they are good and we have good mood, let them be! :)'
2 September 2012 at 18:55

6. FBU1: ke an o Samaras valei patinia ...
'And if Samaras [the then Greek Prime Minister] puts on roller skates ...'
2 September 2012 at 18:55

7. Alkis: ΜΑ <u>ΦΤΑΝΕΙ</u> ΜΕ ΤΗΝ ΑΡΝΗΤΙΚΟΤΗΤΑ <u>ΠΙΑ! ΕΛΕΟΣ</u>!:-D
'<u>ENOUGH</u> WITH NEGATIVITY! <u>MERCY</u>!:-D'
2 September 2012 at 18:56

8. FBU2: KALA!!!!!!!!!!!!!!!! ALLA THN AISIODOXIA POU THN VRISKEIS!!!!!!!!!!!!!!!
'OK!!!!!!!!!!!!!!!! BUT WHERE DO YOU FIND OPTIMISM!!!!!!!!!!!!!!!'
2 September 2012 at 18:56

9. FBU1: siga min exo arnitikotita epidi emina mesa olo to s-k giati den ixa lefta gia ton kafe ke na valo venzina, kseris ti orea pou esiodoksis otan trelenese?
'I don't have negativity at all because I stayed at home all the w/e because I didn't have money for the coffee and to fill [the car] up with petrol, do you know how nice is it to be optimistic when you get crazy?'
2 September 2012 at 18:57

10. Alkis: Αν αρχίσεις να φέρεσαι και να πράτεις σαν να είσαι αισιόδοξος, θα σου έρθει!! Το έχουν δοκιμάσει <u>πολλοί</u> πριν από εμάς κι έπιασε. <u>Ας μας το θυμίζουμε κι ας το εφαρμόσουμε για να το 'πάθουμε' κι εμείς!</u>;-)
'If you start behaving and acting as if you were optimistic, it will come to you!! <u>Many people</u> have tried this before us and it worked. <u>Let's remind this to ourselves and let's practice it so as it can "happen" to us</u> as well!;-)'
2 September 2012 at 18:58

11. FBU1: ne pios tope afto o Joker ston Batman?
'who said this Joker to Batman?'
2 September 2012 at 18:59

12. Alkis: Μπορούσες όμως με σχεδόν μηδέν λεφτά να καλέσεις τους φίλους σου να δείτε μια ταινία και να φάτε ποπ κόρν ή να συναντηθείτε σε άλλου φίλου/φίλης το σπίτι. <u>Για να περάσεις καλά δεν είναι ανάγκη να βγαίνεις έξω και να ξοδεύεις.</u> Κι επίσης, ας παραπονιούνται άλλοι που είναι άνεργοι, όχι <u>όσοι</u> έχουν ακόμα δουλειά, κι ας <u>μην είναι</u> τόσο καλά όσο παλιά στη <u>δουλειά τους</u>!;-)
'You could, however, with almost no money to invite your friends to watch a movie and eat pop corn or meet each other at another friend's house.

<u>To have a good time it's not necessary to go out and spend.</u> What's more, other people who are unemployed should complain, not <u>those</u> who still have a job, even if <u>they are not</u> so well-paid and secure <u>in their job</u> as in the past!;-)'
2 September 2012 at 19:00

13. FBU1: ne alla exo dania pou pira ke me sinesi plirona analoga me ton mistho mou ke tora vazoun ke ta xaratsia ke me miso mistho den mporo na pliroso oute tin Dei ke prepi na pao stin mama ksana ke na mou leei oti den ipia olo to gala mou ...
'yes but I have the loans I took out. I was prudently paying them in accordance with my salary. now they're imposing taxes and with half salary I can't pay the electricity bill. I have to go to mum again who will tell me that I don't drink all of my milk.'
2 September 2012 at 19:01

14. Alkis: Εκεί, λοιπόν, θα πρέπει να χειριστείς τη σχέση σου με τη μαμά και να βάλεις όρια για να μπορέσετε να συγκατοικήσετε αρμονικά και λειτουργικά.
<u>Φαντάσου</u> να μην είχες <u>ΟΥΤΕ</u> τον μισθό να πληρώνεις έστω και μέρος των δόσεων και να μην είχες <u>ΟΥΤΕ</u> τη μαμά να <u>σε</u> περιθάλψει και να <u>σου</u> δώσει στέγη και φαγητό. Δες τα θετικά!
'Well, you will have to handle your relationship with mum and set limits so as to be able to live together harmoniously and functionally.
<u>Imagine</u> you didn't have <u>NEITHER</u> the salary to pay even part of the installments <u>NOR</u> mum to care and give <u>you</u> accommodation and food. <u>See</u> the positive things!'
2 September 2012 at 19:03

15. FBU1: sosta ke naxa genithei stin Afriki ke na min ixa na fao epidi oi Amerikanoi theloun na poulane palia opla gia emfilious ... Trololololol
'right. if I had been born in Africa, I wouldn't have anything to eat because the Americans want to sell old weapons for civil wars ... Trololololol'
2 September 2012 at 19:04

16. Alkis: Είδες; That's the spirit! trololol!
'You see? That's the spirit! trololol!'
2 September 2012 at 19:04

17. FBU1: to na theoroume pleon to fisiologiko politeleia nomizo oti ine arosto. ... Trololololol
'I think it's sick to consider that the normal thing is nowadays a luxury ....
Trololololol'
2 September 2012 at 19:04 · Like · 1

18. FBU3 [female]: Alki paizeis to paixnidi tis xaras?

'Alkis are you playing the glad game?'
2 September 2012 at 19:07

19. FBU1: Xara agnoeite.[9]
'Gladness is missing.'
2 September 2012 at 19:07

20. Alkis: <u>Είναι πολύ άσχημο και δεν το περίμενε κανείς μας</u>. Όμως τι θα <u>κάνεις</u>; Θα <u>μεμψιμοιρείς</u> όλη μέρα ή θα <u>προσπαθήσεις</u> με όσα <u>σου</u> μένουν <u>να έχεις καλή διάθεση</u> ή έστω προδιάθεση και να <u>περνάς</u> όσο πιο <u>όμορφα</u> <u>μπορείς</u> τις μέρες και τις στιγμές <u>σου</u>; Ναι, δεν είναι ό,τι καλύτερο να ανακόπτωνται τα σχέδιά σου και οι προσπάθειες χρόνων αλλά αφού <u>αυτό είναι κάτι που δυστυχώς συμβαίνει</u>, <u>προσπάθησε</u> να κάνεις ότι καλύτερο μπορείς με όσα έχεις. Ή <u>κάτσε</u> και <u>μιζέριασε</u>, τι να σου πω...
'<u>It's very awful and none of us expected it</u>. But what are you going to do? Are you going to <u>whinge</u> all day or are you going to <u>try</u> with all that's left to you <u>to have a good disposition</u> or even predisposition and <u>enjoy</u> as much as you can your days and your moments? Yes, it's not the best to have your plans and lasting efforts thwarted but since <u>this is something which is unfortunately happening</u>, <u>try</u> and do as best you can with what you've got. Or <u>remain miserable</u>, what else can I tell you...'
2 September 2012 at 19:07

21. Alkis: Επειδή το παιχνίδι της λύπης και του άγχους δεν με έβγαλαν πουθενά, λέω να προσπαθήσω να αλλάξω παιχνίδι, ναι.
'Since the grief and stress game didn't lead me anywhere, I'm thinking of trying to change the game, yes...'
2 September 2012 at 19:07 · Like · 1

22. Alkis: <u>Δεν λέω</u> πως πατάς κουμπί και γίνεται αλλά από κάπου ξεκινάς για να αλλάξεις το όλο πράγμα. Και <u>μάλλον ξεκινάς εσύ ο ίδιος από εσένα τον ίδιο. Κλισέ;</u> <u>Δεν ξέρω. Αλλά λογικό.</u>
'<u>I don't say</u> that you press a button and it happens but you <u>start</u> from somewhere to change the whole thing. And <u>you probably start from yourself. Cliché? I don't know. But logical.</u>'
2 September 2012 at 19:09

23. FBU3: se ti diaferei i kali diathesi apo tin kali prodiathesi eeeeeeeeeeeee????????????????????
'What's the difference between good disposition and good predisposition? ahhhhhhhhhhhhh????????????????????'
2 September 2012 at 19:09

24. Alkis: Δεν ξέρω. Βερμπάλισα πάνω στο μεγαλείο του λόγου που έβγαζα.:-)

'I don't know. I exaggerated in the magnificence of the speech I was delivering.:-)'
2 September 2012 at 19:09

25. FBU3: xixixi....
'hihihi....'
2 September 2012 at 19:10

26. FBU1: giati ego den thaxo na valo petreleo fetos ke tha kriono ke tharostiso ke tha gino fimatikos ke den thaxo na doso fakelaki.
'Because I won't have money to get heating oil this year. I'll feel cold and I'll get sick. I'll become consumptive and I won't have to bribe the doctor.'
2 September 2012 at 19:10

27. Alkis: Επίσης το προδιάθεση το είπα με την έννοια ενός προάγγελου της διάθεσης ας πούμε. Αν δεν έχεις την ίδια τη διάθεση, να έχεις ψύγματά της για να ενωθούν και να σε οδηγήσουν στη διάθεση!! (το έσωσα; χαχα)
'Moreover I said predisposition in the sense of a herald of the disposition let's say. If you don't have the disposition itself, you can have nuggets of the disposition that will be linked and lead you to the disposition (is it ok? haha)'
2 September 2012 at 19:10

28. FBU3: asto to kaneis xeirotero
'forget it you make it worse'
2 September 2012 at 19:11

29. Alkis: Αν θέλεις να μιζεριάσεις και να μεμψιμοιρείς κάνε το στο inbox μου. Όχι στον τοίχο μου. Ευχαριστώ. Και βασικά μην το κάνεις καθόλου. Για σένα περισσότερο:-)
'If you want to be miserable and cavil <u>do it on my inbox</u>. Not on my wall. Thanks. And basically <u>don't do it at all</u>. For you mostly:-)'
2 September 2012 at 19:11

Interestingly, Alkis initiates with mere **_phatic communion_** (*Have a nice month and a VERY GOOD mood all the time!!!!!*), emphasized through expressive orthography (capitalization and multiple exclamation marks). Yet, in the course of the interaction, as friends weigh in the thread, he unfurls a range of stances.

The particular date he posts this status, on 1 September, is very crucial as it heralds the end of summer vacations and is usually identified with melancholy. FBU1 and FBU2, in comments 1 and 2, respectively, do not share Alkis's optimism taking an ironic stance towards him (*Leave us alone ...:P, WHAT MONTH????????????, FROM NOW ON ALL MONTHS WILL BE THE SAME!!!!!!!!!!!!!!!!!!!!*). It is comment 6 and the reference to the Greek prime minister's name (*if Samaras puts on roller skates*) that fuels the conversation on crisis. In comment 7, Alkis targets a negative evaluation (*enough, mercy*), expressed emphatically via capitalization, against their sarcastic and cynical attitude.

The remainder of the thread concerns a friendly ruckus between FBU1 and Alkis. FBU1 complains because his salary has been reduced and, as a consequence, he does not have money to go for a coffee, to fill his car with petrol, to pay his loans and bills. On top of that, he lives with his mother who still treats him as a child. Alkis, on the other hand, introduces his friend some hypothetic scenarios of how to partially overcome the difficulties.

The phrase *Many people have tried this before us and it worked* (comment 10) dramatizes his optimistic stance as he attributes the behaviour to many others, so it is not something unattainable. In line with Myers (2004: 152) and Martin and White (2005: 116), this kind of attribution of words and acts to others is a mechanism via which disagreements can be mediated since the credibility of the attributed material lies in the fact that one is speaking of experienced facts and not just personal impressions. To further enforce the boldness of his positioning, Alkis deploys a 'writer-inclusive we' (*Let's remind this to ourselves and let's practice it so as it can 'happen' to us as well!;-*).

In comment 12, he offers alternatives on how FBU1 could have entertained relying on the commonplace *To have a good time it's not necessary to go out and spend*. In a less **face-threatening** light, he employs third-person plural (*those who still have a job, even if they are not so well-paid and secure in their job as in the past*) instead of *you who still have a job even if you are not so well in your job as in the past*. Nevertheless, FBU1 continues to complain. Alkis shifts again to 'specific you' in comment 14 in order to advise and console him (*you will have, your relationship, you didn't have, give you*). He also uses imperative (*imagine, see*) to reinforce his statements as well as a neither-nor coordination (*neither the salary nor mum*) amplified by capitalization. FBU1, though, still does not seem to be convinced and keeps on ironicizing. What he writes in comment 15 is pragmatically incoherent and that is why he adds *Trololololol* at the end, the laugh (analogous to *lol*) users do after they troll (i.e. make fun of or annoy) someone in a cyber environment. Alkis sees *trololol* as an attitude to life (code-switches in English) in general that FBU1 should adopt.

The evaluation underpinning the circumlocution *It's very awful and none of us expected it* (comment 20) targets at the crisis and the general prevalent feelings of misery and insecurity, with the pronoun *us* referring metonymically to all Greeks. Alkis then shifts to an impersonal *you* and formulates a series of rhetorical questions (*But what are you going to do? Are you going to whinge all day or are you going to try … and enjoy as much as you can your days and your moments?*), which presents personal perceptions and experience as shared, or potentially shared, by a whole group of people (Stirling and Manderson 2011). The next instances of *you* apply to FBU1 (*your plans, you can, you have, tell you*). Once again, Alkis tries to knock some sense into his friend by means of imperatives (*try, remain miserable*). His last phrase (*what else can I tell you*), though, shows that he has run out of any further recommendations.

Comment 21 comes as a positive answer to the question posed by FBU3 in comment 18. The *Glad Game* alludes to Eleanor H. Porter's fictional character Polyanna and her attitude of finding something to be optimistic and glad about in every situation. Here Alkis, on the basis of his personal experience of *grief and stress*, expresses the willingness to endorse Polyanna's stance and see life from a more buoyant perspective. In comment 22, he explains how the game can be changed (*from grief to glad*) from a non-authoritarian position (*I don't say that you press*) resorting to commonplaces to invoke a shared understanding of how the world works (Myers 2004: 201): *you start from somewhere to change the whole thing, you probably start from yourself.* Remarkably, he acknowledges the taken-for-grantedness of his statement asking if it is a cliché. He offers an adjusted stance (as he did with the insertion of *sic* in Table 7.2), answering himself, encoded in a claim of ignorance (*I don't know*) which is, however, granted by a concession (*but logical*).

The joke in comment 27 is based on the closeness of the Greek words διάθεση (*disposition*) and προδιάθεση (*predisposition*), a compound word of the preposition προ- (before) and the word διάθεση. Again Alkis pleads ignorance (*I don't know*), yielding a self-sarcastic stance (*I exaggerated in the magnificence of the speech I was delivering*). Obviously, he realizes that he has made wrong usage of the two words giving a rather fluffy explanation (*If you don't have the disposition … to the disposition*) and jocularly questioning if this explanation is adequate.

In his last comment, 29, Alkis becomes more decisive and assertive wishing to give an end to FBU1's constant grumbling through imperatives (*do it, don't do it*) reminding him that if he has problems, these should be discussed privately with Alkis and not publicly on his Wall in the sight of all his friends.

The impact of crisis is an exceedingly unpleasant topic for conversation among Facebook participants and can often lead to confrontations and diametrically opposed opinions. Alkis, however, constructs himself as a mediator and a supporter (see also Norrby and Wirdenäs 2003: 256). By dint of a trove of stance devices (e.g. attribution, inclusive 'we', commonplaces, generic 'they', circumlocution, metonymy, rhetorical questions, non-authoritarian positioning, claims of ignorance), he proposes alternatives, limitations or modifications to his friend's opinions with a view to orienting the discussion towards consensus. The upshot of the foregoing analysis for stance is twofold. First, although it may not have been the poster's original aim at all, stance-taking can be triggered and provoked by friends' comments. Secondly, the way in which its multiple layers are being unfolded is highly dependent on the content of friends' comments.

Expressing the self on Facebook

Stance-taking is 'the primary discursive mechanism by which identity is realized' (Jaworski and Thurlow 2009b: 220). It may index multiple identities, multiple aspects of an identity, a single identity that endures over time, or a privileged 'core' self (Jaffe 2009: 4). The ways in which we communicate how we feel, what we think, what we like or dislike have always constituted a crucial part in our self-presentations. This chapter spotlighted these ways showing how Facebook has stretched our sense of what stance-taking is and how the participants actually mould how we see Facebook via their activities and interactions. Different Facebook affordances steer towards different – familiar, emerging and novel – ways of developing stances within the medium. These stances can be individual, sociocultural, interactional, shared, shareable or shifting. They can come in multimodal, intertextual or interdiscursive ensembles encasing, responding to and/or adjusting already circulated stances. They range from transparent (e.g. explicit emotional disclosures and appraisals) to opaque (e.g. attitudes implied in song lyrics, visuals or expressed through irony and bantering) requiring inferential work from the readers. The users' stances were not necessarily restricted to strict statements and conversations; they could also be inscribed in a single lexical item or a smiley, or choreographed in longer and heated comments, a humoristic comic strip, a meme, an unedited video, an ironic article or a lyric. What is intriguing, therefore, is not that Facebook users take stances but how they do stances to construct themselves as feeling and thinking beings.

Facebook's generic context promotes a good sense of social connection among users (Page 2012: 73). As such, it brings out the interpersonal nature of stance-taking allowing the untangling of identity claims and relations to other people. Users feel the need to talk about, reflect upon and share their emotional experiences and opinions externalizing their weariness, frustration, happiness, satisfaction, anger, disappointment or irritation. At the same time, these stances are vehicles for public performances of identity – they do not fall into the void but are taken so as to be perceived, endorsed, challenged, judged, justified, negotiated, contested or rejected by Facebook audience members. It is a bi-directional process to amuse, influence, validate, claim or disclaim.

As amply evidenced in this chapter, Facebook is not only identified with light-hearted endorsement and affirmation, but it can also function as a terrain for expressive as well as persuasive stance-taking within a period of big sociopolitical upheaval. My participants frequently use Facebook consciously to show and talk about the Greek crisis. At other times, the crisis turns up impromptu in their Facebook interactions, irrespective of their main or initial posting concern. Crisis, as a word, albeit not always overtly specified throughout the data, received highly, negatively charged evaluations such as *destruction, very awful, something which is unfortunately happening*. Crisis, as a general existing situation, was not the sole stance object. The users orient and alternate their stances towards miscellaneous stance objects: the actors responsible for the crisis (politicians), the actors who deepen the crisis (riot police, far right, voters), the repercussions of the crisis (austerity, unemployment, vulnerable welfare system), what the media report about the crisis as well as Facebook friends who take stances in relation to the crisis.

Needless to say, crisis-related stance-taking is seen most obviously in citizens' demonstrations (in placards, banners, slogans and so on). Yet, it can also be seen in these small, daily, often fragmented online gestures. My participants used Facebook to position themselves within the crisis: to express agonies, raise awareness, inform and anti-inform, understand, reflect upon, evaluate, and respond to what is happening. In doing so, they recount reflective and very powerful stories, products of their accumulated stances over time, drawing on shared experience of the crisis. Simultaneously, they point to serious issues in Greek society as well as facets of the crisis often ignored by the official Greek media. Recall Helen's statement in the opening of the chapter saying that Facebook gives 'a picture of what is going on in the world – which is not filtered by the official media'.

In this chapter, we saw that Helen expressed her worries on how politicized she appears in her profile while Alkis, in the very last example, was in favour of continuing the conversation with his friend via private messaging instead of his Facebook Wall. These two cases set the scene for the next chapter, which treats audiences and privacy.

Stance and identity: Why and how

The Greek crisis cropped up and dominated my informants' – as well as many Greeks' – Facebook just as I initiated my research for this book. Subsequently, a considerable bulk of my data dealt with the crisis. The concept of stance proved to be a significant linchpin for the operationalization of these data as 'it offers common ground for researchers interested in the connections between linguistic instances and socio-cultural realities' (Jousmäki 2011: 55). The coding choices for my examples were determined by the use of

- Evaluative adjectives (e.g. *amazing*)
- Evaluative adverbs (e.g. *unfortunately*)

- Affective verbs (e.g. *laugh, cry, love*)

- Cognitive verbs (e.g. *guess, consider, think*)

- Modality (e.g. *probably*)

- Generic versus specific use of pronouns

- Discourse representation (e.g. others' direct/indirect speech)

- Irony

- Rhetorical questions

- References to the 'Like' button

- Usage of song lyrics/titles to imply stances

- Typographical emphasis (e.g. smileys)

- Visual implications of stances (e.g. though memes, profile pictures)

ACTIVITY 7.1: FACEBOOK REACTIONS AND STANCE-TAKING

The 'Like' button functions as a stance-marker of acceptance, affirmation, validation, personal expression, alignment, solidarity and appreciation, and as a confidence booster. In February 2016, Facebook launched a series of new buttons, called 'reactions', which included 'Like', 'Love', 'Wow', 'Haha', 'Sad' and 'Angry', enriching in this way the array of affordances via which users can express their stances towards specific content. Collect some data from personal Facebook Timelines (having obtained the contributors' consent beforehand) and public fans pages and groups and answer the following questions.

1   Are there any users who playfully manipulate 'Like' and other reactions? For what purposes and in what ways?

2   Do users elaborate on their reactions in the comments section to enhance or explain the stance they have taken via the reaction button?

3   Do you detect any instances of miscommunication where the users (deliberately or by mistake) click on a wrong reaction button? Is there any resolution in the comments section?

ACTIVITY 7.2: CRISES AND SOCIAL MEDIA

This chapter as well as Chapter 4 dealt with the Greek crisis. Nonetheless, crises tantalize economies and societies in the European South and elsewhere in the world. Take notes on the following questions.

1 How and why are people using social media venues to talk about crises?

2 Which are the implications for their identities at an individual and collective level?

3 Do you think that changes in a society can affect how people use Facebook and other social media (e.g. fewer posts, different post topics)?

Useful resources

Print

For a panorama of the development of stance as an emerging subject in divergent linguistic strands, see Thompson and Hunston (2000: 1–27) and Damari (2009: 18–20; 2010: 610–13). A compact summary of the various terms used in the literature to describe different types of stance-taking can be found in Jaffe (2009: 6).

The concept of stance has been employed by various researchers in their scrutiny of how opinions and feelings are signalled in digital media. Page (2012, Chapter 4) provides a rigorous analysis on the evolution of an affective style adopted in Facebook status updates. Zappavigna (2012, Chapters 3 and 9) looks at the kinds of evaluative language that people use on Twitter to share experiences and enact relationships as well as to express political views. Evans (2016) examines how stance-taking is particularly enacted in Twitter hashtags. With a focus on Arab Spring and the Occupy Movement, Papacharissi (2014) is concerned with how Twitter is used as a space for political affect where users contribute their emotive declarations. Myers (2010a,b, Chapter 7) explores how bloggers employ stance markers to construct opinions. Interestingly, he also shows how shared evaluations can bring audiences and bloggers together. Taking Flickr as a case in point, Barton and Lee (2013, Chapter 7) investigate multimodality as one of the resources for stance-taking. Moreover, they discuss users' decision to include or exclude a language online as an act of positioning and expression of identity (ibid.: 55–6).

Web

Scott F. Kiesling's work into stance and stance-taking
http://sfkiesling.squarespace.com/stance/

P. R. R. White's website on evaluative language
http://www.grammatics.com/appraisal/

8

Privacy and identity
on Facebook

Editing the self

In trying to reach a consensus regarding a translation issue Carla had posed on her Facebook professional profile, a friend reprimanded her in jest for not starting her sentence with a capital letter right after the full stop. This is Carla's disarming answer to her friend: λυπάμαι. άι μέικ δε ρουλζ ον μάι γουόλ (*i'm sorry. i make the rules on my wall*). Not only does she insist on her use of small letters, despite the remark, but she also encodes her comment in Greek-alphabeted English (Engreek), to even foreground her sole ownership of the profile.

As Papacharissi and Gibson (2011: 86) have observed, self-presentation on SNS involves the production of performances in tandem with the editing of these performances. They claim that such self-editing requires 'acumen for redaction', a kind of literacy that enables users to delete or edit aspects of their identity, presenting thus 'a coherent and polysemic performance of the self that makes sense to multiple publics without compromising one's authentic sense of self'.

Identity online, therefore, is not just something that is 'presented', but it is also 'managed' (Goddard and Geesin 2011: 56). Seeing online identity management as a new and primary responsibility for the internet age (ibid.), this chapter intends to explore how self-presentation on Facebook is regulated by means of privacy. To what extent do privacy issues affect Facebook participants? What kinds of editorial acumen do they apply to their usage of the site in order to safeguard their identity? Do they deliberately exclude any information because of privacy concerns? Do they leave it vague or implied? How do they manage the collapsing of contexts in relation to their intended and unintended audiences? In seeking to answer these questions, I rest on two assumptions: 1) identity performance on Facebook varies according to our audience, and 2) privacy constitutes a function of controlling and managing our audience.

SNS audiences

Identity performance in SNS is audience-specific. Tufekci (2008: 21) has acknowledged that one of the main incentives in being involved in these digital environments is to be seen by those we wish to be seen by and in ways we wish to be seen. In participating in SNS, she asks, 'What exactly do we want to show and to whom? Who can see us?'

For Stutzman and Kramer-Duffield (2010), SNS audiences fall into three categories: intended, expected and unknown. The intended audience refers to the cohorts for whom the online profile is managed and updated. This includes both strong and weak or peripheral ties: current and past intimate friends, relatives, colleagues, occasional acquaintances, people whom the participant barely knows (e.g. friends of friends who have just happened to comment on the same thread and have not met in real life), people with similar music tastes, celebrities and public figures, as well as controversial actors, that is to say, those that the user feels ethically and socially compelled to add as contacts (e.g. parents, bosses, teachers or students in case the profile host is a teacher as occurs with Helen's case with which I will deal later on).

Obviously, just because this collection of people is considered to be the intended public, it does not necessarily mean that it is the actual public. Agents should manage their identity and disclosure behaviour for their expected audience as well, namely their perception of who is actually viewing what in their profile, irrespective of intent and privacy settings.

Finally, there is the general unknown audience on the Web, also called unspecified others (Rössler 2005) and silent listeners (Stutzman et al. 2012), and can include the hosting site (Facebook Inc. in the case at hand), third-party applications that track users' behaviours for targeted advertising, potential employers and love partners, governmental entities, marketing companies and other third parties which use SNS for malicious purposes such as eavesdropping, lurking, even phishing and hacking.

In effect, very few participants think of every possible person to be a member of their audience. On the contrary, they imagine an audience that is often more constrained. Following Bell (1984), Tagg and Seargeant (2014) have proposed an audience design framework for Facebook (Figure 8.1). They posit that if there is no direct addressee on Facebook, status updaters are likely to post their message for their active circle of friends, namely the ones that tend to comment and are expected to comment. Yet, at the same time, their message will also constitute a performance enacted before a broader audience, which does not remain uninvolved and uninterested (the wider circle of friends), as we will see later on. Additionally, beyond their circles of friends, their awareness of the internet as a whole may affect what and how they post.

Any study on Facebook audiences should take into account two parameters. First, as already mentioned repeatedly in previous chapters, in juxtaposition to blogging and other sorts of social media (e.g. Twitter, Flickr), Facebook is to a significant extent concerned with physical friendships and relationships that are initiated offline and then relocated online. Such relocation inescapably involves shared knowledge, views and experiences among members of the audience. Second, the role of the audience is no longer restricted to that of a mere spectator, but now also encompasses producing and socializing (Enli and Thumim 2012). Hence, the value of knowing one's audience is crucial

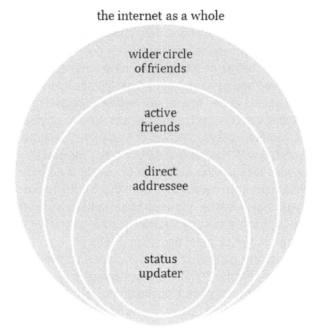

FIGURE 8.1 *Facebook audience design by Tagg and Seargeant (2014) based on Bell (1984).*

when trying to determine what is socially acceptable to post or what will be understood and inferred by the engaged readers (boyd 2010b). Through this prism, selecting who to include in their friends' list becomes both a political and social act for users since they seem more thoughtful of the consequences of excluding or declining a person rather than the advantages of adding them to their list (boyd 2010b: 44). This is exactly where privacy enters the game as a function of one's audience (Acquisti and Gross 2006).

Privacy and personal information

The question of privacy has become central to the agenda of many disciplines within humanities, including law, philosophy and politics, while it has recently constituted a conundrum among social media entrepreneurs, users and researchers. Put it plainly, privacy is a social norm. Rössler (2005: 8) offers an influential definition of privacy: 'Something counts as private if one can oneself control the access to this "something,"' with 'access' being understood both literally and figuratively.

Theorists such as Altman (1976), Nissenbaum (2004), Rössler (2005), Tavani (2008) and Wessels (2012) have classified privacy into:

- **physical/local/territorial privacy:** the right to be left alone; the freedom from intrusion into one's physical space (domestic, workplace or public space);

- **decisional privacy:** the freedom from intervening in one's choices, decisions and actions;

- **psychological/mental privacy:** non-intrusion and non-interference into one's thoughts and personal identity;

- **privacy of communications:** the security and privacy of mail, telephones, email and other forms of communication;

- **informational privacy:** the control over the flow of an individual's personal information, including contact information and personal communication, and control over the contexts in which this information can be used and appear.

What is of special interest in digital environments, and therefore what lies at the core of this chapter, is informational privacy. But what is meant by 'personal information'? The term refers to anything that relates to our name and surname, age, residence, occupation, marital status, physical appearance, education, financial situation, hobbies and interests. It also comprises more sensitive data such as race, nationality, political, philosophical and religious beliefs, health and medical issues, sexual life, prosecutions and criminal records (Hellenic Data Protection Authority 2016). Van der Ploeg (1998 in Rössler 2005: 122) accentuates that the nature of such kind of information should not be taken in essentialist terms but as contextual, for such data acquire meaning and make sense only when occurring in a certain context in which the relevant person can be identified.

The paradox of Facebook privacy

The bulk of personal information that previous generations deemed private, that is, age, politics, income, religion, sexual preference, is precisely what contemporary online cultures display as standard (Livingstone 2008). To Facebook outsiders, disclosing and sharing willingly such information seems like an irrational compromise to their privacy (Raynes-Goldie 2010). For insiders, however, it is a crucial issue of how to be public without being in public (boyd and Marwick 2011). Privacy practices appear paradoxical, as content-sharing behaviour contradicts the need to avoid or reduce potential disclosure-related harms (Stutzman and Kramer-Duffield 2010).[1] On the one hand, users are nudged towards publicizing material that is considered private, while on the other, they are confronted with four technological affordances (boyd 2010b: 45–8) that challenge privacy in their interactions:

1 **persistence:** The online content is automatically recorded and cumulatively archived (e.g. chronological dates in Facebook Timeline).

2 **replicability:** The content is reproducible (e.g. via the facility 'Share').

3 **scalability:** The content can be available to invisible audiences (e.g. the *Ticker* on the right hand-side of any Facebook page, for which Helen has said: *it is as if you're having Big Brother watching you*).

4 **searchability:** The content can be accessed via search engines (e.g. when the profile is public) or by browsing posts from particular dates in Facebook Timeline.

In this light, privacy becomes a socio-technical activity which involves interaction with the technological system and the group context alike (Stutzman and Kramer-Duffield 2010). This activity should be conceptualized as a boundary negotiation process of optimization between disclosure and withdrawal, which ultimately leads to a 'selective access' to the self (Tufekci 2008: 21, 33), what boyd (2008a: 15) aptly calls 'security through obscurity'.

Privacy practices

Facebook users have to make critical decisions on how to come to grips with the sharing of their personal information. Such decisions require an advanced form of literacy – not just digital but sociocultural and ethical as well (Debatin et al. 2009). More precisely, I have found that my participants' privacy on Facebook is shaped by

(a) the underlying architecture of the software;

(b) their personal values (boyd and Marwick 2011) as expressed through specific stylistic and linguistic choices;

(c) creatively combining software affordances with linguistic signals and other textual practices.

Viewing thus privacy as my informants' ability to control access to their identity (cf. Rössler 2005: 111), this chapter will give considerable weight to their textual practices. By textual practices I am referring to a certain sort of literacy practices, namely the practical ways of utilizing written language as well as the sociocultural meanings and cognitions that underlie these practices (Barton and Hamilton 1998; Barton and Lee 2013).

With a view to providing a multi-perspectival view of their privacy practices, my analysis utilizes three sets of data: interview excerpts, Facebook profile information and Facebook posts. The interviews granted me access to my informants' illuminating insights and understandings of their personal policies and (shared) experiences with and around their texts. Facebook profile information and posts, on the other hand, allowed me to trace, frame and analyse their practices in context. Due to the different nature of the data at hand, my focus varies from the description of the users' actions to the regulation of their visibility and the pragmatics of their behaviour.

I start by considering privacy settings and how they have been applied to profiles.

Adjusting privacy settings

As Stutzman and Kramer-Duffield (2010) have pointed out, the customization of privacy settings heralds a shift in users' identity orientation as they can divorce themselves from a large group and social identities. In order to view and customize their privacy settings, users should click on the gear icon in the upper right corner of their Facebook page and select 'Privacy Settings' from the dropdown menu.[2] Figure 8.2 presents an overview of what exactly users can customize in terms of visibility of content and audiences.

Privacy Settings and Tools

Who can see my stuff?	Who can see your future posts?	Custom	Edit
	Review all your posts and things you're tagged in		Use Activity Log
	Limit the audience for posts you've shared with friends of friends or Public?		Limit Past Posts
Who can contact me?	Who can send you friend requests?	Everyone	Edit
	Whose messages do I want filtered into my Inbox?	Basic Filtering	Edit
Who can look me up?	Who can look you up using the email address or phone number you provided?	Friends	Edit
	Do you want other search engines to link to your Timeline?	Off	Edit

FIGURE 8.2 *Customizing Facebook privacy settings (screenshot from my Facebook profile).*

Some of the technical features afforded by Facebook to segment audiences and restrict access and visibility of information include:

- friends-only visible profiles;
- custom uploads for specific audiences within friends;
- locked Walls that disable other users from writing comments on the profile owner's Wall;
- photo and text untagging (I elaborate on this later);
- blocking particular contacts;
- sporadic profile deactivation;
- maintaining separate profiles for different audiences (see next section).

'Possibly I'm a split personality': *Recontextualizing profiles*

In the very first email that Carla had sent me to express her interest in participating in my study, she instantly explained to me how she initiated Facebook networking as a 'doppelganger':

> *I must 'confess' that I have two profiles in Facebook:-) One is strictly personal, a bit incognito, for fun and my friends. I created the other profile when several acquaintances, but not friends, sent me friend requests due to my involvement in a professional association. Therefore, I created a second profile, less active, slightly more 'serious', for PR let's say (possibly I'm a split personality, I know;-)*

According to Table 8.1, multiple profile maintenance has been found to be motivated by four factors: privacy, identity, utility and propriety (Stutzman and Hartzog 2012).

Carla appears to have been motivated by all four factors. For privacy purposes, her personal profile is *a bit incognito* as she describes. When she received friend requests from colleagues in 2009, she decided to craft from scratch a new profile for them, and not include them in her personal one, maintained since 2007, creating at that point distinct personal and professional identities. The circumstances that called for a separate professional profile was *PR* (public relations) as well as information-sharing within a given network of translators as she has explained elsewhere (see also Chapter 6):

> *In my second [the professional] profile, yes, I often feel that I address an audience and I often write stuff like announcements.*

TABLE 8.1 Factors that motivate multiple profile maintenance

Privacy	• Selective withdrawal of access to the self or disclosure.
Identity	• Management of the self in eyes of multiple audiences.
Utility	• Optimizing disclosure for appropriate circumstances.
Propriety	• Normative conformity to prevailing customs and usages.

Source: Stutzman and Hartzog (2012: 773).

Her sense of propriety is related to clear-cut power dynamics (Stutzman and Hartzog 2012): fun versus serious, friends versus not friends, acquaintances. Her self-sarcastic comment on being a *split personality* indicates that even from her initial contact with me, she tried to craft her identity in an amusing way.

To have a more vivid picture, Figure 8.3 shows a graphic representation of Carla's personal profile while Figure 8.4 her professional one. Here I am centring on the recontextualization of her profile for the sake of different audiences since different contexts call for different self-presentations. It is indispensable to take into consideration that Carla's both Facebook personas are not 'friends' with one another preventing thus the discovery of any linkage between the two profiles. Few friends, 24 in total, were found as mutual contacts in both her profiles (out of 113 friends in total in her personal profile and 98 friends in her professional profile in January 2012). Example 8.1 offers a brief insight into how some of them occasionally tease Carla for her two personas:

8.1

FBU1 [male]: χρόνια πολλά και καλά και ευτυχισμένα!!! τα σέβη μου και στην άλλη Κάρλα!!! μαζί θα τα γιορτάσετε?
'very happy birthday!!! my respects to the other Carla as well!!! are you going to celebrate together?'
21 December 2011 at 00:21

If we turn to Figure 8.4, we will notice that Carla mentions her studies (Ionian University, graduation year 1993) and the languages she knows (French, Spanish, English), which lists them along with translation, that is, her job, as her interests. There is no reference to arts and entertainment while the pages she likes are more professionally oriented. Note that atenistas and PlusCorfu are

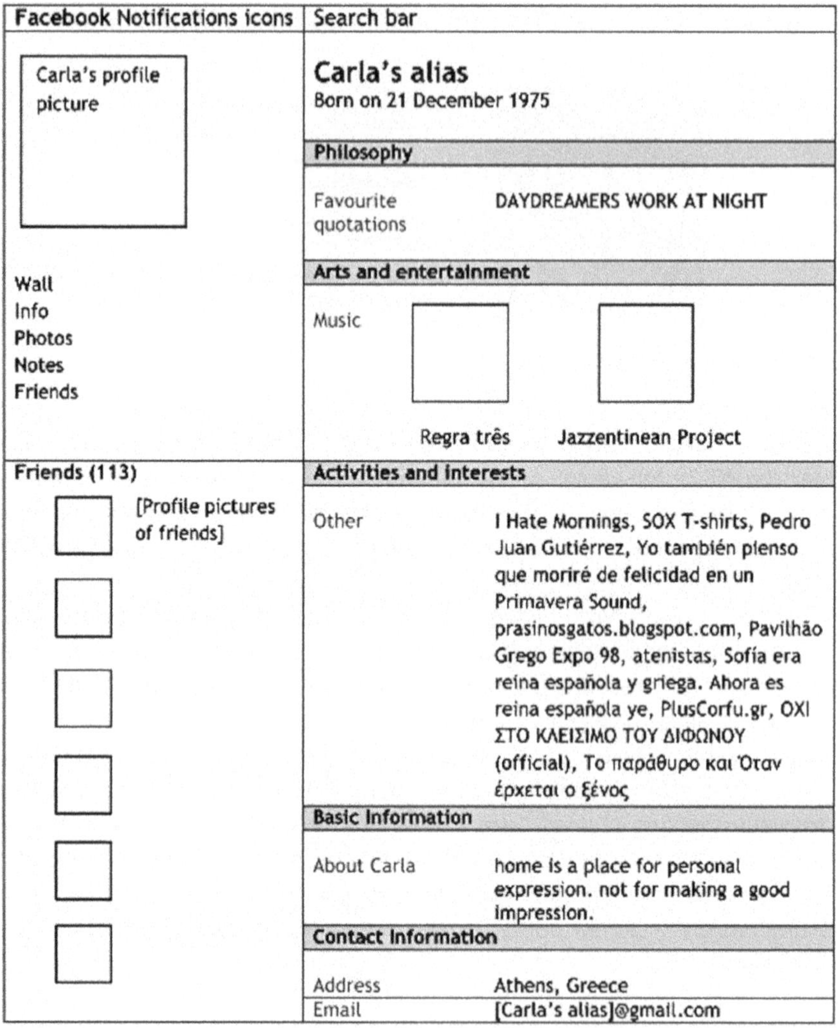

Facebook Notifications icons	Search bar

Carla's profile picture	**Carla's alias** Born on 21 December 1975

	Philosophy
	Favourite quotations DAYDREAMERS WORK AT NIGHT

Wall
Info
Photos
Notes
Friends

Arts and entertainment
Music
Regra três   Jazzentinean Project

Friends (113)	**Activities and interests**
[Profile pictures of friends]	Other I Hate Mornings, SOX T-shirts, Pedro Juan Gutiérrez, Yo también pienso que moriré de felicidad en un Primavera Sound, prasinosgatos.blogspot.com, Pavilhão Grego Expo 98, atenistas, Sofía era reina española y griega. Ahora es reina española ye, PlusCorfu.gr, OXI ΣΤΟ ΚΛΕΙΣΙΜΟ ΤΟΥ ΔΙΦΩΝΟΥ (official), Το παράθυρο και Όταν έρχεται ο ξένος

Basic Information
About Carla   home is a place for personal expression. not for making a good impression.

Contact Information
Address   Athens, Greece
Email   [Carla's alias]@gmail.com

FIGURE 8.3 *A graphic representation of Carla's personal profile (as of January 2012).*

common in both profiles, activating certain place identities: Athens is where she resides, while Corfu is the place where she studied (see also Chapter 4). Looking at the basic information entry ('if you are reading this, you probably know all you need to know'), written in English, one realizes that this profile is indeed strictly specific: people know what to expect from Carla because the majority of them are translators too. Carla's profession allows her to utilize meaningfully multiple linguistic resources in both her profiles, projecting a special kind of identity online, which propels her network to interact with

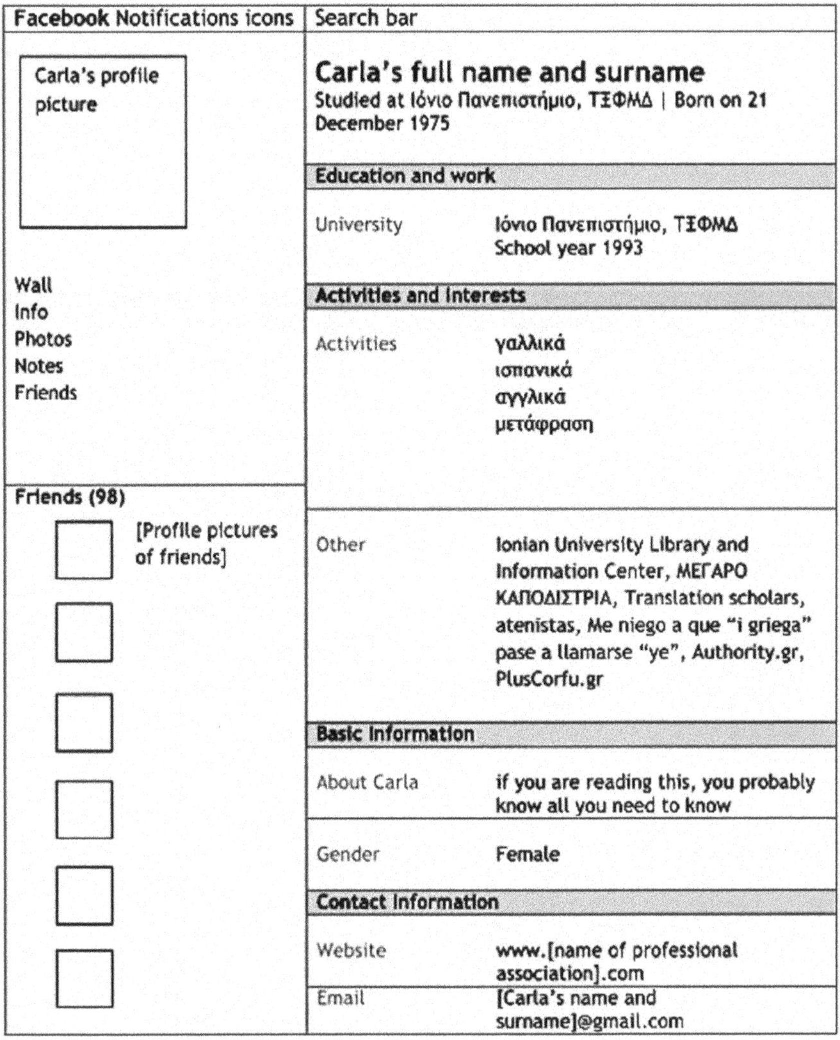

Facebook Notifications icons	Search bar	
Carla's profile picture	**Carla's full name and surname** Studied at Ιόνιο Πανεπιστήμιο, ΤΞΦΜΔ | Born on 21 December 1975	
	Education and work	
	University	Ιόνιο Πανεπιστήμιο, ΤΞΦΜΔ School year 1993
Wall Info	**Activities and Interests**	
Photos Notes Friends	Activities	γαλλικά ισπανικά αγγλικά μετάφραση
Friends (98)		
[Profile pictures of friends]	Other	Ionian University Library and Information Center, ΜΕΓΑΡΟ ΚΑΠΟΔΙΣΤΡΙΑ, Translation scholars, atenistas, Me niego a que "i griega" pase a llamarse "ye", Authority.gr, PlusCorfu.gr
	Basic Information	
	About Carla	if you are reading this, you probably know all you need to know
	Gender	Female
	Contact Information	
	Website	www.[name of professional association].com
	Email	[Carla's name and surname]@gmail.com

FIGURE 8.4 *A graphic representation of Carla's professional profile (as of January 2012).*

her in the languages she knows and they can speak, of course. A relevant example is presented later on in the chapter (Example 8.13). With regard to contact information, she gives the URL of the professional association she belongs to and an email address with her real forename and surname initial as userID as opposed to the playful email userID found in her other profile.

What we have here is a recontextualized self depending on the interests, purposes and values of the professional context. Carla's profile recontextualization involves dynamic textual transformation through the processes of 1) deletion, 2) rearrangement, 3) substitution and 4) addition of information (van Leeuwen and Wodak 1999: 96–8). Table 8.2 recapitulates what happens in both Carla's profiles.

Monitoring two profiles protects Carla to a large extent from the phenomenon of context collapse, namely the flattening of multiple audiences

TABLE 8.2 Carla's profiling recontextualization

Profile entries	Personal profile (since 2007)	Professional profile (since 2009)
Name		substitution (partial name in personal; full real name in professional)
Profile picture	substitution (yet in both smiling)	
Info under name	sameness (date of birth)	
		addition (studies)
Philosophy		deletion
Education and work		addition
Arts and entrainment		deletion
Activities and interests		addition (languages)
Other	sameness (atenistas, corfu.gr)	
		substitution
Basic information		substitution
Gender		addition
Address		deletion
Website		addition
Email		substitution

(intimate friends, relatives, colleagues, occasional acquaintances) into one and the requirement to present in front of them a coherent self (Wesch 2009; Marwick and boyd 2011). Despite the unavoidable overlap of some mutual friends and relocated posts, Carla's networking practices demonstrate profound social awareness of both her intended and expected audience.

'I felt uncomfortable': Handling context collapse and controversial audiences

It follows from the above that the blending of the professional and personal realms on Facebook intensifies the need for active and conscious boundary management. Yet, managing two profiles can be time-consuming, as Carla has admitted, requiring a high level of commitment. Moreover, some users may find it difficult – or even not wish – to make a sharp distinction between personal and professional identity because of their unavoidable overlapping. I will rely on the subsequent quite long interview excerpt[3] with Helen to shine some light upon the challenges and decisions she is confronted with as regard managing context collapse within one and the same Facebook profile as well as upon the strategies she adopts to enact a respectable professional identity in front of her students.

1 **Mariza:** do you have your students as 'friends'?

2 **Helen:** hm.. yes that was an issue

3 **Helen:** I have 2–3

4 **Helen:** from my job in Greece

5 **Helen:** and a great number from England

6 **Mariza:** how do you feel with this?

7 **Mariza:** comfortable or do you have to be careful?

8 **Helen:** for the group [of students] from England, comfortable

9 **Helen:** because we became 'friends' on the last day of the course

10 **Helen:** or after the course had ended

11 **Helen:** so I wasn't their teacher anymore

12 **Helen:** moreover in England I feel more comfortable generally

13 **Helen:** the relationships between teachers and students are different in relation to here

14   **Mariza:** big truth

15   **Helen:** your question is to the point indeed!

16   **Helen:** I feel that it is more comfortable in England

17   **Helen:** in Greece now

18   **Helen:** hm..

19   **Mariza:** have you by any chance deleted anything because maybe for instance it would expose you in front of their [students'] eyes?

20   **Helen:** I have changed the privacy settings

21   **Helen:** so as not to be able to see 2–3 photographs

22   **Mariza:** this is interesting

23   **Helen:** but for the students in Greece

24   **Helen:** not in England

...

25   **Mariza:** has any of your students-Facebook friends ever told you 'ah Mrs. I saw what you posted' or anything similar?

26   **Helen:** no no, because I don't have them anymore

27   **Helen:** as students

28   **Helen:** there are only 2 people now that I'm thinking of it

29   **Helen:** one of them added me towards the end of the academic year

30   **Helen:** and another one – from the MA – had added me in the middle of the year- and I felt uncomfortable

31   **Helen:** because she was a weak student- and I was thinking, hm.. if now she fails the course..

32   **Helen**: I don't know I felt uncomfortable in the particular situation

33   **Mariza:** did you accept her?

34   **Helen:** yes

35   **Helen:** in terms of age the particular student is older than me

36   **Mariza:** ah ok

37   **Helen:** age shouldn't matter

38   **Mariza:** sure

39   **Helen:** but sometimes it makes a difference

40   **Mariza:** your personal life also exists in fb

41   **Mariza:** in several ways

42   **Helen:** of course

43   **Helen:** therefore it's better to become friends with students after the end [of the course]

44   **Mariza:** proper practice

45   **Helen:** or I should customize the settings

46   **Helen:** as I have already done

Helen's account reminded me of an anecdote from boyd and Marwick's (2011) research. In discussing teens' social privacy in online networks, the authors asked a 15-year-old student how she would feel if her teachers browsed her Facebook profile. This is what the girl answered: 'I'd be like "Why are they on my page?" I wouldn't go to my teacher's page and look at their stuff, so why should they go on mine to look at my stuff?' As it can be inferred from what Helen reports, it seems that when students enter college the situation reverses. They send requests for friendship to their instructors with a view to building a more comfortable student-teacher relationship and perhaps being exposed to further intellectual input either in relation to their BA or MA course or in broader terms. Here is precisely where the puzzlement starts for the instructor as students belong to the controversial actors of one's Facebook audience (see above on SNS audiences). Which are students' real motives for wishing to connect with their teachers on Facebook? Which is the most appropriate time to accept a student's request? How much of teachers' personal life should be visible? What kinds of posts are considered proper to be publicized and viewed by students? In order to circumvent potential vulnerability and embarrassment, Helen pursues two main strategies, mentioned twice in the interview: 1) friending her students after the end of the course (turns 9–10, 43) with the reasoning that she is not their teacher any longer, and 2) customizing her privacy settings (turns 20, 45–6).

Remarkably, not only is her offline professional identity dictated to a great degree by place (Greece vs UK), but it is also rendered as such online on Facebook. Having worked for both British and Greek educational institutions, she is entitled from experience to maintain that student–teacher relationships vary considerably across the two countries. Therefore, although she feels at ease within the UK educational context (turns 8, 12, 16), in Greece she is more alert with the material she posts (turns 21, 23–4). The small story with the weak student that Helen recounts in turns 30–2 is indicative of the sea of dilemmas that by and large professionals in asymmetrical relationships (teacher-student, manager-employee) are invited to face. If she had rejected the student's request, having previously accepted requests from other students, this would undermine her professional identity by seeming to be discriminatory and favour particular students. When I told Helen about Carla's case of monitoring two distinct profiles, she appeared reluctant regarding this policy mainly on account of the fact that, to her opinion, identity cannot be put into separate moulds. And indeed, albeit Carla has a separate professional profile, her personal profile is not purely personal but permeated by professional concerns as shown in Chapter 6.

'I don't have to display my history online': Shielding profiles

In contradistinction to Carla's and Helen's practices, Alkis has chosen to moderate context collapse by managing one almost totally bare profile shown in Figure 8.5. To begin with the top of the profile, he has selected an obscure variant of his full name (similarly to Carla in her personal profile), making it difficult for other users to trace him via Facebook's searching facility or other search engines. His profile picture is impersonal, depicting two diving ducks with the motto 'Bottoms up. Wishing everyone a Happy New Year 2012!'. Alkis changes with relatively high frequency his profile picture. I have estimated that almost only 2 out of 10 photos he uploads as profile pictures show directly his face. This is something that does not go unnoticed by his contacts as well:

8.2

FBU1 [male]: Βγάλε το ιμπρεσιονιστικό, βρε χαρά μου, και βάλε τη μουρίτσα σου πια!
'Remove this impressionist picture, sweetie, and put your face+DIM at last!'
7 March 2012 at 15:26

Alkis: Δεν είναι ιμπρεσιονιστικό, είναι πολύ καλοκαιρινοσταλγικό! Ηλιοβασίλεμα, κρυστάλλινο κύμα... Αχ.... Καλά, εσύ τώρα γιατί μου τρολάρεις το thinking tune???!!
'It's not Impressionism, it's very summer nostalgic! Sunset, glassy wave... Ah.... Well, why are you trolling my thinking tune now???!!'
7 March 2012 at 15:32

FIGURE 8.5 *Alkis's profile (as of January 2012).*

8.3

FBU1 [female]: ΕΥΤΥΧΩΣ ΠΙΑ .... ΝΑ ΔΟΥΜΕ ΚΑΙ ΛΙΓΟ ΤΟ ΠΡΟΣΩΠΑΚΙ ΣΟΥ !! :)
'FORTUNATELY AT LAST .... TO SEE YOUR FACE+DIM FOR A WHILE !! :)'
7 April 2012 at 03:33

Alkis: Για λίγες εμφανίσεις!
'For limited shows'
7 April 2012 at 03:33

FBU1: χαχαχαχαχα!!!
'hahahahaha!!!'
7 April 2012 at 03:33

Alkis: (όπως τα τσίρκο, λίγες εμφανίσεις στην πόλη σας!)
'(as in circuses, for limited shows in your town!)'
7 April 2012 at 03:34

FBU1: χαχαχαχαχ τρελοκομειο μου!! οχι μωρε αστην την φωτο αυτη να σε
βλεπουμε!!! αμαν ...εκτος κι αν θα βαλεις καμια πιο προσφατη να σε δω ....!!
εχω να σε δω και καιροο 1!
'hahahahah you crazy!! no, leave this photo so that we can see you!!! oh
my ...unless you upload a more recent one for me to see you ....!! I haven't
seen you for ages!'
7 April 2012 at 03:35

Alkis: Άμα βάλω πρόσφατη θα έχουμε εγκεφαλικά κι εμφράγματα. (Θα με δεις
και θα πάθεις ατύχημααα, βάζεις στοίχημααα!) Αγαπώ τους φίλους μου,
Προστατεύω την υγεία τους! χαχαχα
'If I upload a recent one, we'll have strokes and infarctions. (You will see
me and you'll have an accident, I bet you!). I love my friends, I protect their
health! hahaha'
7 April 2012 at 03:38 · Like · 1

In Example 8.2, FBU1 asks Alkis to put a photo of himself, while in Example
8.3 another user express her gladness for eventually seeing Alkis's face on
a profile picture. The intriguing commonality in both cases lies in the skilful
manner with which Alkis bypasses the issue of why he rarely uploads photos
of himself. In the first case, he refuses to comment at all, retorting that the
picture has nothing to do with impressionism. In the second case, he ironically
draws a parallel between the limited number of shows that a circus typically
performs in a provincial Greek town (the motto 'for limited shows' is used
in circus posters, radio ads and so on) and the days his face will remain as
a Facebook profile picture. This parallelism could be seen as sarcastic since

circuses bear the connotations of freaks, clowns, kitsch, surrealism and chaos. Alkis goes on to further ridicule himself by writing that a recent photo of his will lead to *strokes and infarctions*, alluding to a Greek pop folk song by Antzela Dimitriou (Θα με δεις και θα πάθεις ατύχημααααα, βάζεις στοίχημα αα! – *You will see me and you'll have an accident, I bet you*). He finishes his humorous self-deprecation by saying that he is mindful of his friends' health. Alkis perhaps is modest, shy, sophisticated, or does not want (or need) to show off. Nevertheless, none of these motivations is explicitly stated on why he clearly shrugs off photographs of himself.

Despite his friends wanting him to display his face, he insists on selecting impersonal profile images. His criteria for choosing them are mostly based on

cartoons I like or to express my mood via a picture instead of words, something related to current events, general or personal etc.

We have already seen relevant examples of Alkis's particular practice in Chapters 6 and 7. Let us now return to the rest elements of Alkis's profile page. Contrary to my other informants, he does not provide any basic demographic information (occupation, hometown, marital status, education and birth date), which is prominently displayed at the top of a user's profile. Moreover, he has set his friends' list invisible. The question is plausible: 'Why have a profile if your profile will not say enough about who you are?' (Tufekci 2008: 33). Alkis elucidates:

In the beginning I wasn't so [careful about privacy]. Quite the opposite: I had given much personal data like education, work and much more. In the end, I realized that, since the overwhelming majority of those added to my Facebook are friends and acquaintances of mine, they know such details about me. I don't have to display my history online. My friends' list is invisible even to my friends, as you saw, not only to strangers/not added contacts.

Consider how his views on privacy are voiced in his Facebook interactions as well, in Examples 8.4 and 8.5.

8.4

FBU1 [female]: Ορέ γιατί σου εύχονται?? Σάμπως είχες γενέθλια? Αποκλείεται! Αν είχες γενέθλια το FB θα με είχε ειδοποιήσει! Εκτός αν εκείνη τη μέρα δεν μπήκα FB.... Οοοοοops.... Ορε χρόνια σου πολλά τότενες, για οπότενες κι αν ήτο η επέτειος της γεννήσεώς σου (αλήθεια, πότε ήτο?)
'Why do they wish you?? Did you have your birthday maybe? Certainly not! If you had your birthday FB would have notified me! Unless I didn't login in FB that day.... Oooooops.... Happy birthday then, for whenever the anniversary of your birthday was (well, when was it?)'

4 March 2011 at 00:37
1 person likes this

Alkis's sister: Δεν το έχει γράψει το τσουτσέκι για να μας ταλαιπωρεί!!
'He's sly he hasn't written it to torment us!!'
4 March 2011 at 00:38 · Like · 1

[another 2 comments with bantering between FBU1 and Alkis's sister]

Alkis: 1η Μαρτίου ήτονε! Ευχαριστώ για τις ευχές!! ... Πι. Ες. Είπαμε, <u>τα
πολλά πολλά κομμένα στο facebook</u>. Εγώ κρατάω μια λίστα με τις ημερομηνίες
γενεθλίων όσων θέλω και τελείωσε – <u>δεν εξαρτώμαι από το facebook</u>. Το συνιστώ
ανεπιφύλακτα!
'It was on 1st March! Thanks for the wishes!! ... Pee. Ess. We have said,
<u>not many things on Facebook</u>. I keep a list with birthday dates of the people
I want and it's over – <u>I don't depend on Facebook</u>. I highly recommend it!'
4 March 2011 at 10:01

8.5

FBU1 [male]: kala re poso grafis oti ise stin ilikia???
'well how old have you written that you are???'
19 December 2011 at 13:46 · Like · 1

Alkis: Δεν γράφω τίποτα! Γιατί τι λέει;;;;
'I haven't written anything! Why what does it say????'
19 December 2011 at 13:47 · Like · 1

FBU1: den lei tipota me exis blockarismeno... oreos filos
'it doesn't say anything you have blocked me... what a friend'
19 December 2011 at 13:48 · Like · 1

FBU2 [female]: oxi den se exei blockarismeno... genika den exei grapsei!
oyte se emena to vgazei!
'no he hasn't blocked you ... he hasn't written it in general! it doesn't appear
to me either!'
19 December 2011 at 13:50

FBU1: agapoula tin koukoula
'honey bring the hood [allusion to a Greek ad]'
19 December 2011 at 13:50 · Like · 3

Alkis: Δεν είσαι μπλοκαρισμένος μόνο εσύ. <u>Τα περισσότερα πράγματα στο fb
μου είναι μπλοκαρισμένα από κολλητούς και μη</u> – όσα έχω εισάγει δηλαδή! <u>Όσο
λιγότερα τόσο καλύτερα. Κρατάω ένα μύθο γύρω από το όνομά μου!</u> ;)

'You're not the only one who is blocked. <u>Most things in my fb [account] are</u>
<u>inaccessible to my best and non-best friends</u> – those of the things that I
have filled in I mean! <u>The less the better. I keep a myth around my name!;)</u>'
19 December 2011 at 13:50 · Like · 2

FBU1, in Example 8.4, realizes that she missed Alkis's birthday because
either Facebook did not notify her or because she did not visit the site on that
particular day. Together with FBU2, they jocularly consider him responsible for
this failure (*He's sly he hasn't written it to torment us, it serves him right*).
Once again, Alkis appears careful with privacy matters (*We have said, not
many things on Facebook, I don't depend on Facebook*) proposing a more
traditional way of remembering birthdays. A similar attitude is found in
Example 8.5 where Alkis appears as an advocate of a *less is better* attitude
as regards the dissemination of his personal information. He confides that
most information, from that he has chosen to reveal, in his account is blocked,
and therefore unavailable, regardless of his intimacy with the audience. He
jokingly sees this as *keeping a myth around his name.*

The tension in both the above threads is palpable. On the one hand, since
revealing one's age is one of the most straightforward means of self-identifying
(see also Chapter 5), Alkis's friends reasonably presuppose that they will find
this kind of information in his profile. Alkis, on the other hand, smashes this
taken-for-grantedness by showing that one can indeed efficiently perform
publicly without being in public (cf. boyd and Marwick 2011).

Alkis clarified in the interview that he has tightened (*carefully chosen*) his
privacy settings on account of the general unknown Facebook audience as well.

*All this monitoring by Facebook has got on my nerves. I thought of it a
bit late, of course, especially from the moment that I had given so much
information in the past and although I had deleted it Facebook surely has
backed up copies. But what else can I do apart from at least deleting them?
What's more, despite the privacy settings that I have carefully chosen,
maybe some people can still have access (friends of friends or I don't know
who else) and you don't have to give food for thought to any curious person
that ferrets out. And take note, I'm not a cagey person. The opposite. I
have just been very intensely puzzled over this whole internet issue of our
personal data and how skilfully or even clumsily they spur us (even with
our will, they lure us with other mainly psychological means) on giving 'out
there' everything about us.*

Alkis here deploys the argumentation scheme of comparison. On the one
hand, it is *them*, a conglomerate of several yet not fully specified subjects:
1) the personified Facebook which monitors and keeps copies; 2) friends of

friends; 3) unknown people; 4) any curious person; 5) they, who may refer not only to Facebook Inc. but social media entrepreneurs by and large. These subjects are suspects of evil deeds: monitoring, backing up, ferreting out, spurring and luring. On the counterbalance, it is *him*, not cagey but annoyed (*has got on my nerves*), whose puzzlement is foregrounded with the amplifier *very intensely*. Despite that he presents himself as an agent who takes action by deleting information and instituting strict privacy settings. Alkis's behaviour adds to boyd and Hargittai's (2010) observation that users who regularly post content on Facebook are more likely to modify their privacy settings, especially the more they are conscious of their audience, more than those who share on the site less often.

'You talk in riddles, old man': Encoding meanings in plain sight

Turning now from profile information pages to particular Wall posts, a common tactic to achieve privacy is the uploading of ambiguous statuses like this one:

8.6

Carla [personal profile]
13 December 2010 at 17:34

Tonight we fly
7 people like this

Carla wrote this update, which is actually a song lyric by the Divine Comedy, a Northern Irish band, to suggest that she was going to their concert in Athens, on 13 December 2010. Yet, the lyric was misinterpreted by a female friend who took it literally and commented:

¿Puedo pedir algo del vieje? Quiero que, a tu regreso a Atenas, me mandes un par de fotos: las 2 que te hayan gustado más de TODO tu viaje. Φιλάκια και καλό ταξίδι!!

'Can I ask something from the journey? When you return to Athens I want you to bring me 2 photos of what you liked most from your WHOLE journey. Kisses, have a nice journey!!'

Carla's post is an example of how users can hide information in plain sight and thus segment audiences by anchoring in culture-specific knowledge to provide the right interpretive lens. What we witness here is an instance of 'expectancy violation' (Stutzman and Kramer-Duffield 2010), in other words, an incongruity between the intended audience (those who read and recognize the lyric) and the expected audience (those who read the lyric as being Carla's words).

Vagueness has a similar function to ambiguity. However, while in ambiguity there are two or more competing distinct meanings, in vagueness no meaning can be clearly identified (Channell 1994) as are the cases below:

8.7

Alkis
9 September 2011 at 10:52
μπεζ
'beige'

8.8

Carla
1 February 2013 at 15:10
-17,7!
9 people like this

8.9

Romanos
27 September 2010 at 14:19
Fighting the waves of stupidity

8.10

Romanos
12 April 2011 at 15:59
SaNaVi TeLaRa se nees peripeteies ...
'SaNaVi TeLaRa in new adventures ...'
2 people like this

8.11

Romanos
7 September 2010 at 11:11
QQ Mode: On
1 person likes this

In Example 8.7, there is a mere reference to a colour, meaningful to Alkis though. In Example 8.8, one of Carla's friends made a guess that she had travelled somewhere where the temperature was −17.7°C. Another friend highlighted the vagueness and wrote her *me grifous milas geronta* (*you talk in riddles, old man*) alluding to a punch line from a joke, widely reproduced among speakers of the Greek slang. Actually, what she revealed later in the thread was that she had lost 17.7 kg. Example 8.9 lacks any cue, and clue, on who exactly is stupid and how Romanos is dealing with it. Such updates save a lot of effort for their posters as they express complaints in a discreet manner without directly attacking anyone's face.

Encoded statuses can also contain presuppositions as exemplified in Example 8.10. *New* presupposes that there were old adventures too whereas *SaNaVi TeLaRa* is an acronym made from Romanos's friends' names and can be decoded only by those who are in the know: two people liked the particular update and one wrote *xaxaxaxaxaxaxa!! ξαναχτυπούν!!!* (*hahahahahahaha!! they are back again!!!*).

Another glue that keeps together a private sphere of friends on Facebook is in-group language and inside jokes (Papacharissi 2010: 315). As Romanos corroborates:

> *I often upload on Facebook things that in a way constitute inside jokes with my close friends. ... My language changes depending on whom I'm addressing. In the case of an inside joke, my language will be more 'internetese' and more familiar [to my friends].*

To grasp Example 8.11, we need to bear in mind that Romanos was working in an IT company and studying videogame programming. Here he expresses his inner state via a gaming and geeky reference. QQ initially appeared in massively multiplayer online games to represent either a set of crying eyes or to assert quitting. By recontextualizing this QQ reference, Romanos either wishes to modestly externalize his sadness for something or his thoughts of giving up a person or a situation – once again ambiguity is at work.

A significant cultural depository to which Facebook participants have recourse in order to articulate targeted messages is song lyrics (see also Chapter 7). Although many people dismiss them as fairly trivial (Example 8.6 refers to a rather mundane situation), the foci of lyrics tackle primarily the communication and the signification of underlying cultural values and identities (Machin 2010; Sophiadi 2014). Carla admits that when she mentions a lyric in one of her posts, then this lyric:

> *may be a 'secret' message for a friend (however this is only my intent and the recipient may not get the message sometimes ...;-)*

Such secret messages could, for instance, be hidden in the lyrics read in Figure 8.6, having a very particular *you* in mind.

10 March 2013 · ☀

In the silence of my lonely room
I think of you
Night and day

U2 - Night And Day [High Quality]

High Quality / Please take a look at my other videos.
THX

YOUTUBE.COM

Like · Comment · Share

👍 3 people like this.

FIGURE 8.6 *Posting lyrics with social steganography potential.*

By publishing similar *secret* messages in her Facebook profile, Carla engages in what boyd and Marwick (2011) have diagnosed as social steganography (from the Greek word στεγανογραφία, meaning concealed writing): a privacy strategy – in actual fact, it is a reconstruction of an age-old practice dating back to Ancient Greece and Egypt – used in digital spaces to camouflage information in public view, creating a message that can be read in one way by those who have the inferential capacity to understand the codes and read differently by those who cannot. Social steganography indicates care about privacy, misinterpretation and segmented communications strategies (boyd 2010c). Its power does not reside in strong encryption but in the fact that the audience members do not think to search for a hidden message (boyd and Marwick 2011) unless they are very close ties to the poster. In our first face-to-face meeting, Helen divulged to me that she can recognize particular patterns in lyric and music uploading on Facebook as regards the sentimental situation of her most intimate friends. Similar behaviour is spotted when users do not copy specific lyrics at all – even the title of the song alone can do the whole work of conveying a message (see Chapter 7).

However, this tactic is not always successful; things that are supposed to mean one thing can often be misinterpreted or overlooked. Carla points to this fact in the interview excerpt above: *the recipient may not get the message sometimes …;-).*

The examples thus far have manifested that privacy can be achieved by means of ambiguity, vagueness, presuppositions, in-group language and social steganography. However, situations and addressees do not always have to be so vaguely identified for privacy to be locked up; we will see how in the next section.

████ ████ shared a link.
21 December 2011 🎵

Οι αληθινές φιλίες δεν χάνονται!!
Αφιερωμένο -ξέρεις εσύ!- και μην μου στενοχωριέσαι!
Θα φτιάξουν όλα!

 Oi filoi - Haris Alexiou
www.youtube.com

music: H.Alexiou lyrics: H.Alexiou album: Odos Nefelis '88 label:
Universal

FIGURE 8.7 *Audience-specific reference via pronoun.*

(Translation: True friendships are not lost!! Dedicated – you know! – I don't want you to be sad! Everything will be OK! [Title of the embedded song: *The friends*]).

'Dedicated –you know!–': Making audience-specific references

In Figure 8.7, Alkis's addressee is very specific while unnamed. Alkis perceives the audience as consisting of *you* and *me* (*you know!, I don't want you to be sad!*). His intention is to console a friend via posting a song about the meaning of friendship. Notably, instead of posting the song directly to his friend's Wall (one speculation is that his friend's Wall might have been locked), he does so on his own without revealing the contact's name in all likelihood for reasons of not exposing her or him. In this fashion, Alkis shows concern for his friend's privacy and the incident that has dismayed her or him. This example makes it clear that the protection of privacy does not solely signify the protection from others but also the protection of relations and within relations (cf. Rössler 2005: 192). Furthermore, contrary to Carla's aforesaid statement (*the recipient may not get the message sometimes*), the situation here is too overt for Alkis's addressee not to catch the message.

In Figure 8.8, Alkis has uploaded a video from the American TV series *Beverly Hills* in which one of the female protagonists, Donna, is not allowed to participate in the graduation ceremony. In his opening comment, Alkis introduces an instance of address, that is to say, the explicit mentioning of the intended audience in the text (Myers 2010b: 78) by deploying Facebook's name mentioning/tagging facility to refer to five specific fellow students. In this way, he alienates the rest of his audience encouraging those five participants to respond (three of them indeed responded). His accompanying comment sets in motion an intra-group graduate student identity, using first plural person: μας (*us*) and ξεκινάμε (*we start*). Only the cognoscenti can decipher the meaning

FIGURE 8.8 *Audience-specific reference via tagging.*

(Translation: [name of friend 1], [name of friend 2] [name of friend 3] [name of friend 4] [name of friend 5] etc. etc. I dedicate this to us from today that we start until the graduation!:-))

of the time adverbial phrase *today that we start,* namely the day they started defending their MSc theses.

'*Nagyon nagyon': Reserving a code*

Another practice in which my informants engage to negotiate privacy is code-switching. Helen has a relationship with a Hungarian man. They do not speak each other's language aside from certain words and expressions. They normally communicate in English. Talking about this issue, Helen has said:

> *What you may have seen in my profile*
> *is a lot of code switching*
> *...*
> *and especially as regards interactions with my partner*
> *you may see there something in Hungarian*
> *(which unfortunately I don't speak):-)*

When Helen uploaded the photograph of a landscape she took while travelling by plane, her partner wrote her a comment mixing Greek with English while Helen chose to answer in Hungarian:

8.12

Helen's partner: oxx, agaapi, beautiful picture, alla tora mou leipeis!
'oh love, beautiful picture, but now I miss you!'
9 January 2012 at 23:45

Helen: en is szivem!! nagyon nagyon …
'you too my heart!! very very much …'
10 January 2012 at 15:31

With this choice, on the one hand, Helen frames symmetrical alignment and intimacy, as her partner used Greek in his own comment, while on the other, she reserves a specific code of communication with him which distances her other readership.

The next example illustrates a whole sequence in Spanish between Carla and FBU1, Carla's first Spanish teacher (the same teacher as in Example 6.23 in Chapter 6). The dialogue takes place underneath Carla's London photo album.

8.13

FBU1 [female, Greek]: Cuando viajaste a Londres Carla?
'When did you travel to London Carla?'
10 April 2011 at 01:30

Carla: hace tres semanas mas o menos querida
'approximately three weeks ago my dear'
10 April 2011 at 10:40

FBU1: que bien! cuanto tiempo te quedaste? negocios o placer?
'how nice! how long did you stay? business or pleasure?'
10 April 2011 at 18:32

Carla: 5 dias, nada mas… placer, fui a visitar unos amigos ojala pudiera quedarme mas!
'only 5 days… pleasure, I went to visit some friends:-) if only I could have stayed more!'
11 April 2011 at 02:17

In our post hoc interview, Carla offered a detailed emotionally laden account of the relationship she maintains with her teacher. Back in her undergraduate years in Corfu, Carla was studying translation in English and French, yet she wished to learn a new foreign language. The idea of Spanish, suggested by her mother, immediately thrilled Carla. Together with a fellow student they placed an ad asking for a teacher of Spanish. A young Greek woman, who had grown up in Argentina and was at that time living in Corfu, responded. Carla described me how zealous and inspirational her teacher was. After a certain period of intensive Spanish courses, the teacher decided to return to Argentina for personal reasons. Although Carla felt very sad, she tried not to lose contact with her. Carla now lives in Athens having a career in Latin American literature translation, whereas her teacher moved to the United States where she works as an interpreter. Since both women became friends on Facebook, they communicate more often and almost exclusively in Spanish.

The choice of language in Example 8.13 (of course one can easily copy and paste the excerpt into Google Translate to catch the gist of the interaction) can be seen as a positive politeness strategy which on the one hand indexes an in-group identity, and on the other it minimizes imposition discouraging non-Spanish speakers from intervening with further more or less intrusive questions about Carla's trip. As pointed out by Tsiplakou (2009: 385), such language practice is adopted 'emblematically ... to signal (or construct) ... ingroup solidarity, and, concomitantly, to index overarching in-group rapport'. Apart from generating group solidarity, code choice also cultivates identity-as-performance within localized communities of practice (ibid.: 386); it gums together the two women's collective past and present identities as former teacher and student of Spanish and as current professionals of Spanish who share common history, background knowledge, interpretative frameworks, practices and repertoires.

In both Examples 8.12 and 8.13, participants draw on their available languages in order to contextualize their comments as addressed to very specific members of their Facebook audience. It follows from this that a typical discourse function of code-switching, addressee specification (Gumperz 1982), finds new, fertile ground in SNS blurring the dichotomies between public and private discourse (Androutsopoulos 2013b).

'Why don't you go to another Wall?':
Challenging persistence

Self-censorship: Sporadic deletion of user's own Wall posts

Self-censorship is a textual practice which shows high awareness of privacy issues. This is so because it destabilizes the persistent nature of Facebook converting into a more ephemeral space (Marwick and boyd 2011). One type of self-censorship concerns the sporadic removal of the user's own Wall posts. Alkis below explains why he 'cleans' his Wall:

> *Generally I proceed to 'cleaning' from time to time (and by the way now that you have reminded me I'm about to delete some of them). The reasons are that some things may not express me anymore (rare reason but it has happened) or my Wall has been 'crammed'. Additionally, deleting isolated comments would be equal to some kind of censorship (if we're talking about others' comments). Another important reason is trying to provide the less possible information about me to Facebook or to whoever has access to my Wall against my will (or my privacy settings).*

Alkis here echoes Papacharissi and Gibson's (2011) assertion that an online profile is not a static object but an ongoing process always subject to editing. First, he gets rid of things that no longer express him. Although such a practice seldom happens, it constitutes a token of how fleeting and contingent identities may be. The second, rather vague, reason is that his Wall is full of information which he does not proceed to specify. In one of our first interviews, Alkis had admitted that he sometimes deletes his posts because of the follow-up comments by close friends who reveal personal data that he does not want to be openly publicized. It is useful to remember at this point that comments do not just create a dialogue between two interlocutors; instead they should be seen as 'a performance of social connection before a broader audience' (boyd 2010b: 45). Alkis prefers to delete the whole post rather than individual comments because that would be equal to some kind of censorship. His last reason, the blocking of access to his data, introduces again the comparison of me (my Wall, my will, my privacy settings) against them (Facebook, whoever). What struck me in the above excerpt was the parenthetical and by the way now that you have reminded me I'm about to delete some of them. I do not recognize an **observer's paradox** here; otherwise it would not have been stated that blatantly. That part of the interview took place when Alkis was writing up his dissertation, so it seemed reasonable for him not to have the time or zest to browse older posts on his Wall.

In studying Alkis's case, the ethical challenge for me was that I had to go back and forth his profile checking it every now and then in order not to analyse data that were later deleted. This was never entirely avoidable though. So I decided to make Alkis aware that some data he might want to delete would be 'locked in' and therefore be available after the completion of my study.

Astonishingly, during my observation I noticed that there were no posts at all on Alkis's Wall from 7 December 2007 to 21 October 2010, a quite long time span. In asking him whether he had deactivated his profile during that period or deleted all his posts along with friends' comments, he explicates:

> I didn't face any kind of criticism/bullying or even stalking etc. Simply, when the issue of privacy on Facebook got on my nerves for the first time, I deleted everything (since the date I joined) from my Wall.

What is unfolded here is the tension between 'agency' and 'structure' (Benwell and Stokoe 2006: 10), according to which users construe their identity as they wish while, on the other hand, identity construction is confined by institutionalized power structures. It is the second time Alkis resorts to the emotionally laden expression got on my nerves (see earlier, in Shielding profiles section, where he said: all this monitoring by Facebook has got on my nerves). However, he is still an active member of Facebook's networked topology. Instead of deactivating or shutting down his account, he chooses to sabotage (e.g. by uploading impersonal pictures), contradict and repurpose the very definition of SNS, refusing to abide by the requirements of Facebook's rigid and predetermined architecture.

Self-censorship: Deletion of recent activity

A second type of self-censorship is that of deleting all recent activity, something which can be more easily controlled in the new form of the Timeline (in the sense that only the profile owner can open the whole list of recent activities – other users can just see some of these activities in their News Feed depending on the privacy settings of the given content). Figure 8.9 displays how recent activity appeared on Carla's profile before the Timeline (it was much more detailed; someone could view everything that she had liked as well as comments she had written on other people's Walls), while Figure 8.10 shows recent activity in Gabriel's Timeline.

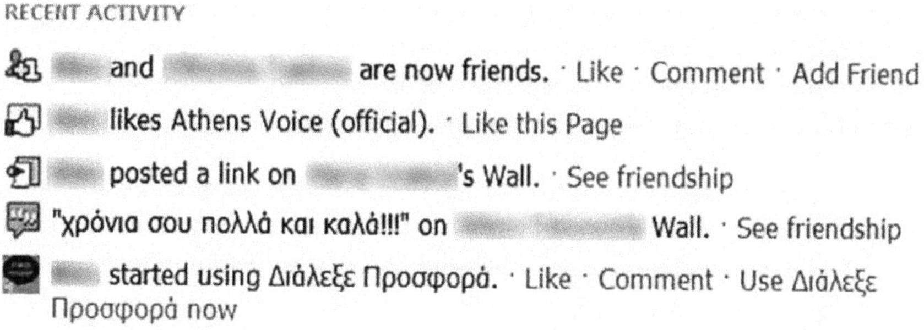

RECENT ACTIVITY
and are now friends. · Like · Comment · Add Friend
likes Athens Voice (official). · Like this Page
posted a link on 's Wall. · See friendship
"χρόνια σου πολλά και καλά!!!" on Wall. · See friendship
started using Διάλεξε Προσφορά. · Like · Comment · Use Διάλεξε Προσφορά now

FIGURE 8.9 *Recent activity before the Timeline (2010).*

Recent Activity
is going to The Atlantic Dialogues 2013.
likes Radical Face.

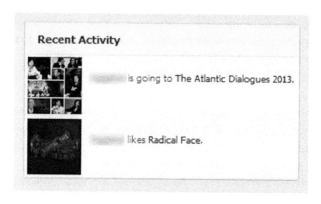

FIGURE 8.10 *Recent activity after the Timeline (2013).*

iel points out in the next extract, he has deleted some of his
vities principally for personal reasons, referring to his grumbling

*It has happened to delete posts or activity (or even untag a photo now that
I'm thinking of it) in the past for personal reasons (i.e. an ex girlfriend who
was complaining with every little thing!) ...*

In a similar vein, Alkis deletes all his recent activity (comments on friends'
status updates, photos and other uploads, likes, profile editing, friending). His
humorous response on why he is doing this comes naturally:

Privacy, privacy, privacy. Ah privacy too!!!!

Other-censorship

Privacy is not solely a function of our disclosures, but of the disclosures about
us by other Facebook members too (boyd 2007). From this perspective, privacy
also refers to the ability to control what is said about us (Raynes-Goldie 2010).
The boundaries between privacy and publicity can be delineated via the practice
of censoring other people's posts. The process of untagging belongs to that category. Consider what my participants say on the issue:

*I have untagged a photograph which was a collage a friend had made in a
stupid application and I didn't like it. I must have untagged one depicting
me in a party because I didn't like the photo at all! and I think that in a bit
joking yet serious enough way I had asked from my friend [in the original he
uses both masculine and feminine inflection] to remove the photograph!*

(Alkis)

*I have untagged a photograph because I didn't like it and it had been
uploaded by someone else ... ah and another photo in which I wasn't
even depicted, you know those photos in which they tag you to something
because you have been to particular bars etc*

(Romanos)

*I have untagged photographs in which my friends have tagged me without
asking me, because I don't want people who don't know me to have
access to who I am and what I do and I think that in this way I somehow
'secure' some personal information/moments*
*I don't remember whether I have deleted a photo. perhaps if someone
uploaded a photo that I considered more 'personal', I would delete it*

(Carla)

A name mention in a post or being tagged in a picture may often lead to disclosure about a user without prior knowledge or consent. In this light, West and Trester (2013: 139) have perceived tagging as a threat to one's positive **face**. In these cases, privacy requires 'interpersonal management' and 'coordination' (Stutzman and Kramer-Duffield 2010) such as untagging the photograph at hand or asking the friend who uploaded it to remove it. After the Timeline launch, Facebook allowed users to review a photograph in which they were tagged before it appeared on their Wall and then decide whether they wanted it to be there or not. My participants provide legitimate reasons on why they have resorted to untagging. Alkis and Romanos put forth an aesthetics criterion (*I didn't like it, I didn't like the photo at all!, i didn't like it*), nevertheless without specifying what exactly had disturbed them, that is, their own appearance, the portrayed situation (if, for instance, they were eating, drinking, smoking, doing a grimace, had a particular pose, did not like their outfit and so on). Romanos mentions he untagged a photo in which he was not depicted but it might have revealed a place he had been and did not wish others to become aware of or considered this kind of tagging as trivial. Alkis does not admit openly he has untagged photographs given his cautious language (*I must have untagged, I think that*). Carla shows major concern for her unknown audience since once she is tagged, she appears to the original poster's network, that is, people she does not know. This kind of censorship, thus, allows her to secure her personal life. Similarly to Alkis, she does not seem to remember specific examples of untagging (*I don't remember*). I do not think of Alkis and Carla as being secretive in the particular excerpts – probably their tagging was not that harmful so as to retain it in their memory forever.

Besides untagging, users can delete others' comments as well. Gabriel understands Facebook as a kind of personal space where he can express political opinions. However, when he receives personal insults that have nothing to do with politics, he opts for removing such comments.

> *I often use Facebook to express political opinions, indirectly or directly, this of course draws criticism, which is welcome. Problems and censorship arise when there are personal references driven mostly from malevolence rather than political opinion. Then I censor and perhaps I delete comments because I don't accept uncalled-for insults in something that even typically is considered my personal space.*

Alkis and Carla, on the other hand, delete friends' comments that may reveal personal information against their will.

> *I have deleted [comments] mainly because close friends of mine have revealed personal data which I don't want to be known to everyone!*

(Alkis)

I may delete a comment which contains private information that I don't want to be published. Otherwise, I would probably delete only something insulting.

(Carla)

I have discerned cases in which my participants do not delete inappropriate comments or irrelevant stuff on their Wall written by their friends but warn or reprimand them to either stop or continue their discussion elsewhere.

8.14

Carla

μαναράκια, <u>δεν πάτε σε κανέναν άλλο τοίχο να τα πείτε λέω εγώ</u>?! ευχαριστώ για το support! νιώθω πολύ καλύτερα, ειλικρινά!
'hey <u>fellas</u>+DIM, <u>why don't you go to another Wall to chat I suggest</u>?! thanks for the support! I'm feeling much better, honestly!'
7 April 2013 at 23:36 · Like · 1

8.15

Gabriel

parakalo tetoiou eidous sizitisis na ginontai se ksexoristo section tou facebook (<u>na figete na pate allou</u> kai ta loipa) ...
'please this type of conversations should take place in a distinct section of Facebook (<u>leave and go elsewhere</u> et cetera)...'
15 December 2010 at 11:32

In one of her statuses, Carla confessed to her network that someone had stolen from her parents' home the copper natural gas pipes. Although her friends expressed their sympathy towards her, a couple of them diverted the conversation to virtually irrelevant topics. Example 8.14 was Carla's response, an indirect plead to stop 'dirtying' her Wall in such a crucial moment. Example 8.15 revolves around a similar theme. Underneath a picture depicting Gabriel preparing a seminar with another friend, two female contacts started writing comments relating to hotel rooms during their pending trip abroad for a conference.

The users perceive their profiles as a holding of theirs. As appears from the preceding examples, they do not delete their friends' comments but deploy witty ways to make them realize that what they do is improper. Carla uses the chatty address *μαναράκια* (*fellas*) to draw their attention as well as the interrobang (?!) to formulate her rhetorical question. Gabriel, on the other hand, makes an intertextual link to a successful Greek ice cream commercial.[4]

'No dirty linen in public': Avoiding comments and changing medium

Avoiding commenting

Another method to assert control over privacy is to avoid commenting. Helen, as also discussed in Chapters 4 and 7, has been very worried about the political and financial situation in Greece since the outbreak of the crisis in 2010. She often uploads photos (e.g. Figures 8.11 and 8.12) she has taken herself from demonstrations held in Athens as well as relevant newspaper articles (e.g. Figure 8.13). Nonetheless, she usually just posts without further comments so as not appear affiliated with a particular political party or being identified with any kind of movement. Consider what she says:

i want to give my own version of an event
to report on an event in my own way
without making an explicit political comment
generally I'm careful with that

By dint of her 'bare' posts, Helen makes wordless yet very powerful statements. Her practice is reminiscent of Georgakopoulou's (2014: 527) remark: 'Implying a position results in an implied selection of a specific audience as the designated one for a particular posting' (on aligning with implied positions and posting with an audience in mind, see Chapter 7). Helen's specific audience includes Facebook members who experience and are concerned about the Greek crisis either from the inside (Greek residents) or from distance (Greeks living abroad) as well as friends from abroad who have knowledge of and interest in the current Greek reality.

FIGURE 8.11 *Posting photos without comments.*

FIGURE 8.12 *Posting photos without comments II.*

(Translation of the placard: solidarity of workers – banks' wealth belongs to us – nationalization without compensation).

 shared a link.

Steve Bell on Greece's euro bailout referendum – cartoon
www.guardian.co.uk

Greek PM George Papandreou stunned Europe's leaders by proposing his country should hold a referendum on the debt deal

Like · Comment · Share · 3 November 2011 at 00:41

FIGURE 8.13 *Posting articles without comments.*

It was touched upon earlier that locking one's Wall is one way of preventing dissemination of personal information. However, Carla's Wall (in both her profiles) is open and friends can post comments and links on it. In learning about Carla's forthcoming business journey to Corfu, FBU1, in Example 8.16, took the opportunity to write on her (personal profile) Wall and ask some further enlightening questions. In the meantime, FBU2 expresses his surprise in learning such news from Facebook. Carla brings him back telling him that he should have consulted a professional website for translators they both use.

8.16

FBU1 [female]: Carla, ematha oti tha ekdramete sto nisi twn Faiakwn me tin ka [όνομα φίλης]. Exw erwtiseis: Pote tha pate, giati tha pate kai kuriws... thelete parea?
'Carla, I've heard that you're going on an excursion to Corfu with [name of female friend]. I have questions: When are you going, why are you going and mainly...do you want company?'
25 November 2010 at 13:27

FBU2 [male]: thee mou, mathainw ta sxedia sas apo to Facebook!!!
'my god, I learn about your plans from Facebook!!!'
25 November 2010 at 15:35

Carla: όχι αν διαβάζεις τις ανακοινώσεις στο site μας;-)
'No if you read the announcements on our site;-)'
25 November 2010 at 17:19

FBU1's disclosure of Carla's upcoming location (Corfu) to her peers is framed as an invasion to her locational privacy (see also Gordon and de Souza e Silva 2011: 137). Notice that Carla leaves unanswered the initial questions, at least in front of her Facebook audience. This practice of leaving messages unanswered because they require personal information to be given publicly is common among my participants. Here are some more examples:

8.17

κάρλα γεια! με αφορμή την αφιξη της [όνομα φίλης] λεω να μαζευτουμε το σαββατο το απογευματακι-βραδακι σπιτι μου. αν βολευεσαι πεσ μου για να σου δωσω νταηρεκτιονσ :). θα χαρω να σε δω. Φιλια

'Carla hi! Due to [name of friend]'s arrival I'm thinking of organizing a gathering on Saturday evening at my home. If it is convenient tell me so that I give you directions :). I'll be glad to see you. Kisses'

(from Carla's Timeline, personal profile)

8.18

που χάθηκες ρε
'hey where have you been lost'

(from Romanos's Timeline)

8.19

popo.. ti kaneis romane..;;;
'well well.. how are you doing Romanos..???'

(from Romanos's Timeline)

Profile hosts leave such invitations for coordination or questions by their friends without any further comments or 'Likes'. This is plausible considering, for instance, that if Carla in 8.17 had responded positively, then all mutual contacts, as well as those who are not mutual but visit Carla's profile, would have been informed on where she would be on that Saturday night. Had she answered negatively, then she would have probably appeared to her network as uninterested in her friend's arrival. Questions in Examples 8.18 and 8.19 should not be considered as mere phatic communion – the one in Example 8.18, particularly, was posed when Romanos had been doing his military service. These questions anticipate a detailed answer from Romanos which he chooses not to give in public. It seems that for both Carla and Romanos the safest way is to continue the conversation elsewhere perhaps via a Facebook message, instant messaging, an email, texting or a phone call (see Example 8.20).

Changing medium of communication

Alkis, in circumstances akin to the above, has the tendency to state the problem explicitly and propose a change of medium of communication recognizing the perforated nature of Facebook. Let me give you one out of the several similar examples I have collected from his profile. A friend had posted a video song on Alkis's Wall. They talked a bit about the song and then their interaction went like this:

8.20

FBU1 [female]: Πώς πάει η ζωή;
'How's life?'
8 May 2012 at 01:58

Alkis: Τα εν οίκω μη εν δήμω
Πάμε inbox!;)
'Let's not wash our dirty linen in public
Let's go to inbox;)'
8 May 2012 at 01:58

FBU1: Πολύ σωστά! :)
'Right! :)'
8 May 2012 at 01:59 · Like · 1

As can be seen, Alkis denies discussing in public his news suggesting to his friend to change their medium of communication, namely to move from Wall comments to their Facebook inbox messages where they can feel more comfortable to chat just the two of them.

Making the rules on our walls

Participation, and concomitantly presence, in Facebook is predicated upon publicness and disclosure which constitute the default (boyd and Marwick

TABLE 8.3 Privacy practices

Practices based on architecture of software	Practices that combine affordances with linguistic signals and textual choices	

• friends-only visible profiles
• custom uploads
• careful friending
• photo/text untagging
• blocking feature
• separate profiles
• hidden friend list
	• recontextualization (addition, deletion, substitution, rearrangement)
	• obscure name
	• impersonal profile picture
	• no demographic info
	• ambiguity
	• vagueness
	• in-group language/jargon
	• audience-oriented references
		• social steganography
		• code-switching
		• self-censorship
		  – removing Wall posts
		  – deleting recent activity
		• other-censorship
		• no comment
		  – own post
		  – other post
		• change medium of communication

2011). Yet, crafting, updating and monitoring a Facebook profile does not necessarily entail that we have to include every single detail about ourselves. In this chapter, I presented some of the – more or less – conscious practices (summarized in Table 8.3) that my informants adopt to control the flow of information on their Facebook Walls in order to enhance and secure their social privacy and hence manage their identity. As the findings suggest, the users appear to deeply care about privacy and 'contextual integrity' (Nissenbaum 2004), namely the nature of information that they think of as appropriate, allowable, expected, or even demanded to be revealed and disseminated within the given context of Facebook. By adopting these practices, my informants showed that

- they are creative;
- they have shared personal and social criteria on what to leave/delete;
- they are competent in manipulating language(s);
- they are skilful in using the system to their advantage;
- they are critical of the system and other users as well (each informant with different forms of criticality).

By valuing privacy, both personally and socially, the users value their identity. Protecting their informational privacy is equal to asserting control over their self-presentation, that is, control of how they wish to present, stage and craft themselves, to whom they want to do so, to what extent, in which contexts and under which circumstances (see also Rössler 2005: 116; Ellison et al. 2011: 20). The analysis provided insights not only on how my participants want to see themselves but most importantly how and by whom they want to be seen, recognized and validated, confirming Papacharissi and Gibson's (2011: 80) observation that 'privacy concerns who partakes in our construction of identity'.

A plausible, yet vexed, question that emerges from the discussion in this chapter is the following: How could we characterize the realm of Facebook: public, semi-public or private? (You may have noticed that throughout this book I mostly employ the characterization 'semi-public'.) I think the most proper answer comes from Enli and Thumim (2012: 92), who regard Facebook as 'a public sphere where individual users contribute with private postings and through their activities negotiate the degree of intimacy'. Put it more minimally, Facebook posts are public by default and private through effort (boyd 2010a). Therefore, partaking in Facebook's networked public trying at the same time not to be public is not an oxymoron (revisit this chapter's section on the paradox of Facebook privacy) but an 'agentic act' (Livingstone 2008: 409) by means of which users protect their identity.

It is useful to bear in mind, though, that the effort to protect privacy can vary enormously among users. Privacy is not the same for everyone. Rössler (2005: 9) posits that 'the dividing line between what is to be regarded as public and what as private is a constructed one and has not been laid down once and for all'. Privacy choices, thus, are expressions of individual subjective preferences, thoughts, feelings, images, self-definitions and self-interpretations also affected by the role of sociocultural norms, asymmetric information, bounded rationality, cognitive biases and the environment by and large (Rössler 2005; boyd and Marwick 2011; Stutzman et al. 2012). So my list of privacy practices should not be taken as exhaustive but as a snapshot. Apart from the users who value privacy in distinctive ways, Facebook too is a 'moving target' with new applications and extra privacy features being developed and implemented incessantly (Debatin et al. 2009: 103). Changes in technology are highly likely to be accompanied by changes in users' attitudes towards privacy. For example, after Facebook's facelift with the arrival of the Timeline, Helen rethought some of her personal information and removed her partner's name from her profile, keeping just the field 'In a relationship' without specifying with whom. As time passes and users become even more dexterous with new technologies, they will invent new, more innovative and witty ways to shield their privacy.

One important caveat needs to be taken into account: privacy is unavoidably predetermined by Facebook's architecture. Participants represent themselves using Facebook's language and frameworks (Enli and Thumim 2012). Even if they have customized their privacy settings, what they achieve is only a compromised or prescribed autonomy negotiated within the terms that Facebook has defined (Papacharissi and Gibson 2011). Of course, users can protest against Facebook's privacy standards by playing with the format and showing that they are critical (Enli and Thumim 2012) as Alkis has opted for doing.

In the end, is it worth it to have a profile on Facebook or not? Grimmelmann (2009) deploys a wonderful metaphor:

> It's true that using Facebook can be hazardous to your privacy, but a hammer can also be hazardous to your thumb. People need tools, and sometimes they need dangerous tools. Hammers are physically dangerous; Facebook is socially dangerous. We shouldn't ban hammers, and we shouldn't ban Facebook.

Facing Facebook as a social tool equips individuals with a multitude of literacies on how to share their personal information, constructing thus meaningful identities and forging reciprocal relationships.

Privacy and identity: Why and how

As previously mentioned, while my observation of Alkis's profile was still inchoate, I noticed he had deleted all his posts from 2007 to 2009. In the follow-up interview, I raised the issue and, as we saw, he provided very personal and insightful commentaries on how he perceives privacy. I kept on combing through my five informants' data, as they were being accumulated, and decided that it would worth exploring privacy through the spectrum of discourse practices extracting implications for identity. The coding of the examples I picked for this chapter involved looking into

- obscure referents (e.g. *-17,7*);
- presuppositions (e.g. in *new* adventures);
- jargon (e.g. internetese/geeky language);
- song lyrics;
- language alternation (e.g. code-switching, code-mixing);
- indexing addressees (e.g. via pronouns or tagging);
- references to Facebook's **lingo**: *Wall, inbox, settings, privacy, personal information, untag, delete, block, hide, friends* (both in posts and in interviews).

ACTIVITY 8.1: FACEBOOK PRIVACY
AND CHALLENGES

Consider the examples and interview excerpts discussed in this chapter as well as your own usage of Facebook and answer the following questions:

1 Do you think that the different levels of privacy, as traced in this chapter, indicate that there could be problems for collecting data from Facebook?

2 Would Goffman's distinction between giving and giving off an impression be relevant to users' privacy practices?

3 Do issues of privacy challenge ideas of personhood and distinctiveness?

4 Is privacy an age-graded matter?

ACTIVITY 8.2: PRIVATE COMMUNICATION
ON FACEBOOK

Towards the end of this chapter, Alkis wrote his friend *Let's go to inbox;)*. A great deal of communication on Facebook takes place privately through messages and/or the medium's messenger app. Skim through your Facebook inbox messages and take notes on the following questions:

1 How is Facebook messaging used for organizing and micro-coordinating life?

2 Has it replaced email or text-messaging? Any reasons for that?

3 In which cases and to what extent do you/your friends favour private messaging to writing public comments on each other's Timelines?

Useful resources

Print

Much insightful work on privacy and social media comes from danah boyd and Alice Marwick (see boyd 2013; 2014, Chapter 2; boyd and Marwick 2011; Marwick and boyd 2014; Hargittai and Marwick 2016). Papacharissi and Gibson (2012) hold an engrossing discussion on the treatment of privacy as a commodity by Web-accessible platforms. If you are particularly interested in the evolution of Facebook privacy features, see Stutzman et al. (2012). Debatin et al. (2009), on the other hand, present a pithy review of Facebook's privacy fails.

Seeing audience as the quintessence of privacy, several recent linguistic and communication studies zoom in on the kinds of strategies that users adopt to signal what is private and what is public, and to directly or indirectly address and exclude particular individuals and groups. Tagg and Seargeant (2014) explore how Facebook users draw on multilingual resources to distinguish between different strands of their potential audience. In a similar vein, Androutsopoulos (2014) draws attention to linguistic consequences of context collapse on Facebook arguing that language style, and more specifically language choice, has an instrumental role in bringing together or separating parts of the networked audience. In her PhD thesis, West (2015) analyses audience behaviours on Facebook in terms of their layeredness (imagined, potential, actual and active audience segments) and overlap. Gershon (2010: 125–30) has a very good commentary on how young adults use song lyrics as second-order information (i.e. information which is 'not actually said' but rather constitutes the 'background knowledge of a situation and expectations of communication' that allows the readership to decipher the meaning of the words) to imply or show that they survive breakups in new media realms. On textual practices, Das and Kramer (2013) discuss a different type of self-censorship, what they call 'last-minute self-censorship', namely content that users typed on Facebook but decided not to publish affected by their perception of audience. From a methodological perspective, Georgakopoulou (2016) talks about the challenges that a researcher may experience in connection with context collapse in social media data bringing forward certain proposals for facing these challenges.

Apart from facilitating new forms of communication, social media have also facilitated new forms of surveillance (recall what Alkis said on this matter in our interview), enabling governments, organizations, corporations and individuals to access our personal information without our prior consent. In his thought-provoking essay, Jones (2016) puts forth a sociolinguistics of surveillance according to which linguists should not only describe and analyse these new forms of surveillance, but also help people develop the literacies needed to confront them.

Web

Facebook Privacy Fail Infographic
http://www.topwebdesignschools.org/facebook-fail/

Video

Person of Interest is an American science fiction crime drama television series which tackles digital technologies, surveillance and privacy rights.
http://www.cbs.com/shows/person_of_interest/

9

Conclusion

Chapter overview

The point of departure of this book was that SNS are dynamic sociocultural arenas which empower users to cement their identities through the meshing of language with other semiotic modes. The aim I set out was to explore the discursive construction of identity within the SNS of Facebook, drawing on insights from Greek users. The following key questions were formulated in setting this aim:

- How do Facebook users construct themselves?

- How are they co-constructed by their Facebook friends?

- What is the role of multimodality in these identity constructions?

- What kind of textual practices do Facebook users adopt to construct their identities?

In Chapters 4–8, I sought to answer these questions embarking on discourse analysis of both verbal and visual modalities employed by five Greek Facebook users: Romanos, Gabriel, Carla, Alkis and Helen. What I identified was the ways in which they

- located themselves in terms of place (Chapter 4) and time (Chapter 5);

- announced activities, shared and broadened their expertise and buttressed solidarity among colleagues and fellow students (Chapter 6);

- communicated emotions, tastes, thoughts, opinions and assessments (Chapter 7);

- controlled the flow of information on their Walls to secure their privacy (Chapter 8).

The analysis was built around five arguments in relation to identity:

- Identity is integrally related to where we are, where we have been and where we are heading towards (Chapter 4).

- Identity is a temporal process (Chapter 5).

- Identity is defined by the work we do (Chapter 6).

- Stance is an essential discursive mechanism via which identity is enacted (Chapter 7).

- Privacy is the ability to control access to one's identity (Chapter 8).

In the rest of this chapter, I summarize my findings and make some overall observations concerning identity on Facebook. I then outline a number of caveats that should be taken into account when researching Facebook discourse. I close with some reflections on the role of Facebook in our lives.

Construction of identity

My first question was concerned with the ways in which Facebook users craft their identities. The analysis shed light on how they claimed a sense of self; indexed their positions within the sociocultural milieu; and projected affiliations to and disaffiliations from people, cultural products, practices, activities, values and ideas. For my summary here, I will start from features that constituted fairly obvious markers of identity, to features that were found to be more novel, creative and surprising.

The most straightforward references to ways of being, doing, feeling and thinking, in statuses and comments alike, were by means of 'I-marked' utterances accentuated by the first person pronoun (or just signalled by the inflection of the verb in Greek) and a verb (either cognitive, epistemic, affective or operative that signalled or announced activity). Some indicative examples included:

- *at a café in Budapest <u>marking</u> students' exams*

- *in <u>my</u> 30s I will <u>become</u> a fan of metal music!*

- *I have (like now) to <u>study</u> all day*

- *Dear politicians, <u>I'm fed up with</u> your dilemmas!*

Utterances of that type, in Chapter 7, were tied to evaluations which could be either quantified (e.g. *Me <u>very</u> happy after so many wishes!*) for reasons of placing emphasis or mitigated (e.g. *<u>I guess</u> I should consider myself lucky*) minding sounding moderate.

'I-marked' utterances came also onstage through the words of someone else. Anchoring in culture-specific knowledge, the users forged intertextual links (I will return to this point in a while) to express stances (e.g. *Σιγά μην κλάψω* – *I won't cry*; song title) and banter (e.g. *I'm a horrible person*; videogame line), among other things. Showing alignment with the I-persona of another text had a double function for them: 1) it articulated more smartly what they were actually feeling, thinking or experiencing in a given moment; 2) it put on display their accumulated cultural capital.

As has been reported by Page (2010) and Lee (2011), Facebook status updates deal in the main with the communication of prosaic and day-to-day topics. My informants were often found to break the mould of banality by being creative and playful, bringing a little bit of excitement to their postings, with 'I' slowly fading. In narrating their autobiographical episodes (Chapters 5 and 7), for instance, they ornamented their personal experiences with vividness and suspense recalling memories and externalizing a gamut of feelings. One way to do so was by deploying tropes to express moods and dispositions such as metonymies (e.g. *addicted to the <u>Greek summer</u>*), personifications (e.g. *I'm in love with this <u>beach</u>*) and hyperboles (e.g. *you see what happens to people in old age?*). Another way was by mobilizing humour. This was attained by rendering ambiguity (e.g. *flower bora bora*), flouting Grice's maxim of quality (e.g. *Don't ask me now how the devil of fb has holed up in here!!!!*), being self-sarcastic (e.g. *as in circuses, for limited shows in your town!*) and playing with typography (e.g. *there's nothing easy(*) in this affair :-)*). Similar effects of unexpectedness were produced in terms of content when the users shared experiences that were utterly different from the average or foreseeable ones, yet they were meaningful to them (e.g. Romanos as a lonely soldier on New Year's Eve).

One distinctive manifestation of identity was the taking up of affordances of multiple languages (e.g. Greek, English, Spanish, French and Hungarian). The users invented neologisms, mixed languages and alternated between scripts (e.g. Greek, English, Greeklish and Engreek). In this fashion, they projected themselves as global or local members of Facebook; they ratified their expertise as language professionals (Helen, Carla and Alkis); they consciously tailored a writing style; they reserved a particular code to exclude or include members of their audience (e.g. international friends) or contributed to the immediate co-text in which another language or script was used.

Co-construction of identity

My second question pertained to the ways in which users' identity is constructed by their Facebook friends. One of Facebook's definite assets, as opposed to the way other social media such as Twitter work, is that the body of communication it hosts is largely structured around offline relationships. In Chapters 6 and 8, I tackled the concept of context collapse, according to which Facebook brings together friends and acquaintances from different backgrounds with different shared pasts and presents and different kinds of shared knowledge. Alkis's Facebook friend list, for instance, comprises colleagues from various jobs as well as fellow students from his undergraduate and postgraduate studies. With each one of them, Alkis shares different prior experiences, yet all of these friends can offer a vital piece to Alkis's identity mosaic. Therefore, paraphrasing Shotter (1993: 6), what makes Alkis, Helen, Gabriel, Romanos and Carla unique is the extensive social Facebook 'seascape' around them.

My initial objective was to examine how my informants were constructed by their friends. But I also found evidence on how they themselves also constructed their friends. This bi-directional process of co-construction was stimulated via

- **'You'-marked utterances.** These could be targeted from a friend to one of my informants (e.g. *how proud you've made us!!*) and vice versa (e.g. *If you want to be miserable and cavil do it on my inbox*).

- **Collective 'we' pronoun.** Depending on the situation and the participants, 'we' could be either writer-inclusive or writer-exclusive and concerned belonging constructions of 'we' as speakers of Greek (Chapter 6), 'we' as Greeks who experience the crisis (Chapter 7), 'we' as Greeks with particular culinary customs (Chapter 4), 'we' as UK residents (Chapter 4), 'we' as translators (Chapter 6), 'we' as fellow students (Chapters 6 and 8), 'we' as members of the same generation (Chapter 5) and 'we' as takers of desired future states (Chapter 5).

- **Labelling.** It involved constructing membership categories relating to profession (Chapter 6) and age (Chapter 5), primarily by means of nominals (e.g. translators, young and old) and adjectives (e.g. wise and mature). Humorous labels were also at play (e.g. *you're the most hopeless awful person*).

- **Evaluation.** The users attributed positive qualities to others' posts (e.g. *So much useful!*) or opted for more indirect endorsement (e.g. *gee what you reminded me of now, Thanx for the post, it's been a long time since I had listened to it..*).

- **Praise.** Facebook friends acclaimed my informants for their achievements within the professional and educational realms (Chapter 6) (e.g. *the reviews are dithyrambic again, Thank you for being such an EAP star again, CONGRATULATIONS!!!!!!!!!!!!!!!!!!!*). A second level of co-construction was traced here as my respondents shifted the credit to a third party (e.g. EAP coordinators and professors). Moreover, it was not only the profile owner who was praised but also the other way round: the profile owner promoted and praised a friend's work in a new post (e.g. *Whoever has 5-10 minutes max to help my friend with the research for her dissertation! The questionnaire is interesting!!*).

- **In-group language/jargon.** The use of a specific code was observed in several different occasions such as discussing a professional issue (e.g. translation jargon), the crisis (e.g. political jargon), in hiding moods in plain sight (e.g. through gaming jargon).

- **Humour.** Humour among Facebook friends functioned as a bridge to shared experience, norms, values and attitudes; it constructed group cohesion and solidarity, exploiting and strengthening the sense of belonging to a group (e.g. *May Ramesses II the Great bless all of you!* that Carla wrote to her colleagues).

- **Direct appeals to the audience.** By asking their audience to do/ answer something, my informants showed that they counted on their friends' opinions and valued them as experts (e.g. *What do you reckon?, Anyone interested in doing consecutive interpreting ...*). Other direct forms of addressing the audience aimed at attracting its attention (e.g. *You'll laugh, you'll cry (from laughing), you'll get moved*).

Significantly, the co-construction of identity was afforded to a great extent by Facebook's technical features. Successive commenting enabled the synergetic activation of a series of identities, individual and collective, in many cases irrespective of the profile owner's original aim. Tagging and name mentioning, on the other hand, were employed to clearly specify members of given 'we' collectives. Clicking the 'Like' button appeared to have a double function:

- my participants were sanctioned for their posts as having shared something useful, interesting or amusing;

- my participants clicked 'Like' to comments made by their friends to espouse and ratify other-constructions of themselves.

Multimodality and identity construction

The third question I addressed related to the role of multimodality in identity construction. Obviously, answers to this question are interrelated to the previous two questions as well. The reason that a separate question was posed, and not incorporated into the other two, was to offer at this concluding juncture a more systematic account on multimodal practices. Below I summarize the main findings under three categories as different modes fulfil different functions: images that the users shot themselves, images they found in the internet and music videos.

Own images

By sharing photographs they have taken themselves, my informants exploited the semiotics of the image allowing it to speak for them. In particular, via their images, they

- validated their experience, namely where they were and what they were doing (e.g. working, having fun, demonstrating, being on holidays, attending conferences) without necessarily posing always in front of the camera;

- gave visual proofs of accomplishments (e.g. having cooked *gemista*);

- showed cosmopolitanism;

- paid respect to other cultures;

- demonstrated artistic photographic skills;

- created professional portfolios;

- invoked regional identities;
- exercised citizen journalism with authentic first-hand material;
- made 'safe' and witty statements without spelling them out in words.

Ready-made images

In my participants' arsenal of images already been circulated online were found memes, comic strips from Greek and foreign artists, mottos typographically enhanced as well as other types of images coming from unacknowledged sources. These images typically had a certain amount of text inscribed in them. Here are some chief reasons why my informants chose to share such images:

- the picture, both visually and textually, encapsulates best what they would like to say;
- to show alignment with the message represented or implied;
- to complement visually the force of their own verbal message (e.g. sleeping dwarf image, Gabriel showing his happiness with photo);
- to suggest an analogy to the situation they were into (e.g. Alkis collecting data for his dissertation – scientist making an experiment as a profile picture);
- to ridicule the self, provoking further comments;
- to amuse their audience;
- to make a nuanced appeal to a collective identity;
- to being attached a label.

Music

My informants did versatile things with music posts, whether these were accompanied by text (own comments or lyrics) or not, such as the following:

- uploading a song just for the sake of it (e.g. because they were actually listening to it on radio, TV, computer playlist and the internet);
- indicating music tastes;
- expressing emotions, dispositions and moods;
- reconstructing memories;

- appreciating aesthetically pieces of music and artists;

- evaluating a situation on the basis of song titles;

- making identity claims on the basis of song titles (e.g. young forever);

- sharing the discovery of a music genre they were not previously acquainted with;

- relaying a covert message to a member of the audience;

- tactfully comforting a friend in front of an audience.

Altogether, multimodal means enabled my informants to articulate facets of their identity more forcefully, convincingly, creatively and indirectly. The same applied to instances in which friends posted images and songs on my informants' Walls to construct their professional, educational and age identities. Crucially, the spectacle as such, be that visual or aural, triggered and spurred rich interactions and collaborative identity constructions in ways that the initial poster could not have foreseen or expected.

Textual practices and identity

My final question sought to identify particular textual practices that users adopted in their identity constructions. Textual practices were understood as practical ways of using texts along with the actions, experiences and socio-cultural meanings affixed to these texts. Although the notion of practice was more systematically covered in Chapter 8 (see Table 8.3), several other occurrences were documented in earlier chapters. These can fall into three board categories: drawing on own/other texts, producing Facebook-afforded texts and concealing texts.

Drawing on own/other texts

- **Copying-pasting.** The users copied – either verbatim or loosely – song lyrics, other people's direct speech, ad slogans, mottos or maxims.

- **Decontextualization, recontextualization and entextualization.** My informants extracted 'instances of culture' (e.g. language forms, textual material and song videos) and relocated them in their discourse activities. In doing so, they invested the original artefacts with new meanings.

- **Mashupability**. This process involved remixing, reappropriating and recasting different modes and resources for meaning-making. With this type of composing, the users created multimodal texts that acquired a new system of signification (as was the case with entextualization). Carla's blending of song lyrics, poetry verses, film titles and lines with photographs in Chapter 4 (Table 4.1) constitutes a properly representative example of mashupability.

- **Recurrent posting**. My participants reproduced exactly the same post (e.g. the EURO.PA.S. event Gabriel promoted in Chapter 6) or referred to the same event with different wording each time (e.g. Carla's and Romanos's countdowns in Chapter 5) or employed a conglomerate of texts, article links and comments (e.g. Carla's reference to the event at the Ionian University in Chapter 4). In the same spirit, each year on 31 December, Alkis enjoys the textual ritual of writing wishes to all of his Facebook friends. A cognate practice was **cross-posting** of professional material in Carla's two profiles.

Producing Facebook-afforded texts

- **Embedding URLs.** Sheer links (i.e. with no opening comments or further clarifications on their content) shared by my informants were found to constitute sites of action that produced textual situations. Readers could draw the main idea from the text appearing in the thumbnail underneath the attached link. It was up to them whether to follow the link up and gain from the recommended source.

- **Clicking 'Like'.** By clicking 'Like' under something a friend has posted is generally seen as the quickest and easiest way to make your contact aware that you enjoy it, without writing a comment. In the data at hand it functioned as a marker of acceptance, affirmation, validation, personal expression, alignment, solidarity and appreciation, and as a confidence booster.

- **Tagging.** As mentioned earlier, the practice of tagging is of cardinal importance in addressing particular individuals and mobilizing collective identities. **Untagging** for reasons of shielding privacy or not feeling flattered by a certain post was reported in the interviews as such a practice could not be visible in participant observation (see also below).

- **Mapping**. My participants selected and pinned on maps (this actually involves a process of tagging the place) specific moments meaningful to their identities.

Concealing texts

- **Obscuring real name.** A practice that reduced traceability and searchability of the self by invisible audiences (see also boyd 2010b).

- **Uploading impersonal profile picture.** The users lean on the semiotic power of images to make alternative identity claims (see previous section on multimodality).

- **Excluding information.** This mainly dealt with the exclusion of demographic details such as date of birth and place of residence.

- **Employing social steganography.** Hiding messages behind copying-pasting lyrics.

- **Self-censoring.** This involved removing one's Wall posts and deleting one's recent activity.

- **Other-censoring.** Deleting friends' comments and untagging (see above).

- **Avoid commenting.** This had to do with one's own post, whereby the image/video was considered to make a statement all on its own without further comments, as well as not answering in public a friend's comment as it would reveal personal information.

The adoption of all these textual practices had major implications for the users' identity facilitating them to

- show identification with a given group of people;

- take social action;

- imply a situation they were into;

- display their linguistic and cultural capital;

- show competence in textual manipulation;

- offer the audience the potential of playful engagement;

- flag the importance of an event to them (e.g. holidays, concert, writing and presenting dissertation);

- keep their audience abreast of information (e.g. by writing regular updates concerning a particular event);

- ask their audience to do something with the information provided;

- issue audience reminders;

- perform emotive action (via 'Like');

- offer latent support to a friend;

- protect their identity.

Identity on Facebook: Overall observations

Identities on Facebook can be deliberately crafted (e.g. promoting one's work), arise impromptu (e.g. after the phatic communion *have a nice month*) or in the course of interaction (e.g. discussing how to prepare *gemista*). The micro-linguistic devices, textual and other multimodal practices traced in my participants' identity crafting give rise to three broader identity issues: audience-centredness, self-continuity and (dis)identification.

Identity on Facebook is necessarily audience-oriented. After having been triggered by an external stimulus (e.g. a beloved song, a trip or a politician's statement), the users felt immediately impelled to share their reflections with others and more often than not initiate discussion and invite their readers to co-construct meaning, as was the case with the stance-taking occurrences (Chapter 7). A similar rationale was applied when users made humour to keep themselves and their audience amused testing and sparking their reactions. They could even resort to sources of fun only as a strategy to elicit the exactly opposite answer. By drawing intertextual links, users addressed Facebook friends that possessed the same background knowledge, presuming that they would be able to disentangle the inferences. 'The enjoyment of intertextuality', Adami (2012: 143) notes, 'rewards those grasping the source with an elitist feeling of being part of a shared semiotics'. The choice of language too indicated deep concern about one's audience, as evidenced by Helen's case, who mostly wrote in English. Such a decision proved to be pivotal in the 'vernacularization'[1] (Georgakopoulou 2014) of the Greek crisis (i.e. the bottom-up discursive representation of the crisis, outside institutions, by ordinary people) because her English message could reach and inform a wider audience.

Another attribute of identity witnessed in Facebook pertained to continuity. Note, however, that this was not transparent at first blush but only after systematic observation largely enabled by the Timeline architecture. Repeated references and/or invocations to places and activities tied to them (Chapter 4) as well as recollections of people, things, events and situations (Chapter 5) across posts could be treated as 'backbones' of the self that bonded together one's identity in the past, present and future into a long-lasting sense of personal identity. Importantly, continuity of one's identity was also generated and ensured by others leading to the collaborative construal of places and memories. However, as manifested in Chapters 4 and 7, the Greek crisis has profoundly shaken my informants' self-continuity. Current and future anxieties with respect to the crisis can have far-reaching ramifications on social media usage too in terms of content of posting and frequency of posting (see also Chapter 5). Whether we are dealing with self-discontinuity or just disruption of self-continuity in times of crisis remains to be seen.

Facebook turned out to be an ideal setting to study how identity is shaped through processes of identification and disidentification (cf. Brubaker and Cooper 2000). My informants located themselves vis-à-vis elements from culture (music, films, literature, ads, internet), ideas, opinions, moments, memories, activities, places, foods, social categories and people. These identifications constituted powerful indices of affiliation, belonging, connectedness, commonality, alignment and groupness. Nevertheless, instances of disidentification were also encountered, dealing mainly with the Greek crisis. The users' disidentification was conceptualized in terms of disalignment, emotional detachment, hostility and bitterness, and was expressed through language typified by low modality, irony, harshness, acerbic evaluation and terms that bore negative load such as *surrealand*, *destruction* and *swamp*. Notice that they did not renounce Greece as a place but Greece as a social entity in crisis, disidentifying themselves from its political system, social organization and the mentality of some of its people.

Researching Facebook discourse: Some caveats

Facebook has disembedded communication from its traditional anchoring in the face-to-face situation of physical co-location and has re-embedded it in a more flexible and complex context (Livingstone and Brake 2009) conflating multimodality, intertextuality, convergence and mashup (Lee 2011). Studying how we use Facebook can provide deep insights into human behaviour difficult to match in most common research settings (Wilson et al. 2012). However, a number of caveats invite consideration while conducting research on Facebook.

First and foremost, it is one thing to say that Facebook has a global potential and another thing that it has global reach. Access, in fact, is not universal and the subjects being studied for their social media usage very often represent a privileged and small portion of the world's western societies (Gilbert 2010).

What is more, the possibilities for identity construction on Facebook, albeit unparalleled, are provided by a private company driven by commercial concerns and interests. This entails that it is typically the software that moulds self-presentation in certain ways, 'limiting or encouraging users to construct their identity along commercially acceptable lines' (Marwick 2005: 95). However, within this book (especially in Chapter 8) we witnessed a range of ways via which users can repurpose the medium and circumvent Facebook's predetermined, commodified assumptions.

We should also be cautious and not hallow Facebook since not all SNS activity is always positive. For instance, personal information in SNS may be used to broker productive interaction, may perpetuate existing stereotypes, may be misused by marketers, or used for evil and dishonest purposes such as stalking, bullying, paedophilia and identity theft (Ellison et al. 2010: 141).

There is a continuing need to bear in mind that Facebook means different things to different people in different contexts (Enli and Thumim 2012). The knowledge and identities that people bring to Facebook shape not only the technology but also how it is used. So, any findings should be taken as adding to cumulative knowledge through qualitative work on social networking (ibid.).

Regarding participants in online ethnographies, it is instructive to bear in mind the degree to which users have incorporated social media into their daily lives. Some users are more tech-savvy, avid and dexterous than others. Moreover, and with respect to my own respondents, the ways in which they used Facebook at the time of conducting this research (e.g. for bantering, tackling professional matters, reflecting upon sociopolitical issues, consuming and appreciating culture) perhaps bears no resemblance to how they are using it now or how they will use it in a couple of years from now. It is not only technologies that develop and change but also users' perceptions and behaviours while plunging into these technologies.

Unavoidably, such changes bear consequences for the sociolinguistic and discursive practices of which these technologies are a part (Thurlow and Mroczek 2011). By the time a book (like this one), an article, a thesis or a university course on social media is completed, users' practices may have changed and the scholarly work will have become outdated (Barton and Lee 2013: 8). This of course does not automatically invalidate our research neither should discourage researchers from continuously taking the social media pulse. Suffice to recall that platforms like Internet Relay Chat may no longer exist or may have disappeared from the limelight, yet the scholars (e.g. see articles in Herring 1996) who investigated them laid solid foundations for later research in CMC.

Another crucial factor affecting users' discourse activities on Facebook is the diverse offline backgrounds they come from: social, cultural, educational, national and so on. A common denominator of my participants' background was that they were highly educated. This uniformity was not a parameter set at the beginning of my research but rather a matter of the way I developed my sample by inviting and snowballing. So this book cannot claim generalizability or representativeness of its findings. This book gives a 'thick description' (Geertz 1973) of what people can do in Facebook communication and how they understand their actions. But it also gives illuminating insights into what Facebook itself can be.

What can Facebook be?

With a focus on discourse manifestations of identity, this book brought to the fore Facebook's significance to our everyday lives, our interpersonal relationships and society by and large. More concretely, it was shown that Facebook can function as:

A space for vernacular literacy practices. Focusing on a wide range of linguistic and multimodal resources utilized by my informants, the analysis shed light on how they delved into a series of vernacular literacy practices (Barton and Hamilton 1998),[2] that is, everyday reading and writing activities on Facebook, related to

- personal communication (e.g. holiday photos, birthday wishes, posting videos to each other's Walls);
- leisure activity (e.g. publicizing music they listen plus its evaluation as in Chapter 7);
- documenting life (e.g. through small stories in status updates, images that imply a situation they are into);
- sense making (e.g. when Carla used Facebook to sort out the transliteration of Abu Simbel in Greek);
- social participation (e.g. through commenting and stance-taking).

A silo of relationships. Voluminous scholarly and popular work has concentrated on how Facebook feeds users' angst to look attractive and show that they lead an interesting, enviable life worthy of receiving copious amounts of 'Likes'. But is it just all about sheer narcissism inflated by new technologies? Findings here evidenced ways that Facebook users step aside self-obsession to connect and be positive to their contacts (e.g. by consoling and comforting each other). This kind of Facebook usage boosts self- and other-esteem and self-confidence in a healthy way.

A digital memory bank. This book has gone some way towards showing that revitalizing the past is an important practice among Facebook friends. So Facebook is not just about staying connected here and now. It can also be a place of nostalgia and remembering good times, and shared experiences and tastes that were there in the past, but are given prominence now. Owing to Facebook's affordances, users can have a persistent written record of their co-authored memories.

A research tool. In this book I focused on Facebook as a rich source of observable ongoing data of discourse behaviour. While observing my informants, it also became apparent that Facebook itself can be used as a tool to collect other types of data. Alkis's case in Chapter 6, where he created a Facebook event to recruit participants for his survey, proved that this novel method of data collection can indeed be very effective for one's research purposes.

A knowledge forum. Facebook facilitates sharing, gaining, broadening and mediating knowledge on a range of topics and by means of various affordances. Knowledge is exchanged in a friendly and casual way (e.g. through humour and conversational devices) fostering participants' socialization in the learning process.

A cardiograph of a society. Studying Facebook proved to go hand in hand with studying Greek society in times of crisis. In observing my informants' Facebook Timelines, I simultaneously dealt with their individualized crisis timelines as those appeared in their posts. What was also brought to light was that changes in society have very much affected their Facebook use (e.g. fewer posts, different post topics; see also Chapter 5).

A grassroots channel. Previous research (e.g. Gerbaudo 2012; Fuchs 2014) has demonstrated how users have exploited Facebook and Twitter for activism and protest (e.g. to coordinate demonstrations). The work reported here showed how people can exploit Facebook as a grassroots channel converting it into a networked 'counterpublic' (Warner 2002) sphere to practice citizen journalism, inform and anti-inform about the Greek crisis.

The final word

Logan Pierce:
Every technology ages, John. The only thing
that never gets old is connecting with people.

(*Person of Interest* 2013)

Facebook's mission has been to give people the power to communicate and stay connected transcending time and distance constraints. As Miller (2011: 217) has vividly described:

[Facebook's] importance lies in its perceived and actual ability to reconstruct relationships, especially within families and with absent friends, that had been gradually fading away due to the attrition of other aspects of modern life, such as increasing mobility. Facebook helps in some measure to reverse this decline in sociality and repair what is viewed as the damage inflicted on people by this loss of close relationships. So the single most important attribute of Facebook is not what is new about it, but the degree to which it seems to help us return to the kind of involvement in social networks that we believe we have lost.

From the very outset of my research, I had asked my informants how they would react in case Facebook suddenly shut down. Here is what they said:

In the beginning it would seem strange to me but I would adjust myself! In any way it would be quickly replaced by something else as is the case with every fashion.

(Gabriel)

I would get sad, maybe I would react strongly in discussions with my friends in any case I would get over it in 1-2 days maximum.

(Alkis)

what are we going to do without it? :) ...
i'm totally reliant on it
it would almost be tantamount to having my email account closed
almost not exactly the same
but even in this case I wouldn't know how to communicate with many people
Facebook has many functions for me ...
I can't believe that I would lose all these

(Helen)

I think I would feel a gap. But it wouldn't be the end of the world. ... We are social animals, we'll find something else to keep ourselves busy.

(Carla)

ok it would piss me off a bit because I would lose something with which I pass some of my time and communicate with people I have known from the past and we no longer see each other but in the end the answer would be 'who cares?'

(Romanos)

We see mixed reactions among my respondents: surprise, sadness, feelings of loss and annoyance. Nonetheless, Gabriel and Carla point to the fact that Facebook is one technological form of our sociality, a form that shapes it and elicits it – it is not unlikely that new platforms will sooner or later undertake this role. In the years to come, and hearkening to the needs of contemporary societies and technologies, Facebook may be revamped, upgraded, transformed, merged, even replaced. It may acquire new roles, functions and practicalities wholly worthy to be assessed and researched. Sure enough though, throughout its life span, Facebook has been well integrated into our daily lives, radicalizing our communication, nurturing our personal relationships and advancing our identity enactment.

Appendix

Timeline of the Greek crisis until the end of my data collection period (April 2013)

2001	Greece joins the Eurozone.
2008	Global economic downturn reaches Greece, which already has heavy sovereign debt from previous years.
October 2009	Social democratic party PASOK (Panhellenic Socialist Movement) wins the elections. George Papandreou becomes prime minister.
December 2009	Government divulges a funding gap in its accounts.
9 February 2010	First austerity measures package (tax increase, pensions frozen, changes to employment regulation, mergers and closures of public organizations, privatization).
January 2010	Greece is on the brink of default.
2 May 2010	Papandreou signs 'Memorandum of Understanding' with Troika, composed of the European Union, the International Monetary Fund (IMF) and the European Central Bank (ECB).
5 May 2010	General nationwide strike. Marfin Bank events in Athens. Three employees are killed.
October 2010	Christine Lagarde (managing director of IMF) sends to Giorgos Papakonstantinou (Greece's finance minister) a list of wealthy Greeks with undeclared accounts in Swiss banks.
May–August 2011	Greek Indignant Citizens Movement (Aganaktismenoi) swarm every evening at Athens Syntagma Square to protest against austerity.
28 June 2011	General strike. Riot police clashes with protesters.
29 June 2011	Government sanctions new austerity measures.

14 September 2011	New tax on property collected through electricity bills.
28 October 2011	Protests on National Day.
31 October 2011	Papandreou announces a referendum on austerity package. The referendum is never conducted.
November 2011	Papandreou resigns. Lucas Papademos, former vice-president of ECB, is appointed interim prime minister.
12 February 2012	Memorandum 2 voted in Parliament. Violent protests in Athens.
6 May 2012	First round of elections. Centre-right party Nea Dimokratia (New Democracy) is first. Left-wing party SYRIZA (Coalition of the Radical Left – Unitary Social Front) is second. Far right-party Chrysi Avgi (Golden Dawn) in Parliament.
17 June 2012	Second round of elections. Coalition government with the participation of New Democracy, PASOK and DIMAR (Democratic Left). Antonis Samaras, New Democracy president, becomes Greece's prime minister.
September 2012	Intense clashes between local residents, who opposed privatization, and police occurred in Northern Greece over the commencement of gold mining by a Canadian company.
9 October 2012	The German chancellor, Angela Merkel, visits Athens. Her visit is greeted with large protests.
November 2012	The parliament votes in favour of new austerity cuts.
April 2013	The government approves a bill for the dismissal of 15,000 public sector employees by the end of 2014, with 4,000 being laid off within 2013.

Glossary

Affordances – the ways in which we understand elements of an environment in terms of their use. Affordances constitute constellations of interface properties (e.g. hyperlinks, navigation buttons, text, images, videos and audio), users' perceptions on how to utilize these properties and for what purposes, and users' wider sociocultural assumptions, beliefs and values. The term was first used by psychologist James Gibson (1977) and applied in technology studies by Ian Hutchby (2001).

Asynchronous – mode of computer-mediated communication (e.g. forums, emails, bulletin boards, Facebook commenting) where the participants do not need to be logged on at the same time, and considerable time gaps can occur between their exchanges.

Circumlocution (or 'periphrasis') – a roundabout way of speaking/writing where the speaker/writer uses more words than necessary so to avoid expressing themselves clearly.

Citizen journalism – a type of reportage in which ordinary individuals temporarily and often spontaneously take the role of a journalist producing and spreading news (e.g. via social media) during a time of crisis, accident or disaster when they happen to be present as the event is being unfolded.

Code-switching – alternating between more than one language or linguistic variety within a single spoken or written conversation.

Coined word – new word that is purposefully or accidentally created.

Comments – a vital feature of all Web 2.0 spaces is their commenting systems via which users can interact writing comments about each other's uploaded content.

Context collapse – the term describes the way in which SNS users present themselves in front of multiple heterogeneous audiences (intimate friends, relatives, colleagues) as well as the challenges they encounter in so doing.

Cover photo – a large image at the top of a Facebook user's profile which represents who the user is or what they care about.

Cultural capital – the accumulation of knowledge, skills, education, tastes, posture, clothing, mannerisms, material belongings, credentials and so on that we acquire and draw upon as we participate in social life.

Curate – collect, catalogue, arrange and assemble content in digital production and social media.

Decisional utterances – when speakers/writers mark their stance towards a certain line of action by proposing it to their interlocutors or committing themselves to it (e.g. I'll keep you posted); also known as 'decisionals'.

Deictics – words and expressions that take their meaning from the particular situation – local, temporal, personal – of the speaker/writer and their audience (e.g. this/that, here/there, now/then, I/you).

Demonstratives – deictic words or phrases (see above) that indicate whether the referent is near or distant (e.g. this/that).

Directives – attempts by the speaker/writer to get the hearer/reader to take a particular action (e.g. via requests, commands and advice).

Discourse – language as a social practice, that is, what people do with language, what language does to them, what language means to them and how language matters to them.

Discourse-centred online ethnography – ethnography which combines the systematic observation of online discourse with the direct engagement with the producers of this online discourse.

Emic – research approach which draws on the perspective of the subjects being studied.

Emojis – colourful glyphs (e.g. winks, **smileys**, love hearts) used in digital communication as a visual representation of a feeling, idea, entity, status or event. The term 'emoji' is Japanese and means 'pictograph'.

Entextualization – the process of extracting discourse material out of its context (decontextualizing) and integrating and modifying (recontextualizing) this material so that it fits in a new context.

Events – a Facebook feature through which members can inform friends and networks about upcoming events of interest. Users can click 'going' to events, invite friends or create events themselves. Events require an event name, network, host name, event type, start time, location and a guest list of friends invited. They are either public or private.

Evidentiality – how speakers/writers mark what they know and what evidence they have for what they believe (e.g. reasoning from personal experience/ knowledge or from what someone else has said or written).

Face – the public self-image that people try to protect. In politeness theory, 'positive face' refers to one's self-esteem (the desire to be liked, admired, ratified, and related to positively), while 'negative face' pertains to one's freedom to act (the desire not to be imposed upon).

Face-threatening – certain verbal acts that have the potential to damage or threaten another person's positive face (e.g. insulting the hearer or expressing disapproval for something the hearer likes) or negative face (e.g. giving an order to the hearer and thereby restricting their freedom) (see **face** above). Such acts are known as 'face-threatening acts' (FTAs). The speaker can save the hearer's face, thus avoiding performance of an FTA, by employing politeness strategies such as indicating in-group identity (positive facework) or using **hedging** (negative facework).

Fave – to favourite, that is, to mark something as a favourite on a social media website to show that you like it or agree with it. The shortened version 'fave' belongs to Flickr's lingo.

Field site – the setting that an ethnographer is observing. The research practice of collecting data from a particular environment is known as 'fieldwork'.

Force – a speaker's/writer's intention.

Graduation – the ways of adjusting the degree of an evaluation (e.g. how intensified or mitigated it is).

Greeklish – the written representation of Greek with Roman characters in computer-mediated environments.

Grounded theory – an epistemological stance that starts with the data, which are then reviewed, enabling the theory to emerge from them.

Groups – separate spaces on Facebook to share information and discuss, either publicly or privately, a range of subjects with specific sets of people like family, fellow students, colleagues or people with common interests.

Hedging – words or constructions that mitigate a speaker's/writer's commitment to a statement (e.g. 'I think', 'quite a bit', 'probably').

Homophones – words that sound the same but have different meanings and spellings (e.g. night – knight).

'Like' button – an image displaying a thumbs-up symbol accompanied by the word 'Like', either in English or in the language in which users have customized their profiles. Users can like status updates, comments, photos, links shared by friends, pages and adverts by clicking the 'Like' button at the bottom of the content. The button displays the number of users that liked particular content and shows a list of them. The 'Like' button is also available in websites outside Facebook.

Lingo – jargon; special terminology used by people who do a particular activity or job or belong to a particular in-group.

Log data – stored, static records of verbal interaction (e.g. characters, words, utterances, messages, exchanges, threads and archives) put into their particular order by a server feature and displayed as a message protocol on users' screens.

Maxim of quality – Grice (1975) introduced a system of 'conversational logic' based on a number of maxims, that is, intuitive principles which are supposed to guide interaction in keeping with a general cooperative principle. Four maxims have been recognized: the maxim of quantity states that contributors should give no more or less information than is required for the current purposes of the exchange; the maxim of quality states that contributions should be genuine and not false; the maxim of relevance states that contributions should be related to the purposes of the exchange; and the maxim of manner states that contributions should be brief, perspicuous and orderly avoiding obscurity and ambiguity. In many circumstances, the maxims are breached or flouted. Any obvious breaching or flouting of the maxims is interpreted by the interlocutor as a conscious act which signals special (implicit) meaning.

Meme – a cultural unit (e.g. idea, joke, rumour, popular tune, catchphrase, fashion trend, architectural style, image and jingle) that spreads rapidly and effectively from person to person via the internet becoming a model for textual (re)production.

Metadiscourse – the ways in which writers reflect on their texts to refer to themselves, their readership or the text itself.

Metonymy – a figure of speech in which a name of a referent is replaced by the name of another semantically associated referent (e.g. 'the President – the White House' in the example 'The White House made known that …').

Microblogging – the act of posting short messages to the internet.

Modality – features in a text that express the speaker's/writer's attitudes towards themselves, their interlocutors, and the topic at hand, that is, what they commit themselves to in terms of truth or necessity. Modality can have high (e.g. 'must', 'always'), median (e.g. 'should', 'probably') or low (e.g. 'may', 'perhaps') levels of commitment.

Neologism – the invention of new words.

News Feed – the centre column of a Facebook user's homepage. It is a constantly updating list of stories from people and Pages that users follow on Facebook. Such stories can include friends' profile changes, status updates, photos, videos, links, 'Likes', posts and conversations between mutual contacts, new friend adds, upcoming events and birthdays.

Observer's paradox – the phenomenon where the researcher's presence itself might influence the participants' behaviour.

Pages – pages allow individuals, companies, brands, organizations, services and celebrities to connect with people on Facebook who just have to click 'Like' on the page they are interested in. Page owners (admins) post information on their page (it behaves like a user's personal profile) which then becomes available to the News Feed updates of the people who have liked their page.

Participant observation – a qualitative method whereby the researcher participates in a group in order to study that group.

Personification (or 'anthropomorphization') – a specific form of metaphor used to give a human form to inanimate objects, abstract entities, phenomena and ideas.

Phatic communion – small talk; the use of language to establish sociability (e.g. greetings, farewells, congratulations and wishes) rather than to convey information.

Post hoc interview – interview that takes place after the ethnography has concluded.

Presupposition – assumption based on background knowledge.

Recontextualization – the process of integrating and modifying discourse material in a new context.

Reflexivity – the term refers to instances whereby language use facilitates forms of conscious reflection on experiences and activities. Social media affordances, such as asynchronous commenting, allow for a high degree of reflection on language use.

Script-switching (also 'trans-scripting') – writing a language using the spelling conventions of another, as in ϑɛνκς, a spelling of English *thanks* according to Greek spelling conventions.

Selfie – self-portraits taken with one's mobile phone or webcam and then posted to social media.

Semi-structured interviews – interviews with a given guide and open-ended questions based on what the interviewee says.

Share – a Facebook button via which users can send another person's or Page's post to friends or reproduce it anew in their own **Timeline** with or without additional comments. Shared content is given automatically credit to the original poster posted in the form of 'FBU1 shared a link via FBU2', 'FBU1 shared FBU2's status', or 'FBU1 shared FBU2's photo'.

Smiley (also 'emoticon') – a symbol used in text-based digital communication to represent a facial expression.

Social media – digital services, such as blogs, microblogging sites (e.g. Twitter), social network sites (e.g. Facebook), content-sharing websites (e.g. YouTube, Instagram), wikis, podcasts, discussion forums, chatrooms, virtual worlds (e.g. World of Warcraft) and livecasting (e.g. Skype), which promote social interaction between participants through the exchange and sharing of user-produced content.

Social network sites (or 'social networks') – websites like Facebook whose prime purpose is to enable users to cement and maintain social and friendship ties. Social network sites have three key features: 1) a member profile, 2) a network of links with other members and 3) the ability to view and search those links (Ellison and boyd 2013). The term 'social network sites' implies that the networks usually consist of people a user already knows, while the term 'social networking sites' places emphasis on relationship initiation, often between strangers.

Status (or 'status update') – a feature which enables users to inform their Facebook friends of their current status, that is, their feelings, thoughts, whereabouts or actions. Facebook prompts the status update with the question 'What's on your mind?' which appears both at the top of the user's homepage and their personal profile. Initially, status updates were exclusively text-based while multimodal content, such as photos and videos, was later allowed to be attached.

Synecdoche – a figure of speech in which the part is used for the whole (e.g. 'a new set of wheels' instead of 'a new car') or the whole is used for the part (e.g. 'this creature' instead of 'this person').

Tagging – Facebook users write the name of a friend, a brand, an event or a group in a post so that it links to the **Wall** of the Facebook page being tagged. Then the post (most often it is a photo depicting the tagged person) appears in the News Feeds of that page as well as in those of selected friends. The main function of tags is to identify who is, what it is or who owns something for reasons of organizing and refining Facebook content, attracting attention, addressing (tagging in this case is also called 'name mentioning') or even teasing particular people. Tagging can also be used in Facebook comments. 'Untagging' refers to the process of removing the tag, therefore the link, between the name and the post.

Techno-autobiography – a journal-style writing in which users describe the digital technologies they first deal when they wake up and how this continues during the day. This practice has been proposed by David Barton and Carmen Lee (2013).

Tellership – whether a story is narrated by a single teller or collaboratively.

Ticker – Facebook feature which was launched in 2011. It appears on Facebook home page next to the News Feed on the right and shows things that users could already see on Facebook but in real time (e.g. friends' comments or 'Likes' on a status, status updates as soon as they are posted and so on). Users can hover over their friends' stories shown on the Ticker and view more details. The Ticker cannot be deactivated arousing major concerns regarding users' privacy.

Timeline – a space in a user's Facebook profile where their content (updates, photos, videos, links and other posts) is categorized according to the period of time in which it was uploaded or created. The Timeline makes it easier for users to jump to stories from their past and view a log of their Facebook activity.

Toponym – a place name.

Toponymic anthroponym – generic reference to people in terms of the place they come from (e.g. the Greeks).

Transgressive semiotics – a sign which violates either deliberately or accidentally the conventional semiotics of a place (e.g. graffiti, trash, discarded items); any sign in the 'wrong place'.

Trope – a figure of speech (e.g. metaphor, synecdoche, metonymy and personification).

Tweet – sending a short message via the microblogging service Twitter; also used as a noun to refer to the message itself.

Wall – the place where each Facebook user's content is posted and displayed. It is visible to anyone granted a permission by the profile owner according to the customization of their privacy settings. Friends' Wall posts appear in the user's News Feed. On 15 December 2011, the Wall was replaced by the Timeline layout.

Notes

Chapter 1

1 Social media researcher danah boyd does not capitalize her name (http://www.danah.org/name.html).

Chapter 2

1 Inspired from the colloquial name of the – printed or online – directory provided each academic year to students by some American university administrations to help them get to know one another. Erstad and Wertsch (2008) note that the name Facebook integrates well the personal expression and the mediational means used.

2 In Greece 4.7 million people were active on Facebook in 2016, of whom 3.8 million on a daily basis. Total population in Greece: 10,773,253 (2016); internet penetration in Greece: 65.6 per cent (June 2016); internet users in Greece: 7,072,534 (June 2016) (Internet World Stats 2016).

3 Since Facebook is constantly being developed and upgraded, the description of its features offered in this book might be different from what is actually in use by the time this book is read.

4 On 15 December 2011, the Wall was replaced by the Timeline layout. The terms 'Wall' and 'Timeline' are used interchangeably in the book regarding data collected from December 2011 onwards as my Facebook participants themselves persisted in referring to the 'Wall'.

5 To enhance interaction with the content, Facebook introduced in February 2016 its 'Reactions' feature, a palette of new buttons, which along with the famous thumb, the icons now include a heart, a laughing face, a surprised face, a tearing face and an angry face.

Chapter 3

1 Once I started gathering enough data from these five informants, I felt I had something interesting and meaningful to say. So, given the time and space constraints, I considered that a sample size of five people was large enough to provide a solid and cohesive foundation for my arguments.

2 According to Facebook Pages Terms: 'If you collect content and information directly from users, you will make it clear that you (and not Facebook) are collecting it, and you will provide notice about and obtain user consent for your use of the content and information that you collect. Regardless of how you obtain content and information from users, you are responsible for securing all necessary permissions to reuse their content and information. You will not collect users' content or information, or otherwise access Facebook, using automated means (such as harvesting bots, robots, spiders, or scrapers) without our permission' (https://www.facebook.com/page_guidelines.php).

3 Glaser and Strauss talk about 'theoretical saturation', namely when no additional data are found that extend or modify the theory developed. They argue that saturation is reached by joint collection and analysis of the data.

4 Relations of participants are discussed when this was considered crucial for the interpretation of the findings, for example references to Helen's partner (Chapter 8), Alkis's sister (Chapters 5 and 7), Carla's sister (Chapters 4 and 7) and Carla's teacher of Spanish (Chapters 6 and 8).

Chapter 4

1 This emphasis might also be related to a Facebook corporate strategy. For instance, if people give their location, it is easier to design ads for them. Many other online services and apps seem to emphasize location, not as identity but as target.

2 Berger (2011) employs the concept of the 'cliché' to describe images that are 'predictable, conservative, and repetitive in both form and content'. Family photographs and tourist photographs are the two par excellence examples of photographic practice defined by the cliché.

3 Booths is a chain of high-end supermarkets in Lancashire, Cumbria, Yorkshire, Cheshire and Greater Manchester, UK.

4 Hala is an area in Lancaster, UK.

5 Single Step is a local wholefood co-op in Lancaster, UK.

6 In Greek *mangas* is used to refer to someone who has guts; in the book it is used as a dog's name – to make a pun – which, after running away from home, is unprepared and weak to confront previously unknown dangers.

Chapter 5

1 Rebetiko is an urban Greek folk music genre which appeared at the end of the nineteenth century. Rebetiko lyrics refer to the experiences of marginalized people (e.g. crime, drink, drugs, poverty, prostitution and violence). Rebetiko is mainly played with long necked bowl-lute, plucked string instruments (bouzouki and baglamas).

2 Lyrics: Gerasimos Tsakalos; music: Vassilis Tsitsanis; singer: Marika Ninou. The song was released in 1953. Alkis's stretches 'now' in an attempt to imitate Ninou's way of singing.

3 However, there are still some traditional cultures, as is the case of Pirahã in the Amazon Rainforest, for which time is not that essential (see Everett 2005).

4 Morrissey is an English singer and songwriter. He was the lead singer of the indie rock band The Smiths (active from 1982 to 1987).

5 Alkis has uploaded one of the film's scenes where a seamstress (played by the Greek actress Rena Vlachopoulou) reprimands her plump client for overeating: 'Σούζι, τρως' (Suzie you've been eating). When the client dismisses this as unfair, the seamstress retorts by saying 'Σούζι, τρως. Και ψεύδεσαι και τρως' (Suzie you've been eating. Not only have you been lying but you have also been eating).

6 Raki is unsweetened, strong alcoholic drink (popular in Greece and Turkey) from fermented grapes, which can sometimes be anise-flavoured.

7 All these references in the status are Greek advertisement slogans.

8 This is a Greek advertisement slogan too.

9 Jennifer Lopez is an American, of Puerto Rican descent, pop and R&B (rhythm and blues) singer, actress, dancer, fashion designer and producer. Lady Gaga is an American, of Italian descent, electronic pop singer, songwriter and actress.

10 Written by Giannis Nikolaou and sung by Pantelis Thalassinos in 1990. The chorus of the song (translated from Greek) is *It's not my fault if I grow older / it's life's fault for being so short*.

11 The commonest Greek wish equally given in birthdays and name days is χρόνια πολλά (chrónia pollá). It literally means many years in the sense of *I wish you to live many years*; hence other-permanence is inbuilt in the wish even if most of the times it is uttered unconsciously. In this chapter, I have opted for translating χρόνια πολλά as *happy birthday*, given that the particular wishes were written on my informants' birthdays. The analysis of name day wishes, which constitute a significant Greek cultural practice akin to birthdays, remained outside my scope (with an exception in Chapter 6) as I considered them problematic for maintaining participants' anonymity. Most of the name day wishes in my corpus revolved around diminutives, puns, proverbs and other cultural references related to participants' real names. All these effects were lost with pseudonymity.

12 Written by the popular Greek folk singer/songwriter Grigoris Mpithikotsis and released in 1955.

13 Madonna is an American singer, songwriter, dancer, actress and businesswoman, often referred to as the 'Queen of Pop'.

14 Anne Murray is a Canadian pop, country and soft rock singer. Papa Winnie is a reggae musician from St. Vincent and the Grenadines in the Caribbean.

15 *Re* is a very common interjection in Greek used to address someone, attract their attention, add emphasis, express astonishment, mark friendly disagreement or hurl an insult.

16 Lyrics from the Greek rap song *Θέλω να γυρίσω* ('I want to go back') written by Nikos Vourliotis and released in 1999.

Chapter 6

1 Kaufman and Feldman do not overlook the fact that there are cases where students feel intellectually deficient when they do not perform well academically.

2 For my participants' full professional and educational details, refer to Chapter 3. For a discussion on Carla's double Facebook presence and Alkis's bare demographics, see Chapter 8.

3 Greek schools were supposedly closed down during the period of Ottoman rule in Greece (between fifteenth and nineteenth centuries). Orthodox clergy taught Greek students the Greek language and Christian tenets at night in secret, thus the name *κρυφό σχολειό*, literally translated as *secret school*. The existence of such schools is today believed to be a national myth (Angelou 1997).

4 From December 2011 until June 2012, Alkis was unemployed. In the meantime, he was preparing his MSc dissertation. This chapter also includes data from the period he was working as a real estate agent (July 2012 onwards).

5 FBU2 puns on the Greeklish homography of *γάμο* (gámo), the accusative case of *γάμος* (wedding), and *γαμώ* (gamó), an offensive verb which means to have sex with someone.

6 Actually, this is a cover version of *My Number One*, the 2005 winning song of the Eurovision Song Contest which was the 2005 Eurovision entrant for Greece performed by the Greek-Swedish singer Elena Paparizou.

7 I had finished my data collection when Alkis told me about his second profile, so I did not include any data from there.

8 Throughout this thread I have employed International Phonetic Alphabet (IPA) symbols that represent the actual pronunciation. For more information, consult the International Phonetic Association website (http://www.langsci. ucl.ac.uk/ipa/index.html).

9 The surname 'Heston' is false friends (i.e. sounds the same) with the Greek phrase 'χέσ' τον' (literally 'shit him') meaning 'ignore him'. Many Greeks prefer to pronounce Heston as í:stən.

10 The Abu Simbel temples are two massive rock temples in southern Egypt carved in the thirteenth century BC.

11 Consistent with the prevalent tradition in Greek tertiary institutions, the oath, namely the text via which students swear that they will practice their discipline ethically and honestly, is always read by the student who graduates ranking first.

12 These are the lyrics of the Greek birthday song:

Να ζήσεις [όνομα] και χρόνια πολλά / Μεγάλη να γίνεις με άσπρα μαλλιά / Παντού να σκορπίζεις της νιότης [ή γνώσης] το φως / Και όλοι να λένε να μια/ένας σοφός (Translation: Long may you live [name of birthday person] and [may you live] many years / May you grow old with white hair / May you spread out everywhere the light of youth [or knowledge] / And may everybody say there [he/she] is a wise man/woman).

Chapter 7

1 I am talking about individual users' profiles and not Facebook Pages or Facebook Groups where people previously unknown to each other can interact.

2 For using song lyrics to hide emotional stances in plain view, see Chapter 8.

3 This is a Greek proverb literally translated as *Everything about the wedding is difficult and the bride is pregnant*. It is deliberately selected by Carla for both its metaphoricity (to refer to a difficult situation) and its literal meaning (to refer to her sister's marriage and pregnancy).

4 Slang.gr (2016) mentions that when someone is boiling in anger κατεβάζει καντήλια (literally: his/her colourful language takes vigil lamps down). The first 'recipients' of this language are usually Christ and Virgin Mary.

5 The word *meme* derives from the Greek *mimema*, signifying 'imitated thing', which was shortened by the evolutionary biologist Richard Dawkins so as to rhyme with *gene*. According to Dawkins, memes are 'small cultural units of transmission, analogous to genes, which are spread from person to person by copying or imitation' (Shifman 2013: 2).

6 Written by Giannis Aggelakas and released in 2005.

7 Written by Loukianos Kilaidonis and released in 1979. As you can probably realize, there is an element of timelessness in the song.

8 Prior to this post, Romanos had already shared a couple of status updates relevant to Portal 2 including: 'Test results: I am a horrible person. And they didn't even test for that.' (19 April 2011 at 23.10) and 'Bye GLaDOS, it's been a blast! ♥' (23 April 2011 at 01.53).

9 FBU1 alludes to a Greek TV series, broadcasted in 2009, entitled *Χαρά αγνοείται* (*Chará is missing*). The story was about a missing teenager girl called *Chará*. In Greek, the name *Χαρά* (*Chará*) and the noun *χαρά* (*chará*), meaning gladness, are homonyms. FBU1 structures his comment punning on these two homonyms.

Chapter 8

1 Facebook has been repeatedly accused of breaches in relation to its users' privacy, for instance from resetting privacy settings without previous warning to allowing unhindered eavesdropping via the Ticker.

2 The process described is in accordance with Facebook's interface as of 2014.

3 Helen was interviewed via Skype's instant messaging facility. Although I had prepared a list of questions intended for semi-structured interviews via email, my discussion with Helen was only partly based on that list. Owing to Skype's synchronous setting and following up Helen's answers, most of my questions emerged impromptu.

4 You can watch the commercial here: http://www.youtube.com/watch?v=6YN72ZsADhg. The plot is as follows: A bunch of young men are rehearsing a rock song on a ground floor. An old man appears outside their window and shouts: 'Μας έχετε τρελάνει. Να φύγετε κύριε, να πάτε αλλού. Και εμείς παίζαμε μαντολίνο, όχι όμως ηλεκτρικό. Ντράγκα ντρούγκα ντράγκα ντρούγκα.' [You've driven us crazy. Leave, sir, and go elsewhere. We were too playing mandolins when we were young, but not electric ones. Twang twang twang twang.]. Gabriel is referring to the underlined bits.

Chapter 9

1 Georgakopoulou draws on what Androutsopoulos (2010) has termed 'vernacular spectacles', that is, multimedia content produced outside media institutions and uploaded, displayed, and discussed on media-sharing websites.

2 According to Barton and Hamilton (1998), these are the areas of everyday life where reading and writing have a key role for people:

- life organization (e.g. checking timetables, writing to-do lists, keeping financial records);

- personal communication (e.g. notes, cards and letters to friends and relatives);

- leisure activities (e.g. practices related to sports and music);

- documenting life (e.g. keeping records of one's own and their family's lives);

- sense making (e.g. researching things related to health issues, legal issues and understanding of one's children's development);

- social participation (e.g. reading and contributing to notices and newsletters, participating in meetings).

References

Aapola, S. (2002). Exploring dimensions of age in young people's lives. A discourse analytical approach. *Time & Society* 11(2–3): 295–314.

Achugar, M. (2009). Constructing a bilingual professional identity in a graduate classroom. *Journal of Language, Identity & Education* 8(2–3): 65–87.

Acquisti, A. and Gross, R. (2006). Imagined communities: Awareness, information sharing, and privacy on the Facebook. In P. Golle and G. Danezis (eds), *Proceedings of 6th Workshop on Privacy Enhancing Technologies*, 36–58. Cambridge: Robinson College. Available online: http://link.springer.com/content/pdf/10.1007%2F11957454_3.pdf (accessed 30 September 2016).

Adam, B. (2004). *Time*. Cambridge: Polity Press.

Adam, B. (2009). Future matters: Challenge for social theory and social inquiry. Keynote paper presented at the Italian Sociological Association Conference, Future Matters for Social Theory, Cagliari University, Sardinia, 29 October 2009. Available online: http://www.cardiff.ac.uk/socsi/futures/sardinia_FM_Conference_Paper_301009.doc (accessed 30 September 2016).

Adami, E. (2012). The rhetoric of the implicit and the politics of representation in the age of copy-and-paste. *Learning, Media and Technology* 37(2): 131–44.

Adami, E. and Kress, G. (2010). The social semiotics of convergent mobile devices: New forms of composition and the transformation of habitus. In G. Kress (ed.), *Multimodality: A Social Semiotic Approach to Contemporary Communication*, 184–97. London: Routledge.

Aguirre, A. and Davies, S. G. (2015). Imperfect strangers: Picturing place, family, and migrant identity in Facebook. *Discourse, Context & Media* 7(1): 3–17.

Allan, S. (2013). *Citizen Witnessing: Revisioning Journalism in Times of Crisis*. Cambridge: Polity Press.

Althusser, L. (1976). *Positions*. Paris: Editions Sociales.

Altman, I. (1977). Privacy regulation: Culturally universal or culturally specific? *Journal of Social Issues* 33(3): 66–84.

Androutsopoulos, J. (2007). Style online: Doing hip-hop on the German-speaking web. In P. Auer (ed.), *Style and Social Identities: Alternative Approaches to Linguistic Heterogeneity*, 279–317. Berlin and New York: De Gruyter Mouton.

Androutsopoulos, J. (2008). Potentials and limitations of discourse-centered online ethnography. *Language@Internet* 5, article 8. Available online: http://www.languageatinternet.org/articles/2008/1610 (accessed 30 September 2016).

Androutsopoulos, J. (2010). Localising the global on the participatory web. In N. Coupland (ed.), *Handbook of Language and Globalization*, 203–31. Oxford: Blackwell.

Androutsopoulos, J. (2011). From variation to heteroglossia in the study of computer-mediated discourse. In C. Thurlow and K. Mroczek (eds) *Digital Discourse: Language in the New Media*, 277–98. New York: Oxford University Press.

Androutsopoulos, J. (2013a). Code-switching in computer-mediated communication. In S. C. Herring, D. Stein and T. Virtanen (eds), *Handbook of the Pragmatics of Computer-Mediated Communication*, 667–94. Berlin and Boston: De Gruyter Mouton.

Androutsopoulos, J. (2013b). Networked multilingualism: Some language practices on Facebook and their implications. *International Journal of Bilingualism*, 1–21. (Published online before print).

Androutsopoulos, J. (2013c). Online data collection. In C. Mallinson, B. Childs and G. V. Herk (eds), *Data Collection in Sociolinguistics: Methods and Applications*, 236–49. London: Routledge.

Androutsopoulos, J. (2014). Moments of sharing: Entextualization and linguistic repertoires in social networking. *Journal of Pragmatics* 73: 4–18.

Angelou, A. (1997). *Κρυφό Σχολειό: Το χρονικό ενός μύθου* [The Secret School: Chronicle of a Myth]. Athens: Hestia.

Antaki, C. and Widdicombe, S., eds (1998). *Identities in Talk*. London: Sage.

Archakis, A. and Tsakona, V. (2012). *The Narrative Construction of Identities in Critical Education*. Basingstoke: Palgrave Macmillan.

Baker, L. R. (2009). Temporal reality. In M. O'Rourke, J. Campbell and H. Silverstein (eds), *Time and Identity: Topics in Contemporary Philosophy*, Vol. 6, 27–47. Cambridge, MA: MIT Press.

Baker, S. (2013). Conceptualising the use of Facebook in ethnographic research: As tool, as data and as context. *Ethnography and Education* 8(2): 131–45.

Baltar, F. and Brunet, I. (2012). Social research 2.0: Virtual snowball sampling method using Facebook. *Internet Research* 22(1): 57–74.

Bamberg, M., De Fina, A. and Schiffrin, D. (2011). Discursive perspectives on identity construction. In S. Schwartz, K. Luyckx and V. Vignoles (eds), *Handbook of Identity Theory and Research*, Vol. 1, 177–99. Berlin and New York: Springer Verlag.

Bamfrod, J., Poppi, F. and Mazzi, D., eds (2014). *Space, Place and the Discursive Construction of Identity*. Frankfurt: Peter Lang.

Barnes, R. (2000). *Losing Ground: Locational Formulations in Argumentation Over New Travellers*. Doctoral dissertation. Plymouth: University of Plymouth.

Barton, D. (2015). Tagging on Flickr as a social practice. In R. H. Jones, A. Chik and C. A. Hafner (eds), *Discourse and Digital Practices: Doing Discourse Analysis in the Digital Age*, 48–65. Abingdon: Routledge.

Barton, D. and Hamilton, M. (1998). *Local Literacies: A Study of Reading and Writing in One Community*. London: Routledge.

Barton, D. and Lee, C. (2013). *Language Online: Investigating Digital Texts and Practices*. London: Routledge.

Baxter, J. (2010). Discourse-analytic approaches to text and talk. In L. Litosseliti (ed.), *Research Methods in Linguistics*, 117–37. London: Continuum.

Baym, N. K. (2000). *Tune in, Log on: Soaps, Fandom, and Online Community*. Thousand Oaks, CA: Sage.

Baym, N. K. (2010). *Personal Connections in the Digital Age*. London: Polity.

Bedijs, K., Held, G. and Maaß, C., eds (2014). *Facework and Social Media*. Münster: Lit-Verlag.

Bell, A. (1984). Language style as audience design. *Language in Society* 13(2): 145–204.

Bell, D. and Valentine, G. (1997). *Consuming Geographies: We are where we Eat.* London: Routledge.

Benwell, B. and Stokoe, E. (2006). *Discourse and Identity.* Edinburgh: Edinburgh University Press.

Berger, L. (2011). Snapshots, or: Visual culture's clichés. *Photographies* 4(2): 175–90.

Bertoni, S. (28 September 2011). Sean Parker: Agent of disruption. *Forbes.* Available online: http://www.forbes.com/global/2011/1010/feature-sean-parker-agent-disruption-napster-facebook-plaxo-steven-bertoni.html (accessed 30 September 2016).

Biber, D. and Finegan, E. (1989). Styles of stance in English: Lexical and grammatical marking of evidentiality and affect. *Text* 9(1): 93–124.

Biber, D., Johansson, S., Leech, G., Conrad, S. and Finegan, E. (1999). *Longman Grammar of Spoken and Written English.* London: Longman.

Blommaert, J. (2005). *Discourse: A Critical Introduction.* Cambridge: Cambridge University Press.

Blommaert, J. and De Fina, A. (2016). Chronotopic identities: On the timespace organization of who we are. *Tilburg Papers in Cultural Studies* 153. Available online: https://www.tilburguniversity.edu/upload/ba249987-6ece-44d2-b96b-3fc329713d59_TPCS_153_Blommaert-DeFina.pdf (accessed 30 September 2016).

Boden, D. and Bielby, D. D. (1986). The way it was: Topical organization in elderly conversation. *Language & Communication* 6(1–2): 73–89.

Boellstorff, T., Nardi, B., Pearce, C. and Taylor, T. L. (2012). *Ethnography and Virtual Worlds: A Handbook of Method.* Princeton: Princeton University Press.

Bolander, B. and Locher, M. A. (2010). Constructing identity on Facebook: Report on a pilot study. In K. Junod and D. Maillat (eds), *Constructing the Self*, 165–85. Tübingen: Narr Francke.

Bolander, B. and Locher, M. A. (2015). 'Peter is a dumb nut': Status updates and reactions to them as 'acts of positioning' in Facebook. *Pragmatics* 25(1): 99–122.

Bourdieu, P. (1984). *Distinction: A Social Critique of the Judgement of Taste.* Translated by R. Nice. London: Routledge (Original work published 1979).

boyd, d. (2002). Faceted id/Entity: Managing Representation in a Digital World. Master dissertation. Cambridge, MA: Massachusetts Institute of Technology. Available online: http://www.danah.org/papers/Thesis.FacetedIdentity.pdf (accessed 30 September 2016).

boyd, d. (2007). Why youth (heart) social network sites: The role of networked publics in teenage social life. In D. Buckingham (ed.), *Youth, Identity, and Digital Media*, 119–42. Cambridge, MA: MIT Press.

boyd, d. (2008a). Facebook's privacy trainwreck: Exposure, invasion, and social convergence. *Convergence: The International Journal of Research into New Media Technologies* 14(1): 13–20.

boyd, d. (2008b). Taken Out of Context: American Teen Sociality in Networked Publics. Doctoral dissertation. Berkeley: University of California-Berkeley. Available online: www.danah.org/papers/TakenOutOfContext.pdf (accessed 30 September 2016).

boyd, d. (2010a). Making sense of privacy and publicity. Paper presented at the South by Southwest Music Conference and Festival (SXSW), Austin, TX,

12–21 March 2010. Available online: http://www.danah.org/papers/talks/2010/ SXSW2010.html (accessed 30 September 2016).

boyd, d. (2010b). Social network sites as networked publics: Affordances, dynamics, and implications. In Z. Papacharissi (ed.), *A Networked Self: Identity, Community, and Culture on Social Network Sites*, 39–58. New York: Routledge.

boyd, d. (2010c, August 23). Social steganography: Learning to hide in plain sight. [Web log post in Apophenia]. Available online: http://www.zephoria.org/ thoughts/archives/2010/08/23/social-steganography-learning-to-hide-in-plain-sight.html (accessed 30 September 2016).

boyd, d. (2013). Networked privacy. *Surveillance & Society* 10(3/4): 348–50.

boyd, d. (2014). *It's Complicated: The Social Lives of Networked Teens*. New Haven: Yale University Press.

boyd, d. and Hargittai, E. (2 August 2010). Facebook privacy settings: Who cares? *First Monday* 15(8). Available online: http://firstmonday.org/ojs/index.php/fm/ article/view/3086/2589 (accessed 30 September 2016).

boyd, d. and Marwick, A. (2011). Social privacy in networked publics: Teens' attitudes, practices, and strategies. Paper presented at the Oxford Internet Institute Decade in Internet Time Symposium, 22 September 2011. Available online: http://papers.ssrn.com/sol3/papers.cfm?abstract_id=1925128 (accessed 30 September 2016).

Brake, D. (2008). Shaping the 'me' in MySpace: The framing of profiles on a social network site. In K. Lundby (ed.), *Digital Storytelling, Mediatized Stories: Self-representations in New Media*, 285–300. New York: Peter Lang.

Brickman Bhutta, C. (2012). Not by the book: Facebook as a sampling frame. *Sociological Methods & Research* 41(1): 57–88.

Brubaker, R. and Cooper, F. (2000). Beyond 'identity'. *Theory and Society* 29(1): 1–47.

Buchanan, K. and Middleton, D. (1995). Voices of experience: Talk, identity and membership in reminiscence groups. *Ageing and Society* 15(4): 457–91.

Buckingham, D. (2007). Introducing identity. In D. Buckingham (ed.), *Youth, Identity, and Digital Media*, 1–24. Cambridge, MA: MIT Press.

Bytheway, B. (2005). Age-identities and the celebration of birthdays. *Ageing and Society* 25(4): 463–77.

Cameron, D., Frazer, E., Harvey, P., Rampton, B. and Richardson, K. (1992). *Researching Language: Issues of Power and Method*. London: Routledge.

Cha, J. (2010). Factors affecting the frequency and amount of social networking site use: Motivations, perceptions, and privacy concerns. *First Monday* 15(12). Available online: http://firstmonday.org/htbin/cgiwrap/bin/ojs/index.php/fm/ article/view/2889/2685 (accessed 30 September 2016).

Chafe, W. L. (1994). *Discourse, Consciousness, and Time: The Flow and Displacement of Conscious Experience in Speaking and Writing*. Chicago: University of Chicago Press.

Chalari, A. (2014). The subjective experiences of three generations during the Greek economic crisis. *World Journal of Social Science Research* 1(1): 89–109.

Channell, J. (1994). *Vague Language*. Oxford: Oxford University Press.

Chouliaraki, L. (2003). Mediated experience and youth identities in a post-traditional order. In J. Androutsopoulos and A. Georgakopoulou (eds), *Discourse Constructions of Youth Identities*, 303–33. Amsterdam: John Benjamins.

Cook, I. and Crang, P. (1996). The world on a plate: Culinary culture and geographical knowledges. *Journal of Material Culture* 1(2): 131–53.

Coupland, J., Coupland, N., Giles, H. and Henwood, K. (1991). Formulating age: Dimensions of age identity in elderly talk. *Discourse Processes* 14(1): 87–106.

Coupland, N. (2001). Age in social and sociolinguistic theory. In N. Coupland, S. Sarangi and C. N. Candlin (eds), *Sociolinguistics and Social Theory*, 185–211. Harlow and New York: Longman.

Creese, A. (2008). Linguistic ethnography. In K. A. King and N. H. Hornberger (eds), *Encyclopedia of Language and Education, Volume 10: Research Methods in Language and Education*, 2nd edn, 229–41. New York: Springer Science and Business Media LLC.

Crowston, K. and Williams, M. (2000). Reproduced and emergent genres of communication on the World-Wide Web. *The Information Society* 16(3): 201–16.

Damari, R. R. (2009). Stancetaking as identity work: Attributed, accreted, and adjusted stances taken by an intercultural couple. *eVox* 3: 18–37. Washington, DC: Georgetown University. Available online: evox.georgetown.edu/evox03/damari.pdf (accessed 30 September 2016).

Damari, R. R. (2010). Intertextual stancetaking and the local negotiation of cultural identities by a binational couple. *Journal of Sociolinguistics* 14(5): 609–29.

D'Arcy, A. and Young, T. M. (2012). Ethics and social media: Implications for sociolinguistics in the networked public. *Journal of Sociolinguistics* 16(4): 532–46.

Darics, E., ed. (2015). *Digital Business Discourse*. Basingstoke: Palgrave Macmillan.

Das, S. and Kramer, A. (2013). Self-censorship on Facebook. Paper presented at the International Conference on Weblogs and Social Media (ICWSM), Boston, USA, 8–11 July 2013. Available online: http://www.aaai.org/ocs/index.php/ICWSM/ICWSM13/paper/viewFile/6093/6350 (accessed 30 September 2016).

Debatin, B., Lovejoy, J. P., Horn, A.-K. and Hughes, B. N. (2009). Facebook and online privacy: Attitudes, behaviors, and unintended consequences. *Journal of Computer-Mediated Communication* 15(1): 83–108.

De Fina, A., Schiffrin, D. and Bamberg, M., eds (2006). *Discourse and Identity*. Cambridge: Cambridge University Press.

DeNora, T. (2000). *Music in Everyday Life*. Cambridge: Cambridge University Press.

Desforges, L. (2000). Travelling the world: Identity and travel biography. *Annals of Tourism Research* 27(4): 929–45.

DiMicco, J. M. and Millen, D. R. (2008). People sensemaking with social network sites. Paper presented at the Sensemaking Workshop, CHI'08, Florence, Italy, 5–10 April 2008. Available online: http://sites.google.com/site/dmrussell2/DiMicco-people-sensemaking-CHI08-fin.pdf (accessed 30 September 2016).

Dixon, J. and Durrheim, K. (2000). Displacing place-identity: A discursive approach to locating self and other. *British Journal of Social Psychology* 39(1): 27–44.

Domínguez, D., Beaulieu, A., Estalella, A., Gómez, E., Read, R. and Schnettler, B. (eds), (2007). Virtual ethnography. *Forum: Qualitative Social Research* 8(3). Available online: http://www.qualitative-research.net/fqs/fqs-e/inhalt3-07-e.htm (accessed 30 September 2016).

Donath, J. (1998). Identity and deception in the virtual community. In M. Smith and P. Kollock (eds), *Communities in Cyberspace*, 27–58. London: Routledge.

Dresner, E. and Herring, S. C. (2010). Functions of the non-verbal in CMC: Emoticons and illocutionary force. *Communication Theory* 20(3): 249–68.

Drew, P. and Heritage, J. (1992). *Talk at Work. Interaction in Institutional Settings.* Cambridge: Cambridge University Press.

Du Bois, J. W. (2007). The stance triangle. In R. Englebretson (ed.), *Stancetaking in Discourse: Subjectivity, Evaluation, Interaction*, 139–82. Amsterdam: John Benjamins.

Du Bois, J. W. and Kärkkäinen, E. (2012). Taking a stance on emotion: Affect, sequence, and intersubjectivity in dialogic interaction. *Text & Talk* 32(4): 433–51.

Dutton, J. E., Roberts, L. M. and Bednar, J. (2010). Pathways for positive identity construction at work: Four types of positive identity and the building of social resources. *Academy of Management Review* 35(2): 265–93.

Dyer, J. and Keller-Cohen, D. (2000). The discursive construction of professional self through narratives of personal experience. *Discourse Studies* 2(3): 283–304.

Eckert, P. and Wenger, E. (1994). From school to work: An apprenticeship in institutional identity. Working Papers on Learning and Identity 1. Palo Alto: Institute for Research on Learning. Available online: http://web.stanford.edu/~eckert/PDF/transition.pdf (accessed 30 September 2016).

Eisenlauer, V. (2013). *A Critical Hypertext Analysis of Social Media: The True Colours of Facebook.* London and New York: Bloomsbury.

Ellison, N. B. and boyd, d. (2013). Sociality through social network sites. In W. H. Dutton (ed.), *The Oxford Handbook of Internet Studies*, 151–72. Oxford: Oxford University Press.

Ellison, N. B., Lampe, C., Steinfield, C. and Vitak, J. (2010). With a little help from my friends: How social network sites affect social capital processes. In Z. Papacharissi (ed.), *A Networked Self: Identity, Community and Culture on Social Network Sites*, 124–43. New York: Routledge.

Ellison, N. B., Vitak, J., Steinfield, C., Gray, R. and Lampe, C. (2011). Negotiating privacy concerns and social capital needs in a social media environment. In S. Trepte and L. Reinecke (eds), *Privacy Online: Perspectives on Privacy and Self-Disclosure in the Social Web*, 19–32. New York: Springer.

Englebretson, R. (2007). Stancetaking in discourse: An introduction. In R. Englebretson (ed.), *Stancetaking in Discourse: Subjectivity, Evaluation, Interaction*, 1–25. Amsterdam: John Benjamins.

Enli, G. S. and Thumim, N. (2012). Socialising and self representation online: Exploring Facebook. *Observatorio (OBS) Journal* 6(1): 87–105.

Erstad, O. and Wertsch, J. V. (2008). Tales of mediation: Narrative and digital media as cultural tools. In K. Lundby (ed.), *Digital Storytelling, Mediatized Stories: Self-Representations in New Media*, 21–40. New York: Peter Lang.

Evans, A. (2016). Stance and identity in Twitter hashtags. *Language@internet*, 13, article 1. Available online: http://www.languageatinternet.org/articles/2016/evans (accessed 30 September 2016).

Evans, L. (2015). *Locative Social Media: Place in the Digital Age.* Basingstoke: Palgrave Macmillan.

Evans, V. (2005). The meaning of time: Polysemy, the lexicon and conceptual structure. *Journal of Linguistics* 41(1): 33–75.

Everett, D. (2005). Cultural constraints on grammar and cognition in Pirahã: Another look at the design features of human language. *Current Anthropology* 46(4): 621–46.

Facebook (2016). Key facts. Available online: http://newsroom.fb.com/company-info/ (accessed 30 December 2016).

Fairclough, N. (1989). *Language and Power*. London: Longman.

Fairclough, N. (1995). *Critical Discourse Analysis: The Critical Study of Language*. London: Longman.

Fairclough, N. (2003). *Analysing Discourse: Text Analysis for Social Research*. London: Routledge.

Fasulo, A. and Zucchermaglio, C. (2002). My selves and I: Identity markers in work meeting talk. *Journal of Pragmatics* 34(9): 1119–44.

Fernbank, J. (1999). There is a there there: Notes toward a definition of cyber community. In S. Jones (ed.), *Doing Internet Research: Critical Issues and Methods for Examining the Net*, 203–20. Thousand Oaks, CA: Sage.

Flaherty, M. G. and Fine, G. A. (2001). Present, past, and future: Conjugating George Herbert Mead's perspective on time. *Time & Society* 10(2/3): 147–61.

Fortes, M. (1983). Problems of identity and person. In A. Jacobson-Widding (ed.), *Identity: Personal and Social-Cultural*, 389–401. Stockholm: Almqvist and Wiksell.

Foucault, M. (1980). *Power/Knowledge: Selected Interviews and other Writings, 1972–1977*. New York: Pantheon.

Friedlander, L. (2008). Narrative strategies in a digital age: Authorship and authority. In K. Lundby (ed.), *Digital Storytelling, Mediatized Stories: Self-representations in New Media*, 177–94. New York: Peter Lang.

Frobenius, M. and Harper, R. (2015). Tying in comment sections: The production of meaning and sense on Facebook. *Semiotica* 2015(204): 121–43.

Fuchs, C. (2014). *OccupyMedia! The Occupy Movement and Social Media in Crisis Capitalism*. Winchester: Zero Books.

García-Gómez, A. (2011). Regulating girlhood: Evaluative language, discourses of gender socialization and relational aggression. *European Journal of Women's Studies* 18(3): 243–64.

Gauntlett, D. (2008). Creative brainwork: Building metaphors of identity for social science research. In K. Lundby (ed.), *Digital Storytelling, Mediatized Stories: Self-Representations in New Media*, 253–69. New York: Peter Lang.

Gee, J. P. (2011). *How to do Discourse Analysis: A Toolkit*. London: Routledge.

Geertz, C. (1973). *The Interpretation of Cultures*. New York: Basic Books.

Georgakopoulou, A. (2002). Narrative and identity management: Discourse and social identities in a tale of tomorrow. *Research on Language & Social Interaction* 35(4): 427–51.

Georgakopoulou, A. (2003). Plotting the 'right place' and the 'right time': Place and time as interactional resources in narrative. *Narrative Inquiry* 13(2): 413–32.

Georgakopoulou, A. (2006). Postscript: Computer-mediated communication in sociolinguistics. *Journal of Sociolinguistics* 10(4): 548–57.

Georgakopoulou, A. (2007). *Small Stories, Interaction, and Identities*. Amsterdam: John Benjamins.

Georgakopoulou, A. (2013a). Narrative analysis and computer-mediated communication. In S. C. Herring, D. Stein and T. Virtanen (eds), *Pragmatics of Computer-Mediated Communication*, 695–716. Berlin and Boston: De Gruyter Mouton.

Georgakopoulou, A. (2013b). Small stories research as a framework for the study of social media practices: Narrative stancetaking and circulation in a Greek news story. *Sociolinguistica* 27(1): 19–36.

Georgakopoulou, A. (2013c). Storytelling on the go: Breaking news as a travelling narrative genre. In M. Hatavara, L.-C. Hydén and M. Hyvärinen (eds), *The Travelling Concepts of Narrative*, 201–24. Amsterdam: John Benjamins.

Georgakopoulou, A. (2014). Small stories transposition and social media: A micro-perspective on the 'Greek crisis'. *Discourse & Society* 25(4): 519–39.

Georgakopoulou, A. (guest ed.) (2015a). Communicating time and place on digital media. *Discourse, Context & Media* 9: 1–72.

Georgakopoulou, A. (2015b). Small stories research: Methods–analysis–outreach. In A. De Fina and A. Georgakopoulou (eds), *The Handbook of Narrative Analysis*, 255–72. Malden, MA: Wiley-Blackwell.

Georgakopoulou, A. (2016). 'Whose context collapse?': Ethical clashes in the study of language and social media in context. *Applied Linguistics Review*. Ahead of print.

Georgakopoulou, A. and Charalambidou, A. (2011). Doing age and ageing: Language, discourse and social interaction. In K. Aijmer and G. Andersen (eds), *Pragmatics of Society*, 29–51. Berlin: De Gruyter Mouton.

Georgakopoulou, A. and Spilioti, T., eds (2016). *The Routledge Handbook of Language and Digital Communication*. Abingdon: Routledge.

Georgalou, M. (2015). Beyond the Timeline: Constructing time and age identities on Facebook. *Discourse, Context & Media* 9: 24–33.

Gerbaudo, P. (2012). *Tweets and the Streets: Social Media and Contemporary Activism*. London: Pluto Books.

Gershon, I. (2010). *The Breakup 2.0: Disconnecting Over New Media*. Ithaca, NY and London: Cornell University Press.

Gibson, J. J. (1977). The theory of affordances. In R. Shaw and J. Bransford (eds), *Perceiving, Acting, and Knowing: Toward an Ecological Psychology*, 67–82. Hillsdale, NJ: Lawrence Erlbaum.

Giglietto, F., Rossi, L. and Bennato, D. (2012). The Open Laboratory: Limits and possibilities of using Facebook, Twitter, and YouTube as a research data source. *Journal of Technology in Human Services* 30(3–4): 145–59.

Gilbert, M. (2010). Theorizing digital and urban inequalities: Critical geographies of 'race', gender and technological capital. *Information, Communication & Society* 13(7): 1000–18.

Gillen, J. (2014). *Digital Literacies*. London: Routledge.

Gilpin, D. (2010). Working the Twittersphere: Microblogging as professional identity construction. In Z. Papacharissi (ed.), *A Networked Self: Identity, Community and Culture on Social Network Sites*, 232–50. New York: Routledge.

Gini, A. (1998). Work, identity and self: How we are formed by the work we do. *Journal of Business Ethics* 17(7): 707–14.

Glaser, B. G. and Strauss, A. L. (1967). *The Discovery of Grounded Theory: Strategies for Qualitative Research*. New York: Aldine de Gruyter.

Goddard, A. and Geesin, B. (2011). *Language and Technology*. London: Routledge.

Goffman, E. (1956). *The Presentation of Self in Everyday Life* (Monograph No. 2). Edinburgh: University of Edinburgh, Social Sciences Research Centre.

Gómez-Cruz, E. and Lehmuskallio, A., eds (2016). *Digital Photography and Everyday Life: Empirical Studies on Material Visual Practices*. London and New York: Routledge.

Goodings, L., Locke, A. and Brown, S. D. (2007). Social networking technology: Place and identity in mediated communities. *Journal of Community & Applied Social Psychology* 17(6): 463–76.

Gordon, E. and de Souza e Silva, A. (2011). *Net Locality: Why Location Matters in a Networked World*. Boston: Blackwell-Wiley.

Grad, H. and Rojo, L. M. (2008). Identities in discourse: An integrative view. In R. Dolón and J. Todolí (eds), *Analysing Identities in Discourse*, 3–28. Amsterdam: John Benjamins.

Grice, P. (1975). Logic and conversation. In P. Cole and J. L. Morgan (eds), *Syntax and Semantics III: Speech Acts*, 41–58. New York: Academic Press.

Grimmelmann, J. (2 October 2009). The myths of privacy on Facebook. Workshop on Federal Privacy Regulation, NYU School of Law. Available online: http://james.grimmelmann.net/essays/FacebookMyths (accessed 30 September 2016).

Gumperz, J. J. (1982). *Discourse Strategies*. Cambridge: Cambridge University Press.

Gunnarsson, B. L. (2009). *Professional Discourse*. London: Continuum.

Hall, S. (1990). Cultural identity and diaspora. In J. Rutherford (ed.), *Identity, Community, Culture, Difference*, 222–37. London: Lawrence and Wishart.

Hall, S. (2000). Who needs 'identity'?. In P. du Gay, J. Evans and P. Redman (eds), *Identity: A Reader*, 15–30. London: Sage.

Hammersley, M. and Atkinson, P. (2007). *Ethnography: Principles in Practice*, 3rd edn. London: Routledge.

Hardaker, C. (2013). 'Uh…not to be nitpicky,,,but..the past tense of drag is dragged, not drug'.: An overview of trolling strategies. *Journal of Language Aggression and Conflict* 1(1): 57–85.

Hargittai, E. and Marwick, A. (2016). 'What can I really do?' Explaining the privacy paradox with online apathy. *International Journal of Communication* 10: 3737–57.

Hellenic Data Protection Authority (2016). Law 2472/1997 on the Protection of Individuals with Regard to the Processing of Personal Data. Available online http://www.dpa.gr/pls/portal/docs/PAGE/APDPX/ENGLISH_INDEX/LEGAL%20FRAMEWORK/LAW%202472-97-NOV2013-EN.PDF (accessed 30 September 2016).

Herring, S. C., ed. (1996). *Computer-Mediated Communication: Linguistic, Social and Cross-Cultural Perspectives*. Amsterdam: John Benjamins.

Herring, S. C. (2004). Computer-mediated discourse analysis: An approach to researching online behavior. In S. A. Barab, R. Kling and J. H. Gray (eds), *Designing for Virtual Communities in the Service of Learning*, 338–76. New York: Cambridge University Press.

Herring, S. C. (2013). Discourse in Web 2.0: Familiar, reconfigured, and emergent. In D. Tannen and A. M. Trester (eds), *Discourse 2.0: Language and New Media*, 1–25. Washington, DC: Georgetown University Press.

Hesmondhalgh, D. (2008). Towards a critical understanding of music, emotion and self-identity. *Consumption Markets & Culture* 11(4): 329–43.

Hine, C. (2000). *Virtual Ethnography*. Thousand Oaks, CA: Sage.

Hine, C. (2008). Virtual ethnography: Modes, varieties, affordances. In N. G. Fielding, R. M. Lee and G. Blank (eds), *Handbook of Online Research Methods*, 257–70. London: Sage.

Hobbs, D. (2006). Ethnography. In V. Jupp (ed.), *The Sage Dictionary of Social Research Methods*, 101–2. London: Sage.

Holmes, J. (2009). Discourse in the workplace: Literature review. Language in the workplace occasional papers. Available online: www.vuw.ac.nz/lals/lwp (accessed 30 September 2016).

Honeycutt, C. and Cunliffe, D. (2010). The use of the Welsh language on Facebook. *Information, Communication & Society* 13(2): 226–48.

Horn, S. (1998). *Cyberville: Clicks, Culture and the Creation of an Online Town.* New York: Warner Books.

Humphreys, L. and Liao, T. (2011). Mobile geotagging: Reexamining our interactions with urban space. *Journal of Computer-Mediated Communication* 16(3): 407–23.

Hutchby, I. (2001). Texts, technology, and affordances. *Sociology* 35(2): 441–56.

Hymes, D. (1964). Introduction: Toward ethnographies of communication. *American Anthropologist* 66(6): 1–34.

Ibarra, H. (1999). Provisional selves: Experimenting with image and identity in professional adaptation. *Administrative Science Quarterly* 44(4): 764–91.

Internet World Stats (2016). European Union. Available online http://www. internetworldstats.com/europa.htm (accessed 30 September 2016).

Ittelson, W. H., Proshansky, H. M., Rivlin, L. G. and Winkel, G. H. (1974). *An Introduction to Environmental Psychology.* New York: Holt, Rinehart, and Winston.

Ivanič, R. (1998). *Writing and Identity: The Discoursal Construction of Identity in Academic Writing.* Amsterdam: John Benjamins.

Jacoby, S. and Gonzales, P. (1991). The constitution of expert-novice in scientific discourse. *Issues in Applied Linguistics* 2(2): 149–81.

Jaffe, A. M. (2009). Introduction: The sociolinguistics of stance. In A. M. Jaffe (ed.), *Stance: Sociolinguistic Perspectives*, 3–28. Oxford: Oxford University Press.

Jaworski, A. and Thurlow, C. (2009a). Gesture and movement in tourist spaces. In C. Jewitt (ed.), *The Routledge Handbook of Multimodal Analysis*, 253–62. London and New York: Routledge.

Jaworski, A. and Thurlow, C. (2009b). Taking an elitist stance: Ideology and the discursive production of social distinction. In A. M. Jaffe (ed.), *Stance: Sociolinguistic Perspectives*, 195–226. New York: Oxford University Press.

Jaworski, A. and Thurlow, C., eds (2010). *Semiotic Landscapes: Language, Image, Space.* London and New York: Continuum.

Jenkins, H. (2006). *Convergence Culture: Where Old and New Media Collide.* New York: New York University Press.

Jenkins, R. (2002). In the present tense: Time, identification and human nature. *Anthropological Theory* 2(3): 267–80.

Jaworski, A. and Thurlow, C., eds (2010). *Semiotic Landscapes: Language, Image, Space.* London and New York: Continuum.

Jenkins, R. (2008). *Social Identity*, 3rd edn. Abingdon: Routledge.

Jewitt, C. (2013). Multimodal methods for researching digital technologies. In S. Price, C. Jewitt and B. Brown (eds), *The Sage Handbook of Digital Technology Research*, 250–65. Los Angeles: Sage.

Johnstone, B. (2008). *Discourse Analysis*, 2nd edn. Malden, MA: Blackwell.

Johnstone, B. (2011). Language and place. In R. Mesthrie (ed.), *The Cambridge Handbook of Sociolinguistics*, 203–17. New York: Cambridge University Press.

Jones, R. H. (2016). Surveillance. In A. Georgakopoulou and T. Spilloti (eds), *The Routledge Handbook of Language and Digital Communication*, 408–11. London: Routledge.

Jones, R. H. and Hafner, C. (2012). *Understanding Digital Literacies: A Practical Introduction*. London: Routledge.

Jones, R. H., Chik, A. and Hafner, C. A., eds (2015). *Discourse and Digital Practices: Doing Discourse Analysis in the Digital Age*. Abingdon: Routledge.

Jousmäki, H. (2011). Epistemic, interpersonal, and moral stances in the construction of us and them in Christian metal lyrics. *Journal of Multicultural Discourses* 6(1): 53–66.

Jousmäki, H. (2014). This is us: multimodal online self-representation of Christian metal bands. In J. Tyrkkö and S. Leppänen (eds), *Studies in Variation, Contacts and Change: Texts and Discourses of New Media*. Helsinki: University of Helsinki. Available online: http://www.helsinki.fi/varieng/series/volumes/15/jousmaki/ (accessed 3 January 2017).

Kaufman, P. and Feldman, K. A. (2004). Forming identities in college: A sociological approach. *Research in Higher Education* 45(5): 463–96.

Kendall, L. (2002). *Hanging Out in the Virtual Pub: Masculinities and Relationships Online*. Berkeley, CA: University of California Press.

Kendall, L. (2008). The conduct of qualitative interviews: Research questions, methodological issues, and researching online. In J. Coiro, M. Knobel, C. Lankshear and D. J. Leu (eds), *Handbook of Research on New Literacies*, 133–49. Mahwah, NJ: Lawrence Erlbaum.

Kiesling, S. F. (2011). Stance in context: Affect, alignment and investment in the analysis of stancetaking. Paper presented at the i-Mean 2 Conference, 15 April 2012. The University of the West of England, Bristol, UK. Available online: http://www.academia.edu/1037087/Stance_in_context_Affect_alignment_and_investment_in_the_analysis_of_stancetaking (accessed 30 September 2016).

King, L. A. and Broyles, S. J. (1997). Wishes, gender, personality, and well-being. *Journal of Personality* 65(1): 49–76.

King, N. and Horrocks, C. (2010). *Interviews in Qualitative Research*. London:

Koteyko, N. and Hunt, D. (2016). Performing health identities on social media: An online observation of Facebook profiles. *Discourse, Context & Media* 12: 59–67.

Kozinets, R. V. (2002). The field behind the screen: Using netnography for marketing research in online communities. *Journal of Marketing Research* 39(1): 61–72.

Kristiansen, T. (2003). The youth and the gatekeepers. Reproduction and change in language norm and variation. In J. Androutsopoulos and A. Georgakopoulou (eds), *The Discursive Construction of Youth Identities*, 279–302. Amsterdam: John Benjamins.

Kytölä, S. (2016). Translocality. In A. Georgakopoulou and T. Spilioti (eds), *Handbook of Language and Digital Communication*. London: Routledge

Kytölä, S. and Androutsopoulos, J. (2012). Ethnographic perspectives on multilingual computer-mediated discourse: Insights from Finnish football forums on the Web. In S. Gardner and M. Martin-Jones (eds), *Multilingualism, Discourse and Ethnography*, 179–96. London: Routledge.

Lakoff, R. (2006). Identity à la carte: You are what you eat. In A. De Fina, D. Schiffrin and M. Bamberg (eds), *Discourse and Identity (Studies in Interactional Sociolinguistics)*, 147–65. Cambridge: Cambridge University Press.

Lampropoulou, S. and Myers, G. (2012). Stance-taking in interviews from the Qualidata Archive. *Forum: Qualitative Social Research* 14(1), Art. 12. Available online: http://nbn-resolving.de/urn:nbn:de:0114-fqs1301123 (accessed 30 September 2016).

Lange, P. (2014). *Kids on YouTube: Technical Identities and Digital Literacies.* Walnut Creek, CA: Left Coast Press.

Larsen, M. C. (2016). An 'open source' networked identity: On young people's construction and co-construction of identity on social network sites. In M. Walrave, K. Ponnet, E. Vanderhoven, J. Haers and B. Segaert (eds), *Youth 2.0: Social Media and Adolescence*, 21–39. Berlin and New York: Springer.

Lee, C. (2011). Micro-blogging and status updates on Facebook: Texts and practices. In C. Thurlow and K. Mroczek (eds), *Digital Discourse: Language in New Media*, 110–28. New York: Oxford University Press.

Lemke, J. L. (2000). Across the scales of time: Artifacts, activities, and meanings in ecosocial systems. *Mind, Culture, and Activity* 7(4): 273–90.

Lemke, J. L. (2008). Identity, development and desire: Critical questions. In C. R. Caldas-Coulthard and R. Iedema (eds), *Identity Trouble: Critical Discourse and Contested Identities*, 17–42. Hampshire: Palgrave Macmillan.

Lemke, J. L. (2013). Thinking about feeling: Affect across literacies and lives. In O. Erstad and J. Sefton-Green (eds), *Identity, Community, and Learning Lives in the Digital Age*, 57–69. Cambridge: Cambridge University Press.

Lenihan, A. (2011). 'Join our community of translators': Language ideologies and Facebook. In C. Thurlow and K. Mroczek (eds), *Digital Discourse: Language in the New Media*, 48–64. New York: Oxford University Press.

Lenihan, A. (2014). Investigating language policy in social media: Translation practices on Facebook. In P. Seargeant and C. Tagg (eds), *The Language of Social Media: Identity and Community on the Internet*, 208–27. Basingstoke: Palgrave Macmillan.

Leppänen, S., Kytölä, S., Jousmäki, H., Peuronen, S. and Westinen, E. (2014). Entextualization and resemiotization as resources for identification in social media. In P. Seargeant and C. Tagg (eds), *The Language of Social Media: Identity and Community on the Internet*, 112–36. Basingstoke: Palgrave Macmillan.

Lewin-Jones, J. (2015). Humour with a purpose: Creativity with language in Facebook status updates. *Linguistik Online* 72(3): 69–87.

Lewis, J. D. and Weigart, A. (1981). The structures and meaning of social time. In J. Hassard (ed.) (1990), *The Sociology of Time*, 77–104. Basingstoke: Palgrave Macmillan.

Lin, M., Hummert Lee, M. and Harwood, J. (2004). Representation of age identities in on-line discourse. *Journal of Aging Studies* 18(3): 261–74.

Livingstone, S. (2008). Taking risky opportunities in youthful content creation: Teenagers use of social networking sites for intimacy, privacy and self-expression. *New Media & Society* 10(3): 393–411.

Livingstone, S. and Brake, D. R. (2009). On the rapid rise of social networking sites: New findings and policy implications. *Children & Society* 24(1): 75–83.

Locher, M. A. and Bolander, B. (2014). Relational work and the display of multilingualism in two Facebook groups. In K. Bedijs, G. Held and C. Maaß (eds), *Face Work and Social Media*, 157–91. Münster: Lit-Verlag.

Locher, M. A. and Bolander, B. (2015). Humor in microblogging: Exploiting linguistic humor strategies for identity construction in two Facebook focus groups. In M. Dynel and J. Chovanec (eds), *Participation in Public and Social Media Interactions*, 135–55. Amsterdam: John Benjamins.

Lockie, S. (2001). Food, place and identity: Consuming Australia's 'Beef Capital'. *Journal of Sociology* 37(3): 239–55.

Long, L. M. (2004). Culinary tourism: A folkloric perspective on eating and otherness. In. L. M. Long (ed.), *Culinary Tourism: Exploring the Other Through Food*, 20–50. Lexington: University of Kentucky Press.

Machin, D. (2010). *Analysing Popular Music: Image, Sound, Text*. London: Sage.

Maíz-Arévalo, C. (2013). 'Just click Like': Computer-mediated responses to Spanish compliments. *Journal of Pragmatics* 51: 47–67.

Maíz-Arévalo, C. and García-Gómez, A. (2013). 'You look terrific!' Social evaluation and relationships in online compliments. *Discourse Studies* 15(6): 735–60.

Mak, B. C. N. and Chui, H. L. (2014). Impoliteness in Facebook status updates: Strategic talk among colleagues 'outside' the workplace. *Text & Talk* 34(2): 165–85.

Markham, A. (1998). *Life Online: Researching Real Experience in Virtual Space*. Walnut Creek, CA: Altamira Press.

Markham, A. (2005). The politics, ethics, and methods of representation in online ethnography. In N. Denzin and Y. Lincoln (eds), *Handbook of Qualitative Research*, 3rd edn, 793–820. Thousand Oaks, CA: Sage.

Markham, A. and Baym, N. (2009). *Internet Inquiry: Conversations about Method*. Thousand Oaks, CA: Sage Publications.

Martin, J. R. and White, P. R. R. (2005). *The Language of Evaluation: Appraisal in English*. London and New York: Palgrave Macmillan.

Martín Rojo, L. (guest ed.) (2014). Occupy: The spatial dynamics of discourse in global protest movements. *Journal of Language and Politics* 13(4): 583–868.

Marwick, A. (2005). Selling Yourself: Online Identity in the Age of a Commodified Internet. Master dissertation. Washington: University of Washington. Available online: www.tiara.org/papersamarwick_selling yourself_mathesis.doc (accessed 30 September 2016).

Marwick, A. and boyd, d. (2011). I tweet honestly, I tweet passionately: Twitter users, context collapse, and the imagined audience. *New Media & Society* 13(1): 96–113.

Marwick, A. and boyd, d. (2014). Networked privacy: How teenagers negotiate context in social media. *New Media & Society* 16(7): 1051–67.

McAdams, D. (1997). *Stories we Live by: Personal Myths and the Making of the Self*, 2nd edn. London: Guilford Press.

McCabe, S. and Stokoe, E. (2004). Place and identity in tourist accounts. *Annals of Tourism Research* 31(3): 601–22.

McLuhan, M. (1974). *Understanding Media: The Extensions of Man*, 2nd edn. Cambridge, MA: MIT Press.

Mead, G. H. (1932). *The Philosophy of the Present*. Chicago: University of Chicago Press.

Meikle, G. (2010). It's like talking to a wall. In D. E. Wittkower (ed.), *Facebook and Philosophy: What's on Your Mind?*, 13–20. Chicago: Open Court Press.

Mendelson, A. and Papacharissi, Z. (2010). Look at us: Collective narcissism in college student Facebook photo galleries. In Z. Papacharissi (ed.), *A Networked Self: Identity, Community and Culture on Social Network Sites*, 251–73. New York: Routledge.

Mendoza-Denton, N. (2001). Language and identity. In J. K. Chambers, P. Trudgill and N. Schilling-Estes (eds), *Handbook of Language Variation and Change*, 475–99. Malden: Blackwell.

Meyerhoff, M. and Niedzielski, N. (1994). Resistance to creolization: An interpersonal and intergroup account. *Language and Communication* 14(4): 313–30.

Miller, D. (2011). *Tales from Facebook*. Cambridge: Polity.

Miller, D. and Sinanan, J. (2017). *Visualising Facebook*. London: UCL Press. Also available online: http://discovery.ucl.ac.uk/1543315/1/Visualising-Facebook.pdf.

Miller, D. and Slater, D. (2000). *The Internet: An Ethnographic Approach*. Berg: Oxford.

Miller, H. (1995). The presentation of self in electronic life: Goffman on the Internet. Paper presented at Embodied Knowledge and Virtual Space conference, Goldsmiths' College, University of London, June 1995. Available online: http://citeseerx.ist.psu.edu/viewdoc/download;jsessionid=8379489 69F307A89C366C0507F0B1AAA?doi=10.1.1.110.190&rep=rep1&type=pdf (accessed 30 September 2016).

Molz, J. G. (2007). Eating difference: The cosmopolitan mobilities of culinary tourism. *Space and Culture* 10(1): 77–93.

Moore, E. (2006). Educational identities of adult university graduates. *Scandinavian Journal of Educational Research* 50(2): 149–63.

Musser, J., O'Reilly, T. and the O'Reilly Radar Team (2007). *Web 2.0 Principles and Best Practices*. Sebastopol, CA: O'Reilly Radar.

Myers, G. (2004). *Matters of Opinion: Talking about Public Sssues*. Cambridge: Cambridge University Press.

Myers, G. (2006). Where are you from?: Identifying place in talk. *Journal of Sociolinguistics* 10(3): 320–43.

Myers, G. (2010a). Stance-taking and public discussion in blogs. *Critical Discourse Studies* 7(4): 263–75.

Myers, G. (2010b). *The Discourse of Blogs and Wikis*. London: Continuum.

Myers, G. and Lampropoulou, S. (2012). Impersonal you and stance in social science research interviews. *Journal of Pragmatics* 44(10): 1206–18.

Nikander, P. (2002). *Age in Action: Membership Work and Stage of Life Categories in Talk*. Helsinki: The Finnish Academy of Science and Letters.

Nikander, P. (2009). Doing change and continuity: Age identity and the micro-macro divide. *Ageing & Society* 29(6): 863–81.

Nishimura, Y. (2017). Age, gender and identities in Japanese blogs: Analysis of role language as stylization. In S. Leppänen, E. Westinen and S. Kytölä (eds), *Social Media Discourse, (dis)Identifications and Diversities*, 263–86. London: Routledge.

Nissenbaum, H. (2004). Privacy as contextual integrity. *Washington Law Review* 79(1): 119–58. Available online: www.nyu.edu/projects/nissenbaum/papers/washingtonlawreview.pdf (accessed 30 September 2016).

Norrby, C. E. and Wirdenäs, K. (2003). Swedish youth discourse: On performing relevant selves in interaction. In J. Androutsopoulos and A. Georgakopoulou (eds), *Discourse Constructions of Youth Identities*, 247–78. Amsterdam: John Benjamins.

Ochs, E. and Capps, L. (2001). *Living Narrative: Creating Lives in Everyday Storytelling*. Cambridge, MA: Harvard University Press.

Ollier-Malaterre, A., Rothbard, N. P. and Berg, J. (2013). When worlds collide in cyberspace: How boundary work in online social networks impacts professional relationships. *Academy of Management Review* 38(4): 645–69.

O'Rourke, M., Campbell, J. and Silverstein, H., eds (2009). *Time and Identity: Topics in Contemporary Philosophy*, Vol. 6. Cambridge, MA: MIT Press.

Page, R. (2010). Re-examining narrativity: Small stories in status updates. *Text & Talk* 30(4): 423–44.

Page, R. (2012). *Stories and Social Media: Identities and Interaction*. London: Routledge.

Page, R., Barton, D., Unger, J. and Zappavigna, M. (2014). *Researching the Language of Social Media: A Student Guide*. London: Routledge.

Painter, C. and Martin, J. R. (2011). Intermodal complementarity: Modelling affordances across image and verbiage in children's picture books. In H. G. Wen (ed.), *Studies in Functional Linguistics and Discourse Analysis*, 132–58. Beijing: Higher Education Press.

Papacharissi, Z. (2009). The virtual geographies of social networks: A comparative analysis of Facebook, LinkedIn and A SmallWorld. *New Media & Society* 11 (1–2): 199–220.

Papacharissi, Z. (2010). Conclusion: A networked self. In Z. Papacharissi (ed.), *A Networked Self: Identity, Community and Culture on Social Network Sites*, 132–58. New York: Routledge.

Papacharissi, Z. (2014). *Affective Publics: Sentiment, Technology, and Politics*. Oxford: Oxford University Press.

Papacharissi, Z. and de Fatime Oliveira, M. (2012). Affective news and networked publics: The rhythms of news storytelling on #Egypt. *Journal of Communication* 62(2): 266–82.

Papacharissi, Z. and Gibson, P. (2011). 15 minutes of privacy: Privacy, sociality and publicity on social network sites. In S. Trepte and L. Reinecke (eds), *Privacy Online: Theoretical Approaches and Research Perspectives on the Role of Privacy in the Social Web*, 75–89. New York: Springer.

Papacharissi, Z. and Yuan, E. (2011). What if the internet did not speak English? New and old language for studying newer media technologies. In N. Jankowski, S. Jones and D. Park (eds), *The Long History of New Media*, 89–108. New York: Peter Lang.

Papen, U. (2005). *Adult Literacy as Social Practice: More than Skills*. London: Routledge.

Parks, M. (2010). Social network sites as virtual communities. In Z. Papacharissi (ed.), *A Networked Self: Identity, Community, and Culture on Social Network Sites*, 105–23. New York: Routledge.

Person of Interest (2013) [Television series]. *One Percent* [Television series episode]. Dir. C. Fisher. CBS, 7 February 2013, 22.00.

Pettijohn, T. F. and Sacco, D. F. (2009). The language of lyrics: An analysis of popular Billboard songs across conditions of social and economic threat. *Journal of Language and Social Psychology* 28(3): 297–311.

Placencia, M. E. and Lower, A. (2013). 'Your kids are stinking cute': Complimenting behaviour on Facebook among family and friends. *Intercultural Pragmatics* 10(4): 617–46.

Poulios, A. (2011). *The Construction of Age Identities in Everyday Talk: The Case of the Elderly*. Doctoral dissertation. Thessaloniki: Aristotle University of Thessaloniki. Available online: http://hdl.handle.net/10442/hedi/28567 (accessed 30 September 2016).

Proshansky, H., Fabian, A. K. and Kaminoff, R. (1983). Place-identity: Physical world socialization of the self. *Journal of Environmental Psychology* 3(1): 57–83.

Puri, A. (2007). The Web of insights – The art and practice of webnography. *International Journal of Market Research* 49(3): 387–408.

Raynes-Goldie, K. (4 January 2010). Aliases, creeping, and wall cleaning: Understanding privacy in the age of Facebook. *First Monday* 15(1). Available online: http://firstmonday.org/ojs/index.php/fm/article/view/2775/2432 (accessed 30 September 2016).

Relph, E. (1976). *Place and Placelessness*. London: Pion.

Rheingold, H. (1993). *The Virtual Community: Homesteading on the Electric Frontier*. Reading, MA: Addison-Wesley.

Ricoeur, P. (1984). *Time and Narrative*. Translated by K. McLaughlin and D. Pellauer, Vol. 1. Chicago: University of Chicago Press.

Robards, B. (2013). Friending participants: Managing the researcher-participant relationship on social network sites. *Young* 21(3): 217–35.

Robinson, L. (2007). The cyberself: The self-ing project goes online, symbolic interaction in the digital age. *New Media & Society* 9(1): 93–110.

Rose, G. (2001). *Visual Methodologies*. London: Sage.

Rössler, B. (2005). *The Value of Privacy*. Translated by Rupert D. V. Glasgow. Cambridge: Polity Press.

Russell, T. and Stutzman, F. (2007). Self-representation of online identity in collected hyperlinks. *Proceedings of the American Society for Information Science and Technology Annual Meeting (ASIST 07)*. Available online: fredstutzman.com/papers/ASIST2007 Stutzman.pdf (accessed 30 September 2016).

Rybas, N. and Gajjala, R. (2007). Developing cyberethnographic research methods for understanding digitally mediated identities. *Forum: Qualitative Social Research* 8(3). Available online: www.qualitative-research.net/index.php/fqs/article/view/282/61926/12/32011 (accessed 30 September 2016).

Salmons, J. (2015). *Qualitative Online Interviews: Strategies, Design and Skills*, 2nd edn. Los Angeles: Sage.

Schaap, F. (2001). *The Words that Took us there: Ethnography in a Virtual Reality*. Amsterdam: Aksant Academic Publishers.

Scheibman, J. (2007). Subjective and intersubjective uses of generalizations in English conversations. In R. Englebretson (ed.), *Stancetaking in Discourse: Subjectivity, Evaluation, Interaction*, 111–38. Amsterdam: John Benjamins.

Schein, E. H. (1978). *Career Dynamics. Matching Individual and Organizational Needs*. Reading, MA: Addison-Wesley.

Schiffrin, D. (2006). From linguistic reference to social identity. In A. De Fina, D. Schiffrin and M. Bamberg (eds), *Discourse and Identity*, 103–32. Cambridge: Cambridge University Press.

Schnurr, S. (2012). *Exploring Professional Communication: Language in Action*. London: Routledge.

Scollon, R. and Scollon, S. W. (2003). *Discourses in Place: Language in the Material World*. London: Routledge.

Seargeant, P. and Tagg, C. eds (2014). *The Language of Social Media: Identity and Community on the Internet*. Basingstoke: Palgrave Macmillan.

Shifman, L. (2013). Memes in a digital world: Reconciling with a conceptual troublemaker. *Journal of Computer-Mediated Communication* 18(3): 362–77.

Shotter, J. (1993). Becoming someone: Identity and belonging. In N. Coupland and J. F. Nussbaum (eds), *Discourse and Lifespan Identity: Language and Language Behaviors*, 5–27. Thousand Oaks, CA: Sage.

Sidiropoulou, M. (1999). *Parameters in Translation: English vs. Greek*. Athens: Parousia 46.

Slang.gr (2016). *Καντήλι*. Available online: http://www.slang.gr/lemma/show/kantili_2001#lemma_3717 (accessed 30 September 2016).

Sophiadi, A. (2014). The song remains the same..or not?: A pragmatic approach to the lyrics of rock music. In N. Lavidas, T. Alexiou and A. M. Sougari (eds), *Major Trends in Theoretical and Applied Linguistics: Selected Papers from the 20th ISTAL*, Vol. 2, 125–42. London: Versita de Gruyter.

Stæhr, A. (2015a). Normativity as a social resource in social media practices. In L. M. Madsen, M. S. Karrebæk and J. S. Møller (eds), *Everyday Languaging: Collaborative Research on the Language use of Children and Youth*, 71–94. Berlin: Mouton De Gruyter.

Stæhr, A. (2015b). Reflexivity in Facebook interaction: Enregisterment across written and spoken language practices. *Discourse, Context & Media* 8: 30–45.

Stirling, E. (2014). Using Facebook as a research site and research tool. In *Sage Research Methods Cases*. Available online: http://methods.sagepub.com/case/using-facebook-as-a-research-site-and-research-tool (accessed 3 January 2017).

Stirling, L. and Manderson, L. (2011). About you: Empathy, objectivity, and authority. *Journal of Pragmatics* 43(6): 1581–1602.

Stutzman, F. and Hartzog, W. (2012). Boundary regulation in social media. *Proceedings of ACM Conference on Computer Supported Cooperative Work (CSCW'12)*, 769–78. Available online: http://fredstutzman.com.s3.amazonaws.com/papers/CSCW2012_Stutzman.pdf (accessed 30 September 2016).

Stutzman, F. and Kramer-Duffield, J. (2010). Friends only: Examining a privacy-enhancing behavior in Facebook. *Proceedings of the 28th International Conference on Human Factors in Computing Systems*, 1553–62. Available online: fredstutzman.com/papers/CHI2010_Stutzman.pdf (accessed 30 September 2016).

Stutzman, F., Gross, R. and Acquisti, A. (2012). Silent listeners: The evolution of privacy and disclosure on Facebook. *Journal of Privacy and Confidentiality* 4(2): 7–41.

Sundén, J. (2003). *Material Virtualities: Approaching Online Textual Embodiment*. New York: Peter Lang.

Tagg, C. and Seargeant, P. (2014). Audience design and language choice in the construction of translocal communities on social network sites. In P. Seargeant and C. Tagg (eds), *The Language of Social Media: Identity and Community on the Internet*, 161–85. Basingstoke: Palgrave Macmillan.

Tagg, C. and Seargeant, P. (2016). Facebook and the discursive construction of the social network. In A. Georgakopoulou and T. Spilioti (eds), *The Routledge Handbook of Language and Digital Communication*, 339–53. Abingdon: Routledge.

Tavani, H. T. (2008). Floridi's ontological theory of informational privacy: Some implications and challenges. *Ethics and Information Technology* 10(2–3): 155–66.

Taylor, S. (2003). A place for the future? Residence and continuity in women's narratives of their lives. *Narrative Inquiry* 13(1): 193–215.

Taylor, Y., Falconer, E. and Snowdon, R. (2014). Queer youth, Facebook and faith: Facebook methodologies and online identities. *New Media & Society* 16(7): 1138–53.

Thelwall, M. (2008). Fk yea I swear: Cursing and gender in a corpus of MySpace pages. *Corpora* 3(1): 83–107.

Theodoropoulou, I. (2015). Politeness on Facebook: The case of Greek birthday wishes. In M. A. Locher, B. Bolander and N. Höhn (eds), Special issue: Relational work in Facebook and discussion boards/fora. *Pragmatics* 25(1): 23–45.

Thompson, G. and Hunston, S. (2000). Evaluation: An introduction. In S. Hunston and G. Thompson (eds), *Evaluation in Text: Authorial Stance and the Construction of Discourse*, 1–27. New York: Oxford University Press.

Thorne, S. L. (2008). Transcultural communication in open Internet environments and massively multiplayer online games. In S. S. Magnan (ed.), *Mediating Discourse Online*, 305–27. Amsterdam: John Benjamins.

Thurlow, C. (2011). Determined creativity: Language play in new media discourse. In R. H. Jones (ed.), *Discourse and Creativity*, 169–90. London: Pearson.

Thurlow, C. and Jaworski, A. (2011). Banal globalization? Embodied actions and mediated practices in tourists' online photo-sharing. In C. Thurlow and K. Mroczek (eds), *Digital Discourse: Language in the New Media*, 220–50. London and New York: Oxford University Press.

Thurlow, C. and Mroczek, K. (2011). Fresh perspectives on new media sociolinguistics. In C. Thurlow and K. Mroczek (eds), *Digital Discourse: Language in the New Media*, xix–xliv. New York: Oxford University Press.

Thurlow, C., Lengel, L. and Tomic, A. (2004). *Computer Mediated Communication: Social Interaction and the Internet*. London: Sage.

Tommaso, L. (2015). The construction of age identity in an online discourse community: The case of Boomer Women Speak. In G. Balirano and M. C. Nisco (eds), *Languaging Diversity: Identities, Genres, Discourses*, 163–75. Cambridge: Cambridge Scholars Publishing.

Tracy, K. (2002). *Everyday Talk: Building and Reflecting Identities*. New York: Guilford.

Tsiplakou, S. (2009). Doing (bi)lingualism: Language alternation as performative construction of online identities. *Pragmatics* 19(3): 361–91.

Tuan, Y. F. (1991). Language and the making of place: A narrative-descriptive approach. *Annals of the Association of American Geographers* 81(4): 684–96.

Tufekci, Z. (2008). Can you see me now? Audience and disclosure regulation in online social network sites. *Bulletin of Science, Technology & Society* 28(1): 20–36.

Turkle, S. (1995). *Life on the Screen: Identity in the Age of the Internet*. London: Weidenfeld and Nicolson.

Twigger-Ross, C. L. and Uzzell, D. L. (1996). Place and identity processes. *Journal of Environmental Psychology* 16(3): 205–20.

Tyrkkö, J. and Leppänen, S., eds (2014). *Studies in Variation, Contacts and Change in English: Texts and Discourses of New Media*. Helsinki: University of Helsinki.

Urban Dictionary (2016). *Story of my Life*. Available online http://www.urbandictionary.com/define.php?term=Story%20Of%20My%20Life (accessed 30 September 2016).

van der Ploeg, I. (1998). *Keys to Privacy: Translations of 'The Privacy Problem' in Information Technologies*. Maastricht: Shaker.

van Dijck, J. (2013). 'You have one identity': Performing the self on Facebook and LinkedIn. *Media, Culture & Society* 35(2): 199–215.

van Dijk, T. A. (2009). *Society and Discourse: How Social Contexts Influence Text and Talk*. Cambridge: Cambridge University Press.

van Leeuwen, T. (1996). The representation of social actors. In C. R. Caldas-Coulthard and M. Coulthard (eds), *Texts and Practices: Readings in Critical Discourse Analysis*, 32–70. London: Routledge.

van Leeuwen, T. and Wodak, R. (1999). Legitimizing immigration control. A discourse-historical analysis. *Discourse Studies* 1(1): 83–118.

Varis, P. (forthcoming). *Ethnographic Fieldwork and Digital Culture: A Beginner's Guide*. Abingdon: Routledge.

Warner, M. (2002). *Publics and Counterpublics*. Cambridge: Zone Books.

Wenger, E. (1998). *Communities of Practice: Learning, Meaning, and Identity*. Cambridge: Cambridge University Press.

Wertheim, M. (1999). *The Pearly Gates of Cyberspace: A History of Space from Dante to the Internet*. New York: Norton.

Wesch, M. (2009). YouTube and you: Experiences of self-awareness in the context collapse of the recording webcam. *Explorations in Media Ecology* 8(2): 19–34.

Wessels, B. (2012). Identification and the practices of identity and privacy in everyday digital communication. *New Media & Society* 14(8): 1251–68.

West, L. (2015). Responding (or not) on Facebook: A sociolinguistic study of Liking, Commenting, and other reactions to posts. Doctoral dissertation. Washington, DC: Georgetown University.

West, L. and Trester, A. (2013). Facework on Facebook conversations on social media. In D. Tannen and A. Trester (eds), *Discourse 2.0: Language and New Media*, 133–53. Washington, DC: Georgetown University Press.

Widdicombe, S. (1998). Identity as an analyst's and a participant's resource. In C. Antaki and S. Widdicombe (eds), *Identities in Talk*, 191–206. London: Sage.

Wilson, R. E., Gosling, S. D. and Graham, L. T. (2012). A review of Facebook research in the social sciences. *Perspectives on Psychological Science* 7(3): 203–20.

Wittkower, D., ed. (2010). *Facebook and Philosophy*. Chicago: Open Court.

Woodward, K. (2002). *Understanding Identity*. London: Sage.

Wooffitt, R. (2005). *Conversation Analysis and Discourse Analysis: A Comparative Critical Introduction*. London: Sage.

Yus, F. (2011). *Cyberpragmatics: Internet-mediated Communication in Context*. Amsterdam: John Benjamins.

Zappavigna, M. (2012). *Discourse of Twitter and Social Media: How we use Language to Create Affiliation on the Web*. London: Continuum.

Zhao, S., Grasmuck, S. and Martin, J. (2008). Identity construction on Facebook: Digital empowerment in anchored relationships. *Computers in Human Behavior* 24(5): 1816–36.

Index